Majority Rules

Roger Fleming

Elderberry Press

OAKLAND

Distributed to the trade by
Elderberry Press
1393 Old Homestead Drive
Oakland Oregon, USA 97462
Tel: 541.459.6043
editor@elderberrypress.com
Our books are available from your favorite bookseller in print and ebook.
Publisher's Catalog-in-Publication Data
Majority Rules / Roger Fleming.—2nd ed.
ISBN: 9781934956649 [soft cover]
ISBN: 9781934956632 [hard cover]
Library of Congress Control Number: 2013951205
1. Congress—fiction.
2. Politics—fiction.
3. Washington D.C.—fiction.
4. Political parties—fiction.
5. Immigration—fiction.
I. Title.

For my friend, Louise Rockwell, whose tireless help and encouragement allowed me to write this book despite my lack of skill

This is a work of fiction. All the names and characters are either invented or used fictitiously. Although most of the events depicted are imaginary, the narrative draws on federal legislative efforts debated or voted on in the U.S. Congress in the 1980s. In that regard, where the novel touches close to reality I have provided endnotes in an attempt to explain at least some of what, in fact, took place there. Neither this story nor the notes are intended to address these issues in any comprehensive manner or account for all the many different political or historical perspectives on these sometimes controversial subjects.

Majority Rules

Why give up? Why despair? Undoubtedly there is injustice and deceit in this world ... One has to live, therefore, with one's enemies, since one cannot have everyone for a friend, to take men for what they are, to be content with the virtues one finds in them, to endeavor to see that their vices do you the least possible harm ...

— Alexis de Tocqueville

Prologue

December 2013   El Paso, Texas   86 Degrees Hazy

Twenty-five years later nothing had changed. The local paper headline read, "U.S. Border Agent Shot by Juarez Drug Cartel." The story detailed how two presumptive immigrants were also injured, but escaped and were recouping at a local hospital. On an outdoor patio, an Hispanic waiter placed three margaritas on a tile top table next to the newspaper and disappeared as quietly as he'd appeared. Nick Taft would have preferred ice water and inside air-conditioning but was helping a friend quietly celebrate the conviction of a gang member.

The U.S. Attorney for West Texas – who referred to his friends by their Spanish names raised a glass to his Washington colleagues – Nick and an official from the Justice Department. "Here's to you guys. Successful prosecutions on this border are difficult. Efforts by our new task force, Tomás, and information you dug up on the Immigration Act, Nicolás, drew attention to our arguments. Thanks for coming out." They sipped the chilled margaritas as if they'd earned them. "Maybe we'll finally start making some progress down here," he said with a touch of remorse.

"Over fifty thousand people murdered near border cities in the past few years, and we *may* start making some progress?" Nick's hand shaded his eyes, "Congressman Palmer knew it would come to this. We're so far behind the curve, it's laughable."

The prosecutor had asked Nick before how he became involved in border politics. "Taft, tell me in truth, how did you and that Congressman get involved in this never-ending battle in the first place?"

Nick nodded. As he began to launch into his twenty year old

tale of Washington politics, the piercing noise of a car backfiring shook the air. His eyes instinctively followed the sound to a black truck where a gun barrel rested on the passenger door. Thomas slumped forward onto the table. Wait staff scrambled in every direction. Nick looked down at the blood on his sleeves and his murdered colleague. A woman pleaded to 911 from under a counter.

Nick was helped to the men's room. He leaned over the sink and listened to the familiar moan of emergency vehicles in the distance. He stared into a water-stained mirror and reflected back wondering how he had become so involved in this political war. There wasn't a day when at some point, he didn't still wonder why he ever left the routine security of his hometown in Florida.

1

November 1984   Florida   79 Degrees Sunny

Was there a worse way to make a living – anchored under dull fluorescent lighting while the Florida sun blanketed miles of ocean and beaches? A *litigator*. It didn't sound as cool as lawyer and it wasn't. He wasn't sure if he was an uninspired lawyer or if the practice of law had become uninspiring, but Nicholas H. Taft, Esquire was long sure of one thing. He needed to get out of that firm and out of that town.

He tried explaining to the doctor who'd paid his tuition, "The dark suits and mahogany library make you feel the part, but this endless legal process isn't helping anybody."

Flamingo Beach wasn't bad, and the local politics were intriguing. Once an outpost to renegade movie stars visiting Palm Beach just up the road, it later became known as a "city of recovery," overflowing with substance abuse clinics. On its journey from martinis for breakfast to a cash-rich tourist town, Flamingo grew into a fledgling commercial hub. Still, as part of Florida's Gold Coast, heavy partying played a strong role. Women wore lucent dresses, and businessmen were defined as much by their liquor tolerance as their ability to navigate office warfare.

Office politics, of which Taft had witnessed plenty, seemed childish. But, the electoral process that put people in office felt meaningful; and party activists were so welcoming he dove in headfirst. Presiding over a political youth organization in a coastal city fueled by tourism and drinking would seem to have few advantages. But it gave credibility to a young lawyer who'd sell his soul for a new career. After walking dozens of precincts for an array of candidates, Nick found one who kept winning

3

despite the odds, U.S. Congressman Sanderson Palmer. He was a likable man who appreciated Nick's few political skills, which at the time were a subtle blend of enthusiasm and desperation.

The Congressman once complimented him during a local fundraiser, "Nick, you've done a hell of a job growing the Young Patriots here to over 300 young folks. Nice work."

"Well, I just invited all my friends and all their friends and the best looking women we could find to our meetings, ensured the drinks kept coming and charged everyone membership dues."

"Very resourceful," Palmer replied, clapping Nick on the shoulder.

The '80s began two decades of greed and excess, and expensive white dust from Colombia replaced the carefree love of the '70s. Studio 54 and Warhol carried the social scene and national politics began to see a new wave of partisanship. In the 1984 elections, everyone played their part. President Reagan was reelected in a landslide, carrying forty-nine states to only one for Walter Mondale; Palmer was reelected to the U.S. House and Florida had an incumbent Republican in the Senate for the first time in a decade. The Reagan Revolution was a reality, and having a different opinion than the predominant popular culture, while not cool, was becoming acceptable.

Conveniently, Nick's disillusionment with the law and growing attraction to politics coincided with an opening in Palmer's Washington office. Apparently there was a buyer's market for souls, but it was a unique opportunity to learn the world of federal power and a perfect exit. He gave his firm notice and vowed to stay out of trouble during his last days.

Born and raised on the Florida coast, Taft was accustomed to the social circuit. Sonny Hughes hosted the best parties in Flamingo Beach. They were always full of beautiful women and vodka-doused ice sculptures that wouldn't melt in the Florida heat. Sonny, a high school friend, was now Flamingo's best caterer. Nick shifted in his leather desk chair and looked at the perfect row of Florida Statute books on his credenza, then left his law office relishing interaction with anyone but another lawyer. He and his sometime girlfriend, Karen, headed to Sonny's fall soirée for just one drink. He had a hearing the next morning and couldn't be late. It was only a motion hearing, but the plaintiff's lawyer was green and hungry and had some law on his side.

As with any good event, this started with an excellent cocktail and went from seeing some old friends to talking of fishing offshore in the Atlantic to just one more rum and tonic. They recounted how two weeks prior a rickety wooden sailboat had washed ashore on Flamingo Beach with seventeen Haitians onboard. While police waited for federal INS agents to arrive, Nick and two friends delivered twenty McDonald's hamburgers, fries and colas to the exhausted but grateful and polite seafarers. His friends speculated and Nick hoped the tired travelers would end up in the hands of a clever immigration lawyer who could draw out the legal process and allow them to stay. But unlike others who'd survived similar voyages to remain as political refugees, these brave souls would be returned immediately to Haiti.

The party conversation meandered from the latest gossip about whomever to Nick's pending move to Washington. After countering debate with a Florida Atlantic University professor who argued that any form of government was the same as any other government and irrelevant to reality anyway, Nick headed back to the bar.

He argued across the pass through bar from the kitchen, "You know the difference between some governments, professor? Ask the brave people who've left behind everyone they know and risked their lives to escape to a country they know almost nothing about."

Karen with a raised eyebrow at the end of the counter, "Another drink and you'll regret it."

By midnight he was having the best discussion with a retired judge or once practicing attorney, he couldn't remember which no matter how many times he was told. Drinking their way through the political landscape, he praised Nick for giving up the law to work in Congress. "Ramifications of federal decisions may render our criminal process irrelevant anyway – the exclusionary rule for one." He passed a joint off someone handed him, "Go try and make a difference, kid." Nick talked about him the entire drive home down A1A until he saw the blue lights. That it was a state trooper was unmistakable; that Nick had too much to drink, undeniable; that the lights blew right past them and kept going, unbelievable.

Most hangovers are at their worst in the beginning. He managed some cereal while choosing a dark suit for his court appearance and told Karen, "There's no way I can go to what's her name's party tonight. I can't even function."

"Spare me," she mumbled from the covers. Her blond hair sliding across white sheets, "I'll go by myself. I usually do when it's my friends' parties. Just go to work, stop obsessing about politics, and don't get pulled over – you'd probably still blow over a point one."

Those words stuck in his head as he drove into a glaring coastal sun. Karen didn't care about politics; it was all just a game to her and so many others to whom it didn't matter which party was in power. Heat waves were wafting from the hood of his car and it was only 7:30 am. *But why does she say obsessing?* He blew through a just-turned red light and panicked as he scanned the landscape in his rearview mirror, however quickly faded back to his quandary. *He'd admit to being in politics barely a year and that it was the only thing that seemed to give his life meaning.*

After buying a double-brewed, he found his way to the court house elevators hoping the usually chatty cashier ladies weren't so unusually quiet due to his damaged appearance. He walked the halls toward the courtrooms attempting to stride purposefully – hallways which seemed to get longer every year as they added more judges to that ever-growing circuit. There was a time when lawyers knew a fair percentage of judges in the county but now they were just unfamiliar names on pleadings. Suffering the usual hellos to nameless litigators awaiting their respective hearings, his eyes focused on the only one he actually recognized, Porter Oliver, the plaintiff's lawyer in his case.

Porter hadn't seen him, so he sat on a bench along the wall. To regroup he tried both slurping some caffeine and opening his brief case, but then clumsily spilled his coffee. It flowed on the terrazzo floor beneath him except for a few puddled drops in the holes of his worn wingtips. As he nudged the cup under the bench with his foot, his only bleary thought was, *Could I get away with doing nothing about that?* Before anyone noticed the door to Judge Quartel's chambers opened.

The litigants entered and sat on opposite sides of a long oak table. The judge entered. He was an oddly familiar man in his sixties, distinguished in his black robe, but otherwise a mess. His hair was askew, his lean face haggard and gray with – was that stubble? They respectfully stood and looked toward the judge. When His Honor nodded at Nick, he squinted with surprise and recognition and a slight smile crossed his face.

The evening's mystery was solved on the pleadings right in front of him; apparently he was, in fact, a judge and not retired. Nick was suddenly feeling better. Even if he couldn't argue well in the next few minutes, at least the presiding judicial officer would understand why. Judge Quartel acknowledged the plaintiff's motion for summary judgment and recognized Porter to begin. Porter's enthusiasm stunned both Nick and the judge. He began well, but then stumbled and got nervous, then grew much louder. Nick closed his eyes trying to focus on the words.

With eyes open again, he noticed Quartel looking at him almost humorously, "Mr. Taft, I would entertain a motion for cloture about now."

Nick struggled to conceal his confusion. Cloture, he thought, was a parliamentary device used to cut off debate in a political body. He'd never seen it used in a court of law. Yet, he had no better ideas.

He offered with some authority, "Your Honor, I move for cloture."

Porter tried to keep talking, but the judge waved him off, "Motion granted."

Porter looked up as if to ask, *What the hell does that mean?* Nick looked back with an expression that said, *Don't you know? It was a motion for cloture, and you lost.*

Judge Quartel closed the hearing, "Plaintiff's motion for summary judgment is denied. Mr. Taft, please prepare an order for my signature with copies to all parties. Thank you, gentlemen."

The last hearing he would ever argue was over. He'd hardly said a word and his opponent had spoken too many. As they walked out of his chambers, the judge smiled, "Good luck in Washington, Taft."

After exiting the building, Nick looked back at the sun-drenched county court house where he'd been sworn into the Florida Bar a few short years before and wondered if he would ever return.

2

January 1985   Washington, DC   21 Degrees Snowing

Driving in ignorant bliss through the nation's highest ranked murder city was the start to his first imperfect day. Nick caught brief glimpses of the Capitol dome through half defrosted windows but it kept disappearing behind distant buildings.

He found a side street and pulled over to get his bearings. The icy roads weren't helping and his gloved hands made it difficult to hold a map.

After spotting someone who might point him in the right direction, he rolled down the passenger side window, "Excuse me, sir, sir? Could you tell me how to get to the Capitol?"

Leaning a little too far into the window, "Sure. I got you covered. I'll show you."

"Show me?"

"Jus' down the road, I'm goin' that way," as he pulled the car door shut and tucked a swing-blade into his boot.

In his relatively sheltered life, Nick had never seen such bloodshot, wired or empty eyes nor experienced quite the combined odor of alcohol, tobacco and wet socks.

"Nice ride. What are you, a lawyer or somethin'?"

Mentioning he'd been a prosecutor in the State Attorney's Office had a sobering effect on some. This guy was out of the car before Nick could finish his sentence. In reality he'd only been an intern there during law school, but the experience was helpful and being able to mention it had proven more so. Fortunately, he turned down an unplowed side road and looked straight up at the Capitol dome – the ghost of a majestic white crown peering through a thick gray sky.

His next encounter was with a U.S. Capitol Police officer

who provided the first clue of the attitude of his new boss. Holding up a parking sticker, Nick motioned the officer over, "Excuse me, I'm here to start work with Congressman Palmer. Can you tell me which garage this is for?"

The officer wearing an official blue leather Capitol Police emblazoned jacket had a friendly, but no-nonsense expression, "That's in parking lot 6. It's about a quarter mile down this road on your right, partially underneath I-395."

"Officer, with all due respect, that can't be right."

"Son, with all due respect, I'm quite certain that's right. Now, keep it moving."

After locating the remote lot 6, he trudged uphill through ice-crusted puddles to his office in the Cannon Building – the oldest of the House buildings. But as he began to cross the intersection at First and C Streets by the Library of Congress, he heard an angry voice, "Hey! Watch your light, watch your *light!*" He turned in the middle of the intersection to look back at a U.S. Capitol Police officer who was grimacing at him. Nick sheepishly returned to the curb.

He eventually reached the Cannon Building, an impressive-looking structure with a subtly ornate exterior. Nick breezed through security, his wool socks and new wingtips now wet and cold. He was certain just by the building's grandeur that meaningful debate took place inside its walls. He walked unassumingly down the corridors squinting at the room numbers. He hadn't found contact lenses yet that actually worked and was too embarrassed to wear his nerdy glasses. Finally, he recognized the Florida state flag and could make out Palmer's name on the door.

Then were the words he would hear a thousand times a day for the next year. In a slightly southern accent, "Good mornin', Congressman Sanderson Palmer's office. How may I help you?" However, she wasn't actually speaking to him, but to her headset. So when he started to respond, she politely put two fingers toward him as if to say, on the one hand, "Please wait while I take this call," and on the other, to say, "Can't you see I'm on the phone?" He looked around at the pictures on the wall of South Florida, and photos of the Congressman with the President at the White House and on Air Force One.

The front entrance to the office was small with a desk on either side as one walked in the door. A chest-high shelf in front of each desk required one to look over it onto the person sitting there. There was one black leather couch facing the entrance doorway with a gold framed mirror above it. Three doors led from the foyer into interior offices; two of which were closed and one open just enough to partially see desks and almost hear conversations.

She reached over and pulled the slightly open door shut. "Sorry, you were saying?"

"Hi, I'm Nick Taft..."

"I'm sorry," she pointed a finger toward him again, her gaze went into the middle distance, "Good mornin', Congressman Sanderson Palmer's office, hold please. Good mornin', Congressman Sanderson Palmer's office, how may I help you? Yes sir... well, the Congressman is not voting in favor of gun control... no, no sir he isn't. Yes, he does own guns of his own... now sir, I really don't think that's an appropriate thing to say. Well, then you have a nice day now, okay."

Turning back toward Nick, "I'm sorry, are you here for the tour of the Capitol?"

"No, I..."

At this point they were interrupted by Valerie Raney, whom Nick would learn was the Administrative Assistant or "head" of the office. They'd never met since Palmer had hired Nick in Florida. She was a Capitol Hill veteran in her fifties who appeared long past ready to retire. Valerie donned a brightly-colored but stiff-fitting business suit, and her jet black hair was perfectly coiffed. She wore makeup that highlighted her cheeks like little red apples and a Republican elephant pin on her lapel. She took up a position by the receptionist's desk.

With her back to Nick, she said, "You make sure I'm RSVP'ed to that Energy Institute luncheon today and there's a printed name tag for me – it's very important."

The receptionist, Barb, lowered her eyes, "Yes, I know, I've responded twice to the invite."

Valerie glanced at Nick as if he was eavesdropping, "Okay, but if I show up and have to write out my own name tag again, we're going to discuss it at length."

"Okay." Barb continued in a softer voice, "Now then, sorry. Are you with a larger group?"

"No, I'm a lawyer. My name's Nick Taft. The Congressman hired me to handle his Judiciary Committee issues."

"Oh. Hey everyone look, it's our new Legislative Assistant!"

The "assistant" tag didn't sit well with him from the first instant. However, he soon discovered why his title didn't reflect his legal training. The pecking order among congressional staff was paramount to those who'd either worked or waited their way to the top of the ladder, such as the Chief of Staff (COS) or Administrative Assistant (AA). Everyone below either of those titles was less powerful as in Legislative Director (LD), Legislative Assistant (LA) or Legislative Correspondent (LC).

After he was introduced to the office manager, he asked to see his office. She smiled a wide toothy grin, "Sure, it's right here – your desk." He thought *desk? You must be joking. Where're the crayons?* He'd just traded an office and secretary at a prestigious law firm for a desk where he was now an "assistant" something.

He suppressed that glaring contrast for the moment, and after a quick rundown of his duties, was determined to short-circuit his bureaucratic chores. The apple-cheeked Valerie or Val, as she preferred, described to him the time-consuming drudgery of constituent mail. As she was advising on how important it was he read each letter carefully and come to her with questions, he was looking past her at the bizarre print hanging from her office wall. He'd recently talked to a friend who'd once worked on the Hill and explained how ninety percent of constituent mail could be disposed of in minutes with form letters. From his Cub Scout days to his law practice, Nick had always played it by the book, but he'd come to Washington to work for Sandy Palmer, not for anyone else.

3

Inauguration Day   The Capitol   17 Degrees Snowing

The second Monday of his new job was Inauguration Day. The office bustled with the Congressman's Florida friends who flew in for the ceremonies. At nine-thirty, a savvy auto dealer from Boca Raton handed him a Bloody Mary and said, "Welcome aboard, young man, I know your dad, great guy, good doctor. Say, didn't you go to medical school?" Nick hadn't had time to hustle any passes to the swearing-in, so would watch it on TV with other staffers. It was 17 degrees with a foot of snow on the ground and still blowing. With the wind chill, it was so cold the Inaugural Parade had to be cancelled.

The office didn't seem at all the same with so many friends and supporters of the Congressman milling around with Mimosas in hand. Instead of stacks of constituent mail on each counter or desk, there were colorful plates with sweet rolls and ham biscuits and red, white and blue napkins. In lieu of nervous murmuring and policy talk, there was laughter and celebration.

Without tickets to any Inaugural Ball that evening, Nick had a less celebratory dinner with his only Washington acquaintance – his cousin's college roommate, Regina Moxley. She was an unusually well-tanned redhead, originally from Australia, and a lifelong liberal in no fine mood since *the dimwit* Ronald Reagan was beginning his second term. Her outlook improved when Nick paid off a $20 bet they'd made on the Super Bowl just the past Sunday. He'd bet with his heart on the Miami Dolphins, she on San Francisco – for the city, not the team. Although the Dolphins lost 38 to 16, they'd at least earned the right to play in the game. His demeanor improved as well when other Hill staff at the restaurant announced that due to the extreme weather, all government buildings would be closed the next day.

Daylight brought a clear blue sky and sparkling quiet snow everywhere. It felt like a Sunday morning, few cars braved the snowy streets. Smiling along the way, Nick slid down the sidewalks to a local diner for breakfast. He liked the anonymity his new city provided. He was temporarily put off to discover the antenna assembly on his car had been removed while parked in front of his building. Around one o'clock, he headed to his office to read up on some issues. Despite being a political science major, he lacked actual knowledge of the legislative process. He was no Ivy League lawyer, but his stint at the State's Attorney's office had sharpened his legal understanding of right and wrong. He hoped a little extra effort would make the difference.

Due to the weather-induced shutdown, Nick couldn't directly enter the Cannon Building. Instead he had to go through the entrance of the largest House office building two blocks down the street. The Rayburn Building, named after Texan, Sam Rayburn who served twenty-four terms in Congress – seventeen as Speaker – was the newest of the three House buildings. It was an imposing structure with wide halls and tall doorways where most of the committee rooms were located and most committee staff as well.

Nick showed his new Congressional ID to the security guard who gave directions through a maze of underground tunnels to the Cannon Building. But Nick took his time wandering the halls of Rayburn hoping he might come across the infamous Judiciary Committee room. He remembered when he was in high school that the impeachment proceedings against President Richard Nixon had taken place there. He recalled being awed by how important the people in that room seemed who held the President's future in their hands and struck by how critical the process was there. He remembered the hesitancy in President Nixon's voice during televised press conferences when his allies in Congress slowly turned on him.

As he scanned the many congressmen's names on a roster by the elevators, he leaned over and pushed the call button. Nick marveled at the idea that he belonged in this place and was no longer just another outsider. The elevator doors opened within seconds and revealed a slim blonde woman in jeans giving him an annoyed look.

She tilted her head, "What are you doing?"

His weight shifted to his back foot, "Well, actually, I was just looking for the Judiciary Committee room."

"You're in the basement." It wasn't her words so much as her attitude that made him feel stupid.

"Oh, I didn't realize. I just started working for Congressman Palmer and was coming in today to do some reading."

She gave him an appraising look and he thought her face softened a little. She stuck out her hand formally, "Hi, Lisa Castile, Majority Counsel on the Judiciary Committee."

"I'm Nick Taft," he said trying to hide how impressed he was by her title. "You've worked up here a while...?"

"Three years, right out of Harvard Law. You want to see the committee room? I'm headed there now, it's on the first floor."

"Yeah," he said, but just stared. Somewhat attracted to her at first, he was now definitely interested. She was so polished, even in jeans – especially in jeans.

Lisa held back the door, "Well, you'll have to step in. You see, the elevators move, the hallways pretty much stay put."

When the elevator doors opened again, she strode off down the corridor without a look back. He hustled after her. She was different – a fine featured woman with a relaxed air of authority, not forced. As he came alongside her, she looked straight ahead, as if fixed on some worldly goal only she could see.

"You just started working here? My advice is don't let any political hacks in this place mess with your substantive work product."

"Okay," Nick responded, although unsure of what she meant. "What are you working on today?"

"It's not really my issue, but immigration reform – trying to figure out what we can do for all those poor people who've come in mostly through Mexico."

"You mean illegal immigrants?"

"Well, we basically let them in, didn't we?"

"So, they're not illegal?"

"First, they're called people. Second, it's a very complicated issue."

"I know. Beyond those who've come in from Mexico, many land on or near the shores of Florida and while some are allowed to stay, others are sent back immediately. It must be quite complicated to them."

Lisa impatiently looked at her watch. So he impatiently looked at his too. She hurried him through the committee's law library. The chestnut table dividing the room was thirty feet long. Law books were stacked from floor to ceiling with legal reporters of every federal dispute in the country going back two hundred years. Lisa put her papers down next to a stack of books and motioned Nick to follow her.

They walked down an interior corridor through a doorway which opened onto a view of the hearing room from behind the dais where the Members sat. It was the highest spot in the room which looked down onto the witness table, the press table and chairs from where the public is allowed to view hearings. Lisa pointed to the benches behind the congressmen's leather and wood chairs and said, "That's where committee counsels hang out during meetings. There's not much room to maneuver when everyone's lugging their research, memos, and statistics."

The very high-ceilinged room was mostly dark with faint light filtering through tall windows draped by enormous floor-to-ceiling thick, dark blue curtains. Nick had never seen a committee room where the real work on legislation actually happened nor did he have a clue what took place there, but he asked no questions. He followed her down the aisle behind the chairs.

When they reached the center, she swung the tallest chair around and said, "Sit down in the Chairman's seat. Go ahead – you can pretend you're in the majority."

The prestigious chairmanship of that committee overseeing the country's justice system was held by Texan, John Staunton, who first experienced the legal process as a defendant. During a fuel stop his senior year in college, while hitchhiking to Lubbock, a cash-desperate young Staunton lifted the wallet of a ranch hand who had picked him up, then caught another ride with a trucker. The trucker testified against him, and young Johnny pled out to a misdemeanor. His defense attorney's investigator, Judd Traynor, was so good at digging up dirt on the rancher that Staunton was disappointed they never got to use it in trial. But he and Judd became friends and their paths would cross again.

Nick declined to sit in the tall chair. Something about her offer made him feel uncomfortable. "That's okay. Thanks for showing me the room, though."

"Are you handling Judiciary issues for Palmer? He's a bright Member. You're lucky to work for him. Florida needs congressmen like him."

For many years Florida had survived on a predominantly agriculture and tourism based economy. But with the rapid growth of the '70s and '80s combined with extensive Cuban and Latino immigration, Miami had become an international city and South Florida especially had become more politically important. Nick had gone to school with students who were becoming a part of that new economy and political base.

"Yeah, he's a really good guy. I'd like to help him get some legislation passed."

Lisa laughed. She'd paid too many dues to tread lightly.

"Are you serious? You're in the minority, my friend. You're not going to get any legislation passed unless, of course, you want to cosponsor one of our bills."

"I'm sure if we work well together, we can get something through," Nick said, stung.

"You really don't get it, do you? Look, we've controlled the House for 30 years, we have a 70 seat majority over you. The D to R ratio on this committee alone is 21 to 14." She lectured on while fiddling with her pearl necklace, "You and your Members have no power here. Don't bang your head against the wall, just enjoy learning the process."

Unsure what to make of Ms. Castile's advice, he continued his journey through the empty halls wondering whether she was being honest with him. If she was right, the job was going to be worse than it already appeared. He got lost again in the underground tunnels and asked directions from a guard in the Longworth Building, the second oldest, and some say dreariest of the House buildings due to its construction during the Great Depression. The dimly lit tunnel from Longworth to the Cannon Building was lined with drab white brick walls and dingy gray-brown well-worn floors.

Finding his office, he opened the first of his underwhelming government pay checks, then made coffee and began reading files on the upcoming crime and immigration issues. But his mind wandered to Ms. Castile's discomforting words, *The rules couldn't be that draconian? Every elected Member must be able to get legislation at least voted on. She must have been bluffing, right?* Another possibility lingered, *She might have been flirting.* Feeling optimistic, he returned to his reading. He'd learn the process inside out and be ready the next time Majority Counsel Castile merely blinked in his direction. When finished, Nick drove the slippery roads back to his sunny apartment in Georgetown – an apartment he was lucky to have found.

In November when Congressman Palmer offered Nick the job in DC, he'd set out for a weekend there to find a place to live. His cousin's friend, Moxley, who was traveling, offered her studio as long as he would feed and walk her Welsh Corgi puppy, Sir Winston. It was a rumpled one-room apartment near Georgetown University. He and Winston became fast friends despite the fact there was no sign of any dog food in the place. Nick fed him taffy from her coffee table so he wouldn't just sit and stare at him. A woman he'd dated in school who lived in Virginia agreed to have dinner while he was in town. It was a cold December evening. She showed up in a full length mink, blond strands spilling over a turned-up collar, and slender legs bracing her fur against the wind.

Having hit many popular spots in DC where he didn't know a soul, Nick opened up about his impending changes. After listening to him equivocate on leaving his hometown, she encouraged him to make the move.

"Look around you," she said, "at the historic buildings and cobblestone streets, the people dressed so nicely in wool suits. Feel the cool, fresh air. Look at the fall leaves still left on the old oaks. Are you kidding me? You don't have this in Florida. Flamingo's got one season, and it's either really hot and humid, or it's just hot. I can still hear you complaining about the climate there and how practicing law was so tedious. You're going to love it here."

They made it back to Moxley's apartment on Churchill Street and woke up the neighbors for old time's sake. She first required he coax the ever-present puppy out into the hallway with several pieces of taffy but it was worth it for all of them. She made him feel at home in Washington if only for a night.

Early the next morning he and Winston walked to a local diner for breakfast. Winston ate eggs and toast while Nick sipped coffee and scanned the rental ads in the Washington Herald. From his brief visit, he was convinced he wanted to live in Georgetown but all he'd seen listed was one studio apartment, and the ad was explicit – No calls before 9:00 a.m. Monday. It was 8:00 Sunday, his flight back to Florida departed that afternoon and he hadn't found a place yet he'd pay ten dollars to live in, so he called the number from the diner pay phone.

The gentleman who answered was not happy: "The ad says Monday after 9:00!"

"Yes sir, I know, but I'm from Florida. I'm moving here in four weeks to work for my Congressman and my flight home leaves in a couple of hours."

"Who's your Congressman?" he asked with an edge.

For his second time in Washington, Nick was reminded that politics played a role in everything. He knew the Democrats had dominated the U.S. House for decades and that they controlled about half the U.S. Senate as well as most law firms in town. What were the odds that his intended landlord in high society Georgetown would be a Republican?

But the question left little room for a diversion so he just told him, "Congressman Palmer from Flamingo Beach."

"A Republican? And a good one at that."

Relieved at the response, he'd quickly added, "Yeah, and I'm involved in party politics down there. I'm just kind of in a jam and don't know the DC area very well."

He met the owner who agreed to rent the place at a better price than he'd seen all weekend. He was Major Eugene Ity, a dapper gentleman in a conservative suit, long since retired from the War College but still consulting for the CIA. He sat on several bank boards and had considerable family money. The apartment was a unique studio on the top floor of an ivy covered brick building with big double-paned glass windows. Nick wrote a rent check and began contemplating how to get all his stuff there from Florida.

––––––––––

If we're lucky in life, we have one friend we can count on to help with our less than desirable worldly tasks. For Nick, that was Rennick McGregor, better known to Nick and his family as Ren. They grew up a few blocks from each other and became best of cronies in junior high.

Ren was learning the construction business of South Florida. For a guy with little more than a high school education he was doing well. He owned his house and boat and owed the bank nothing. Although Nick was younger and a lawyer, he had mounds of credit card debt and seldom paid his rent on time. While Nick continued his academics into graduate school, Ren became more street smart – he could overhaul an entire house in months and get paid more than the original builder. They were an unlikely pair, but complimented each other well. And although Nick outgrew his South Florida neighborhood, he always came back to Ren for advice.

After some enticing, his friend agreed to help load a moving truck and drive with him to Washington. Considering their past, it was not surprising that within minutes of struggling to lift heavy furniture they got into it.

Ren complained, "You think I don't know you're arranging these so I'm left carrying the heavy end every time? Now, we're switching on this one." He was a stocky Scotsman with blonde to white hair and a ruddy complexion.

Nick had a swarthier black Irish look with hazel eyes, and

was of slighter build, "Whatever you say tough guy – but you just switched to the heavy end."

They finished loading the truck on a Thursday night and headed for the highway to DC the following morning. Since the Ryder Rental truck was not new, it rattled and sputtered until reaching a speed somewhere between sixty-five and seventy.

If we're unlucky in life, we have one friend we can count on to talk about absolutely nothing but sex and who, given the chance, would talk about nothing else to a captive audience for hours on end. Oddly, the friend Nick was lucky and unlucky to have was one and the same.

They hadn't made it onto I-95 that morning before Ren started in, "I'll tell you what Taft, maybe it's a good thing you're leaving Flamingo. Too many women to chase down here. Just a matter of time before they all run us out of town on a rail anyway. You do like 'em blond, blue-eyed, and scrawny though." He crossed his thick ankles onto the dashboard, "Me, I like a girl with a little meat on her bones – you know – somethin' to hold on to."

Thinking this couldn't possibly go on for seventeen hours, Nick indulged his friend, "Sure Ren. So how's that bodybuilding bank teller chick working out for you? Can she bench press *you* over her head yet?"

"Funny Taft." But, at least he paused and drifted off for a while. The moment Ren awoke from a nap, he asked a different question, "Taft, why you movin' to Washington? You're leaving a pretty good thing here."

"It could be a mistake, but anything would be better than the law. Our legal process is about trickery and deception, Ren, and the rules can disallow a jury from even hearing the most relevant evidence. In Congress it's like the issues are about what's best for the country, not just the parties in front of a judge. I think in Congress our representatives are sort of like

24

the jury and the American people are the judge – at least every two years. You know what I mean? Our political process allows open testimony at Congressional hearings where witnesses can say whatever they want, and a public vote in the House and Senate. And it's not a never-ending process; you either win or lose the vote in the end. I'm so tired of the law, I couldn't do it another day."

"Oh fuck you, Taft. You're tired of your job, so you're just quitting? Who's not tired or bored with their job?"

"It's not like that. I've created an opportunity for myself in Washington by getting involved in politics."

"Can you create an opportunity up there for me? I want to quit my job too. What happens when you get tired of politics?"

Nick, who only smoked when he drank, lit a cigarette, "I'm not sure one ever gets bored of politics, there's always something interesting happening. You know, Renny, they say in order to be successful, a person has to have a mentor. Maybe I'll find one up there."

Nick wanted to be a doctor like his father who'd helped so many people, but struggled terribly through pre-med in college. Switching to pre-law allowed him to follow in the footsteps of his grandfather, who was a successful lawyer in the early days of Palm Beach County. Though no great student, he landed a job with a decent law firm in Flamingo. His dad seemed proud of him following his grandfather's career path, but was quietly disappointed when he moved to Washington. Nick believed he could still be a successful lawyer, if not in Florida, maybe in Congress. His grandfather had served in WWI and his father in WWII. There was no war to fight when Nick came of age, but he believed his new career might also be a way of serving.

As the landscape darkened from a sun-bleached green to the rich pines of Georgia, the only conversation other than women was a debate over the choice of music on the radio. "Ren, this country music is just too sad."

"Oh, Taft, you need to mellow out, man. That's good music – it's about people's feelings. Better than that top-forty crap."

"People's feelings? Sorry, but this George Jones song about how he stopped loving her one day is just flat out depressing. I have to change it."

"You don't even get it – the guy in the song is dead. That's why he stopped loving her."

"And *that's* not depressing?!"

Their eventual compromise was a station reviewing a decade of Crosby, Stills and Nash. At the North Carolina border the radio news allowed Nick to distract his friend again, "Why does the news keep talking about the Iranian hostages from 1979? There've probably been a half dozen political kidnappings or murders since then that never come up – why?"

"I don't know my friend, but it's getting cold in here. Where's the heat? What's up with you and Karen anyway? She want you to leave?"

"We're just friends with benefits. It doesn't feel legit to me. I almost feel guilty."

"Oh man, are you on drugs? You need your head examined."

Nick turned the radio up seeking to switch the subject back. "You realize the press could report on the Ohio couple kidnapped in Sri Lanka or the U.S. political officer kidnapped and killed by Islamic radicals in Beirut in March. I still don't get why they never covered the 'Boat People' who fled the killing fields of Vietnam after we pulled out – a million people murdered for political ends. Who makes those decisions?"

"Sounds like a great question for somebody else."

The temperature dropped again as they entered Virginia and the heater didn't work. Once in DC they rode in tired silence, maneuvering the bumpy streets of Georgetown.

After unloading the truck, they had a beer with Moxley

who complained about many things, but mostly that Ronald Reagan was just stupid. She'd grown up in southern California where border issues mattered; and Reagan, while often talking of it had accomplished nothing on immigration reform in his first term. Regardless, it was fashionable in liberal Washington to talk about how dumb any Republican president was, and equally chic to speculate on how bright the most recently failed Democratic presidential candidate had been. So, Ronald Reagan was a moron, Walter Mondale and Jimmy Carter were brilliant, and Richard Nixon and Gerald Ford had been incredibly stupid. National politics were really quite simple.

Nick flew back to Florida the next day where he wrapped up his affairs at his law firm, and enjoyed an Atlantic Avenue bar crawl with friends as a going away party. When January began, he said good-bye to his life in Florida and drove to a snow-covered Washington.

4

Late March 1985   Capitol Hill   45 Degrees Raining

The months following inaugural week proved discouraging for Nicholas H. Taft, the onetime real lawyer, even litigator, turned congressional minion. First and foremost, Majority Counsel Lisa Castile hadn't been bluffing, nor, and most unfortunately, flirting with him either. Congress's rules were debilitating to any member of his party who tried to serve their constituents. Nick learned that his Members had no right to call a hearing, invite a witness to testify, or use a committee room for any reason. Furthermore, the majority had so stacked the ratios in their favor that even if a minority Member offered the most practical amendment, the vote would be the same against it every time: 9 to 5 in subcommittee and 21 to 14 in full committee.

By the end of March, Nick was totally disheartened. Not only did one party control every aspect of debate, but when he'd paired up with a Democrat to cosponsor important legislation, hardly anyone was there to listen. They'd drafted a common sense amendment for the immigration bill based upon language in the Senate-passed version. But as he learned the hard way again, the majority used a demoralizing tactic called "proxy voting" to ensure the outcome of votes. It allowed Members to transfer their voting privileges to the Chairman so he could vote for them by proxy. Consequently, once the Chairman established a quorum (enough Members present for committee business), Members could simply leave and allow the Chairman to control everything.

Because immigration reform was not the sexiest issue in the winter of 1985, and more celebrated hearings were happening elsewhere, the committee markup of that bill eventually became sparsely attended. In fact, by the time Palmer, a junior Member, had an opportunity to offer the amendment to secure the U.S.-Mexico border, those senior to him had abandoned the room. Among the few people remaining were the Chairman, the clerk, and the Democratic cosponsor of the amendment. Palmer gave Nick a look that said, *You really want me to offer this?*

Nick shot back, "Sandy, our borders are wide open. This amendment, though not politically popular, may help secure our border and save future immigrants from this illegal limbo trap. Even if we lose, at least you'll have something on the record to refer to during House floor debate." Nick believed the amendment was worthwhile, but was also anxious to test this legislative process for his own edification.

Most politicians are optimists in the face of brutal reality – Palmer, a realist, was the exception, "Much debate on it? Fat chance! Mr. Chairman, I have an amendment at the desk."

Chairman Staunton took the cigar out of his mouth and peered down to the lower row on the Republicans' side of the dais as if he barely recognized Palmer, "What?"

Palmer motioned toward the clerk's desk and repeated, "I have an amendment at the desk, Palmer amendment number one." Staunton shook his head in futility and waved for him to go ahead.

He argued: "Mr. Chairman, your bill to grant amnesty to illegal immigrants present in the U.S. is popular with our agricultural and service industries. But, we don't even know how many illegals are coming across the U.S.-Mexico border. This amendment would require we withhold amnesty to anyone until we can determine that our borders are secure. It seems to me, Mr. Chairman, that if we're going to say it's okay for all the people who have come in illegally to stay, and become citizens with no legal consequences, then we're just encouraging more to cross illegally and wait for the next amnesty deal."

Palmer was interrupted by the Democratic cosponsor of the

amendment, "Will the gentleman yield?"

Representative Sedgwick began: "Mr. Chairman, to ensure that illegal immigration does not mushroom into an uncontrollable situation we must commit the resources to control our border first. Without that, this move to allow amnesty to illegals already here is meaningless. Our border agents are virtually overrun. In just the 66 miles of border under the San Diego office of the U.S. Border Patrol, we apprehended over 270,000 illegal aliens in only six months. The fact of the matter is we've got a serious problem on our border. Assaults upon our border patrol are increasing every day. We see exploitation of illegal aliens in robbings, rapes, and drug trafficking. We have more than a cottage industry brewing; we have a growing threat to our own security..."

Chairman Staunton interrupted, "Vote!"

Palmer reacted, "What?"

"Vote!" Staunton bellowed again with a look that said, "Don't test my patience, son."

Palmer looked at Nick, threw up his hands, and rolled his eyes.

The Chairman scoffed, "The clerk will call the roll."

The clerk began, "Mr. Talley." "Proxy no," said the Chairman. "Mr. Bowers." "Proxy no," repeated the Chairman. "Mr. Peck." "Proxy no," continued the Chairman while reading a newspaper.

On down the line it went, no one there to read the amendment or hear the arguments. Nick glanced over toward Lisa who was sitting behind the Chairman as the vote continued. She was fingering her pearls and caught Nick looking at her, but returned him a half-smile-half-frown. When Chairman Staunton finished voting for the absent Democrats, the amendment had already been defeated, but the clerk dutifully continued down the roster to the Republicans. Members strolled in from the Republican anteroom and despite President Reagan's full support for amnesty, voted with Palmer to delay it when their names were called.

The clerk announced the tally, "Mr. Chairman, there are 15 *ayes* and 20 *nays*; the amendment fails."[1] Staunton asked perfunctorily, "Are there any other Members seeking recognition for the purpose of offering an amendment?" The Republicans in the room looked blankly at each other, then sheepishly back toward the Chairman.

Staunton particularly relished this control over vote counting. He'd barely won his first race many years before for the Texas State House by a handful of ballots. His chance to run for the U.S. Congress came when an elder Texas statesman became gravely ill. Most other politicians, out of respect, refused to speculate about the potential open seat; but Staunton jumped in as if the funeral was already over and locked up early support. That initial lead gave John the edge, but again he won by less than one percent.

Nick walked back to his office lugging his files with all the research and counter-arguments he'd prepared for the amendment. Political reality was enticing him to abandon the fundamentals of his political science education. Congressional process was perhaps not always about the parties working together for the greater common good.

While absorbing his first legislative defeat, Nick was interrupted in front of the entire staff by the most cheerful tone he'd heard from Val since he'd been there, "So, how'd it go with your big amendment?"

That first of many political losses to come would prove to be a defining moment of Nick's career, and motivated him into regrouping for the next fight when he'd be a little wiser.

––––––––––

The weekend came with an invitation to accompany his pal Moxley to a party in Virginia. She explained during their drive into the country how the horse people in Middleburg were some of the most fun folks near Washington. "They have money, like to party and you just might learn something." Nick wasn't sure what that meant, but was game for a change of scenery. He cautiously confided on the way that he'd recently called his ex-girlfriend, Karen, and she was back with her ex-boyfriend – and they were already very serious. He asked for her female take on how realistic that was. Moxley offered no advice but instead enthusiastically launched into her own bizarre dating challenges. His new city quickly felt like a lonelier place.

Everyone at the party was dressed like a country squire, or as if they'd recently dismounted their horse. Nick was wearing just his gray pants and blazer. But the farm's early spring lawn was perfectly manicured and the colorful guests presented a refreshing change of attitude from button-downed Capitol Hill. One thing was certain, they all liked to drink and drink a lot. He was beginning to feel like he was back in Florida, albeit among strangers.

He enjoyed meeting Ashley Gentmore, the widow who owned the place. She was previously married to a Democratic power-broker and knew something about everyone. She had prematurely silver-white hair, a lean equestrian's body and appeared to be made for that hundred year old farmhouse. As Nick was beginning to relax and admire the architecture of the old home, Moxley stumbled to the back porch with a vodka-tonic loosely in hand and introduced Nick as her wayward Floridian friend who worked on the Hill. When the squires asked for whom he worked, Moxley couldn't contain herself.

In her enthusiastic if waning British/Australian accent, "My friend works for Sandy Palmer, another moronic Republican and they both think that *fucking-numb-nuts* Reagan is a great President!"

The group politely snickered and turned back to their cocktails.

Moxley gave Nick a look, "Sorry, I couldn't help it. But why do you work for Palmer and all those stupid Republicans, you're such a bright lawyer, and they're all just so ...you know ...stupid – *capesce?*"

He liked Moxley but was convinced she suffered from political Tourette's. Her extensive education failed to allow her coherent debate, she usually resorted to emotional vitriol. Considering his experience that week though, Nick began to wonder if she was right. Sipping his drink he looked at the rolling hills and wondered: *How had his party managed their power such that no one in the majority would even listen to their ideas? Would his party treat the minority the same should they ever regain power again? What a vicious cycle that would be – each majority party locks out the minority's ideas so the country never benefits from the collective wisdom of both.*[2]

As he was leaving, Mrs. Gentmore took his hand and whispered, "You handle yourself well among the cynics. It's important to stay focused in politics, Nick, and learn to listen."

5

Early April 1985   Georgetown   47 Degrees Cloudy

Late one Saturday after reviewing bills he had no way of paying, Nick got a panicked call from Moxley. Sir Winston had gone missing again. The last time he'd escaped, he was at Booeymonger's deli. Moxley was within earshot calling Winston's name, but the little ingrate was hiding behind a door begging for food. For one with a double major in Communications and Marxian Economics, she wasn't the keenest sleuth on the street. Nick agreed to help look and set out down the block. He noticed the house on his corner was preparing for yet another party. It was a palatial Georgetown home surrounded by old brick walls. Mexican men were unloading trucks out front beneath an array of shiny new spring leaves.

After crisscrossing several streets he spotted Sir Winston at Sugars Café near the University. Students were coaxing him to stand on his short hind legs for a piece of cheeseburger. Nick fashioned a leash from some twine the waitress offered and led Winston away with a foiled again expression on his grease-laden whiskers. As they walked back toward Nick's building along the old trolley-railed streets, he passed the party palace again where he heard a familiar voice among Spanish conversations inside the gate. He looked to see an attractive woman wearing a black cocktail dress giving instructions to one of the bartenders.

"Lisa, is that you?"

"Hey, Nick. What are you doing here?"

"I live down the block."

"Nice neighborhood."

"Wow, nice dress," he quickly looked up from the low cut neckline.

"Thanks."

"What's going on?" He looked past her into a secluded courtyard with a gurgling stone fountain. "I've often wondered who lives here."

Lisa smiled, "One of your favorite people, Chairman Staunton."

"You're kidding. He's the one having all the parties?"

Lisa stepped from behind the wrought iron gate, "Yeah, fundraisers actually. Is this your puppy? Corgis are my favorite dogs in the world! They're so cute. What's his name?"

"Sir Winston...yes he's...mine, he uh, was actually a friend of mine's, but she...died."

"Wow, that's horrible."

"It was really...sad." Nick was stunned himself at the morbidity of his story.

"But that's okay now, isn't it Winston? Does Mr. Winston have a birthday coming up?"

"Well, next month. Why?" Nick was thinking, *It's actually Sir Winston, but she could call him anything she wanted.*

"Because I'm going to buy him a new leash, as in a *real one*."

"Oh, we just lost his the other day."

"Well, I'm getting him a cool new leash soon. Okay, Winston?"

They were interrupted by an olive skinned guy in a Brooks Brothers suit who barked at Lisa, "Are you actually going to help us out here or what?"

"Yes Alec, I was just talking with Congressman Palmer's counsel. Nick, have you met Chairman Staunton's Chief of Staff, Alec Sivore?"

"No, nice to meet you."

"Same to you," he replied, as if returning an insult. "We're in a bit of a hurry."

Money is the matter of any given moment to a politician and

Alec Sivore was the quintessential scavenger. He could take the glass eye from a blind man and swear he looked better without it.

"No problem. Nice seeing you, Lisa."

Lisa was embarrassed by Alec's attitude, "Sorry about that. He gets really uptight before fundraisers, at least until the lobbyists show up with their checks in hand. You know how it goes."

"Sure. I'll see you around."

He headed down the street to his place and after impatiently yanking another $20 DC parking ticket off his car windshield, went upstairs to call Moxley with the news that he'd found Winston. She wasn't home, so he left her a message that Sir Winston was safe and could stay the night with him. Nick had dinner and was out like a light when his head hit the pillow.

Around midnight distant voices awoke him from a deep sleep. He was surprised to look out his window and see Lisa Castile arguing with Alec Sivore. It was obvious things were heating up as Lisa threw her shoes and purse onto the hood of a car. Nick opened his window just enough to hear their words.

"You bastard, how dare you say that in front of those people. I work with them too, you know, except I do real work."

Alec, slightly slurring, "Hey, I was doing my job. It's why I get paid."

"Paid to treat me like wait-staff?"

"Come on – those politicos took to you like a saltlick. Can we just go home?"

"No, we can't. I'm sick of your bullshit and your scam fundraisers."

Alec leaned in as if to push her, then ripped her dress as he stumble-stepped sideways. "Don't ever say that again, damn it. I do good work!"

"To hell with you and your so-called work."

"Sanctimonious bitch!"

Alec's car sped away scattering Lisa's shoes and purse onto the street and sidewalk. She picked up one shoe and put it on, but then sat on the bumper of a parked car.

Nick opened the window and spoke just loud enough, "You all right?"

"What?" She looked up at the window. "Oh, great," as she turned away, wiping her cheek with the back of her hand. "What are you doing?"

"I live here – remember?"

"Sorry. Did we wake you?"

"Hang on. I'll be right down." He was up, into his jeans and sweater and scrambling down the stairs within seconds. He opened the door to his building and walked to her.

Lisa, mumbling to herself, "Sanctimonious bitch, who does he think he is? Yes, I'm all right. But he's an ass."

"Agreed. So, you two are dating?"

"Hmm...I guess you heard a lot?"

"Not that much – some."

Lisa, straightening her dress, "We *were* dating, if you could call it that."

"Well, it happens."

"No, I should never have dated him. He's the Chairman's Chief of Staff. We work together. I'm just stupid."

"Hey, we all make mistakes."

"Not like me."

"Why don't you come up and wash your face? I'll make you a cup of coffee."

Lisa looked at Nick for a few seconds, "Sure, that would be nice."

He handed Lisa her other shoe while she gathered her purse, then followed him into his building. Once in Nick's apartment, Lisa's mood changed completely when she saw Winston. "Mr.

Winston, hello little boy, how are you?" Winston perked up and wagged his tail. "Aren't you the best little dog?"

Nick gave her a wash cloth and towel and pointed toward the bathroom.

She came out with her dress back together, a little lipstick and her hair pulled back. He poured strong coffee and Lisa sat at the wood counter that constituted half the kitchen. He thought he detected just the slightest hint of perfume. She looked around at the sailing prints on the wall, the bookshelves dividing the quasi-living room and bedroom area and the dusty oriental rugs.

"Like the way you did this place. Do you actually own a vacuum?"

He just smiled.

She set the subject, "So how is it being in the minority?" She muffled a laugh, "I have to admit I almost felt sorry for you and Palmer at the markup Thursday. That was pretty sad." Laughing again, "I'm sorry, that's really rude of me."

"You have a sadistic sense of humor, don't you? I'm up here busting my hump just to pass one legitimate amendment and you guys run the place like a prison camp to ensure that never happens. It's ridiculous."

"Oh Puhleese – you're in the minority! Don't say I didn't warn you."

"That's not my point."

"Well, what's your point?"

"We're lucky enough to live in a democracy where people choose who will represent them. Their elected members represent a majority of those peoples' votes. Members of the minority party in Congress under this process aren't allowed to fully participate in legislation and that precludes those voters from being fully represented."

"Taft, that's why they're called the minority party. The

majority rules and we get to govern – get it?"

Lisa's allegiance to the majority party regardless of its blind spot on equality within its own halls impressed Nick. It reminded him of his allegiance to his party's collective indignation at its self-inflicted minority status.

"Well, I've seen how Congress governs and I don't like it. The majority isn't ruling here, Lisa, the majority party is – it's different. Doesn't it seem the least bit hypocritical to you?"

"What?"

"That the party in charge oversees a set of rules in *The People's House,* of all places, that discourages debate and allows only one group to hold hearings, call witnesses and determine what is even voted upon? Don't the minority's ideas deserve to be heard as much as the majority's? Why not let the ideas of both parties in and take the best of both? We're not the enemy."

"Oh give me a break. You just haven't been around long enough. Now there's a little boy that looks thirsty. Where's your water bowl, MR. WINSTON?"

Nick thought, *Water bowl?*

"Well, let's see where Mr. Righteous is hiding your water."

"Uh... actually I broke Mr. Winston's bowl yesterday, I mean this morning. Didn't I Winston? I forgot to put a new one down tonight before we went to bed."

"No water? What kind of master are you?"

He found a soup bowl and handed it to her. She filled it and placed it on the kitchen floor. The corgi slurped like a parched desert rat; the bowl was licked dry in thirty seconds. Lisa gave Nick a dubious look and filled it again.

"Thirsty little bugger, isn't he? I mean, I've never seen him so thirsty. Do you always have this effect on animals?"

She leaned back and tilted her head slightly, "Yeah, mostly male animals – they tend to drink a lot when I'm around. Hey, thanks for the coffee and company, but I should get going."

If Lisa kept a list of those thirsty male animals, it would include her now immediate ex-lover, her very first boyfriend in college – a linebacker for the Texas Longhorns – and her former constitutional law professor at Cambridge.

"Where's your phone, can I call a taxi?"

"I'll drive you. Where do you live?"

"No, no, you've done enough. I live on the Hill. I can get a cab."

"Really, I can drive you there in fifteen minutes. My car's right out front."

"Great."

He was fond of his second-hand BMW. Although its front grill recently went missing, the sleek car was a five speed stick with softly faded leather interior, and fast. They wheeled through the side streets of Georgetown onto Rock Creek Parkway and hit 50 mph under the over-hanging terrace of the Kennedy Center along the Potomac. It was after one o'clock in the morning so few cars were on the road. It seemed like just the two of them driving in the city.

"Nice car, did you get this up here?"

"I got it in Florida when I was practicing law."

Running her fingers along a stash of parking tickets in the passenger door pouch, "You practiced law?"

"For two years, a litigator at a firm in Flamingo Beach."

"Hmm, most lawyers on the Hill never practiced law. By the way, collecting these," she pointed to the stash of tickets, "is not wise in this town – they will catch up with you."

"Sometimes I wonder how they write legislation without having been in a courtroom persuading a judge how to interpret a statute. Some of the legislative drafting I've seen isn't that great."

"How old are you?" she asked.

"Twenty-seven. And you?"

"Don't you know, you never ask a woman her age?"

"No. You just asked *me*."

"You're not a woman, are you?"

"Definitely Not!"

Before she got out of the car, she looked him in the eye, "Thanks, Nick." She put her hand on his arm as she pushed out of the car.

"Hey, no problem. I'll see you on the Hill."

"Yes, you will."

He watched until she got in her door and thought of what it would be like to kiss her.

—————————

After another few hectic weeks Congress shut down for recess. He learned that when Congress recessed the place cleared out. Anyone who was anybody high-tailed it out of town except for newcomers. As Val said (she was leaving on a trip to Palm Springs), "Well, it is a Congressional office after all. Someone has to be here." An energy institute was paying for her trip and she was to speak on a panel at their four day retreat.

Nick figured he'd enjoy the slower pace, and he did for a day or two. The hallways were disarmingly empty. He wore jeans to work and actually answered some constituent mail. But the fact was he had time on his hands and missed Florida and South Floridians.

6

April 1985   Capitol Hill   68 Degrees Sunny

The halls were buzzing again the first week back from recess. Val, looking a little rosier than usual, had an announcement to make. The Congressman had finally hired a new press secretary. Alexi Tehaus, a local TV reporter from WTZF in West Palm Beach, walked into the gathering. She was 5'7", tan and thin with sun-drenched brown hair, green eyes and long legs. She had both North and South American features, wore a white blouse, khaki skirt, high-heels and a sly smile. Nick was thinking *now this is more like it.* Compared to the wool-skirted aficionados he'd been dealing with, this chick was a rock star!

There was a party that Friday night at another Florida Congressman's staffer's apartment to celebrate the arrival of spring. Only staffers from Florida Hill offices were invited. Nick arrived late, grabbed a beer, and headed to the balcony to take in what little sunlight was left. Alexi showed up next to him on the railing with a white wine in hand and asked, "You're from Flamingo Beach, right?"

"Yep, born and raised."

"Please tell me this isn't supposed to be fun. Please tell me our nation's capital has something a little more exciting to offer on a Friday night."

"Well, yes, this is supposed to be fun, but Washington does have a little more to offer."

Alexi looked back through the sliding doors to the party, then past Nick across the landscape toward Georgetown, "What do you say we blow this place and go get a real drink?"

"I'm right behind you."

He drove her to his favorite bar in the heart of Georgetown.

Forever known as Billy Martin's Tavern, it had a dark mahogany interior set off by Tiffany-inspired lamp shades, an antique mirror backed bar and English hunt prints. Alexi, flirting with the bartender, ordered a Tanqueray gin martini straight up with a twist. He'd never had a martini but was game to go head to head with the brazen brunette from West Palm Beach, so she ordered him a dirty Absolut martini with a couple of olives.

Nick took a big sip. *Good Lord! Was that grain alcohol? Was she trying to kill him?* "That's quite a drink." Trying not to cough, "I like the dirty part, it reminds me of..."

But Alexi cut him off, "I know what it reminds you of..."

Coughing, "How's that?"

"I'm a reporter – I know all about you, Nick."

"I doubt it."

"You want the Cliff's notes? You're 27 and your father's a successful doctor. You didn't follow in your father's footsteps, opting instead to become a lawyer and you went to work as a litigator at Minter, Candler & Ferrell, which you hated. But you were good at political law like zoning and lobbying and you were a precinct captain for the Palm Beach County Republican Party. And you're kind of struggling here because you don't really have any power and Val doesn't like you and is trying to make your job miserable."

"Wow, that's impressive."

Nick appreciated Alexi's interest. He'd quit telling his story in DC after a short time because everyone there seemed uniquely more important from somewhere else more impressive. However, he would learn that many in Washington actually had no proud history to be told and their stories in fact only began the day they'd arrived.

"Val doesn't like me, huh? I thought so. But why?"

"That'll cost you another martini. Aren't these the best?"

"Yeah, but they're kind of strong."

"Kind of strong? I call them liquid Quaaludes – cheers!"

He leaned back from the bar and tried to get a read on Alexi and her appetite for alcohol, "How'd you know all that?"

"I hear things, Nick. And, I listen."

Nick was unsettled by Alexi's knowledge and her flippant attitude about where she got it. He understood that political reporters were aggressive and brash, but trustworthy?

"So what do you do around this town on the weekends?" she asked.

"Well, usually, I go to the Folger and read up on a little Shakespeare..."

"Oh, bullshit."

"But, this weekend the Palmers asked me to stay at their house in Virginia to watch the place and feed the dog. It's a really cool..."

"Are you fucking kidding me? You're staying at Palmer's house – tonight?"

"Yeah, it's great. It's got a hot tub, a heated pool and..."

"Okay, honey. Finish your drink, let's go. You're showing me Palmer's house."

"Well, I don't know if I should."

"Trust me, you should – now pay the tab and let's get out of here."

He wheeled up Potomac Lane past the old farms recently subdivided into colonial style homes. The house was an impressive stone and wood structure with an expansive lawn bordered by old maple trees. Alexi loved checking out everything in the place. She was like a cat burglar sizing up the Chippendale, the hand-painted etchings, and the Steuben on the coffee table.

"You want a drink?" Nick asked, walking toward the bar.

"I'll tell you what, I make great drinks. You just crank up the fireplace, it's freezing."

They sat on the wrap-around couch watching the fire as they

critiqued her bar skills. After a few cocktails, they were sitting closer. His Washington tales got better with each sip of rum; like when he'd met the President at the White House (where he'd actually never been) or when he'd debated the Chairman of the Rules Committee on an amendment (whom he'd only met briefly at a reception). You'd never know if Alexi wasn't buying any of it. Her eyes were well fixed on his and every time she laughed, she kept grazing his arm with her hand.

The drinks were done, and they were leaning on each other. There was a long pause, then Nick stood up and took an out-of-character stab at discipline, "You know, this probably isn't a good idea."

They both suspected where they were headed. After another pause, Alexi stood next to him, "Well, I suppose one kiss wouldn't end the world."

It was a stunningly good kiss. As their clothes dropped to the floor, a very different evening began to unfold until the telephone rang. Nick started to pick it up, then let it go to the answering machine. They managed one more kiss until they heard the congressman's voice leaving a message on the machine. After the interruption, they made one more drink, sat out by the pool and avoided looking at one another. Alexi stayed the night, but slept in the guest bedroom.

The next morning in the Palmers' kitchen, they casted blame on each other with their eyes.

Alexi finally broke the silence, "Well, I think you were right."

Nick, waiting for coffee to brew, "What, that this was probably not a good idea?"

"No, that our nation's capital did have something more exciting to offer on a Friday night," she said laughing. "I wonder what the Congressman would think if he knew you were seducing women in his house. I wonder what Mrs. Palmer would think?"

"That's hysterical," he nodded, "but who exactly was seducing whom?"

"That depends on where you draw the line now doesn't it, Nicky?"

"Okay, look, we're attracted to each other, but we're working together. I'm barely learning enough to get anything done in that socialist encampment. You just started working here..."

"Yeah?"

"So let's not . . . you know . . . screw it up. Let's just make a pact that we're going to be good friends – all right?"

"Sure thing Opie – whatever you say."

There was a long silence on the drive down GW Parkway from Virginia, but it may have simply been because it was a warm spring morning, the windows were down, and brilliant sunlight shone through a blue sky. Nick wasn't sure what Alexi's silence meant. But experience had taught him one thing about those circumstances – to keep his mouth shut.

When they were back on Capitol Hill, close to Alexi's apartment, she opened up, "How the hell am I supposed to get any press for this honest Congressman?"

"Well, I'm glad you asked. I've been struggling to get a bill introduced that had some chance for a Democratic cosponsor so it might actually get a hearing."

Once parked in front of her place, he continued telling her all he'd learned about being in the minority, Lisa Castile's advice about wasting his time, and Chairman Staunton's arrogance. He described his own legislative failures so far regardless of the merits of the amendments, the party line votes every time, and his frustration with the whole process.

He turned off the engine, "Alexi, this place is a rigged casino."

In one gesture she touched up her lipstick and opened the

car door, "Well, you just get something introduced. I can get press on almost anything if it has some credibility. It would help if Palmer introduces a bill with some sex appeal. And, forget illegal immigration. Don't you read the headlines? Crime and drugs, drugs and crime, that's all any law-abiding Floridians care about. Remember, even in a casino, though the house always wins in the end, there's usually one cocky dealer you can beat."

––––––––––

The next days required focus for the Legislative Counsel, as Nick's new title described him. He'd won that upgrade despite the office bureaucracy's resistance. The Congressman invited him to meetings in South Florida with federal prosecutors. They arrived with their shirts sticking to their backs at the federal building in a hot, humid downtown Miami.

A very matter-of-fact Assistant U.S. Attorney described how frustrated the government had become, "We watch drug runners arrested just beyond U.S. waters walk free time and again."

She was tall and thin, and her auburn hair was pulled back in a small bun. Slight creases at the sides of her eyes tightened as she explained, "Even if the Coast Guard tracks a suspected drug ship and obtains permission from its country to board – seizes illegal drugs and arrests the crew – defendants are sliding because of a procedural gimmick. We could use some help."

Criminal defense attorneys had discovered a loophole in federal law that was leaving judges with no choice. Under the current statute which was written eons ago, any permission from a country to allow a foreign sovereign to board a ship flying under its flag had to be *in writing*. The modern technologies of radio and telephone used in the 1980s – radio from ship to shore and telephone from U.S. to foreign embassy – were insufficient pursuant to the words of the antiquated statute. Consequently, high seas dealers bringing thousands of pounds of cocaine into the U.S. were not able to be convicted on the few occasions when they actually got caught.

Nick, whose favorite subject in school was criminal procedure, dug in for a battle. He interviewed federal prosecutors, got the statute's history and case law down, and would draft a bill to allow modern communications to suffice to board a foreign ship. He had lunch on the beach with a law school classmate turned criminal defense attorney to get his perspective. The Port of Palm Beach was one to which drug ships were sometimes towed to begin prosecutions. Although he now lived and worked in DC, opportunities like this to employ political skills for the benefit of Floridians allowed him to feel tethered to his hometown. He wished, but doubted he'd get the chance to boast about this effort to his father.

He did get the chance that afternoon at his parents' home to talk about it with their housekeeper who'd worked for his family for thirty years and practically raised Nick. Maleva, who had the sweetest smile, was a 65-year-old dark skinned Guatemalan woman who'd done everything from change Nick's diapers, to walk him by the hand to kindergarten, to teach him the basics of life. They'd spent countless hours playing *Go Fish* and *Crazy Eights* in his early years while she taught him how to appreciate the simpler things in life. During those years, he called her Ma Leva thinking they were somehow related – he had a grandmother that went by the name, Grandma Leah. Maleva was very impressed with Nick's work on the drug dealer issue and emphasized how proud she was of him working for their congressman. Her pride meant a lot to Nick.

Later that afternoon, on a whim, he drove west to visit his favorite former client, a farmer in western Palm Beach County who grew garden vegetables on several hundred acres. Nick had helped him win some local political and zoning battles.

They talked politics as they drove around the farm in Hendrick Woods' truck through the laser-guided rows of crops. His cowboy-booted client was a serious conservative. Nick explained what he'd learned so far about illegal immigration and the opposing debates about amnesty and securing the border.

Farmer Woods stopped the truck every twenty yards, "Lupe, are them peppers all going to fit on that truck? Matia, those cucumbers goin' to get picked today?"

When Nick said he was becoming convinced the country needed to essentially close the U.S.-Mexico border, Woods stopped the truck again.

"Nick, you see these people out here? They work hard. This is back-breaking work, mi amigo, and they're the only ones who both know how to do it and who will do it. You shut down that fuckin' border and this farm will go out of business in a matter of months."

"Why don't you hire Americans?"

"Look, I've tried to hire Americans to do this work. They'll last three days on average and they're gone. These folks here live together, support each other, know how to get things done and are loyal. Tell that to your Washington politicians."

Nick thought about Hendricks's advice as he drove back toward the ocean early that evening. He was surprised by the farmer's admonition and suddenly lacked confidence in his understanding of the practical impact of the current immigration law and guest worker programs.

His last night in Florida, Nick went out with friends. Some were still complaining about the stupidity of their least favorite judge, others about the real-estate market. Nick was living off a government paycheck in the insulated economy of Washington; he couldn't relate. They pumped him for information on DC. He told them of his adventures and tried to explain how bitterly partisan Congress was, but still living in the real world, they couldn't relate. One thing they all agreed upon was that the *New Coke* that had just come out sucked and they all wanted the old *Coke* back. After midnight, the once Young Patriots closed out their favorite bar on the intracoastal and drank too much, but laughed most of the way home.

Nick looked down from 5,000 feet onto a checkerboard landscape en route back to Washington and thought of how different it had been in Florida doing policy-related work. His new job was more interesting and he was less hassled on a daily basis, but the consequences of his actions weighed heavier on him. Though he longed for his place within the camaraderie of his home town, he couldn't help but reflect on how much he'd already learned about issues like crime and immigration and how they impacted everyday cities like Flamingo Beach.

──────────

Just one week back on the Hill, Nick had drafted legislation, a memo explaining the history of the statute, and a statement for the record prepared for Congressman Palmer. He sought advice from the Republican counsel on the subcommittee regarding proper drafting and a strategy for introduction. Unfortunately, the majority had had their way with this counsel one too many times. The lifeless staffer, Chuck, spent twenty minutes of their half hour meeting trying to talk him out of introducing the bill because it wasn't going anywhere, anyway.

Chuck explained how the majority had no interest in plugging loopholes in federal statutes to crack down on crime, but preferred hearings showcasing how the criminal justice system was biased or its prisons too crowded. Chuck, who was an Ivy League lawyer, said Nick wouldn't even get a hearing on his bill much less a committee markup, and not to waste his time.

Nick refused to be dissuaded. He needed someone

trustworthy to assess whether he was close on the "credible legislation" front. He'd only seen Lisa Castile once since their fateful evening on his street. She was sitting in the cafeteria with several staffers from her office who Nick didn't know. She'd smiled and waved as he walked by. Nick always ate alone there and his counterparts always seemed intent on collective dining. He questioned whether this was simply because there were so fewer Republican staff. He would call her later that afternoon.

Lisa agreed to help. They met at the carryout diner in the basement of the Rayburn Building and got through the niceties. She started by thanking him for his kindness a few weeks back and asked how Mr. Winston was doing. Nick made up something lighthearted about the dog and then described his drug dealer issue as laid out by the prosecutor, the history of the law, and the statutory construction.

She listened and reviewed his memo, "It's a decent issue and you've tailored the legislation narrowly – that's good. Your problem is the only congressmen who care about border drug smuggling are those from the few states most affected by it: Florida, Texas, Arizona and California; and the only of those on the committee with *any* power is Staunton."

The growth rate in Florida during the previous decade was unparalleled, but it wouldn't pay off politically until the decennial census of 1990 added congressional seats there due to population shifts – creating more power for the fast-rising Florida Congressional Delegation. Lisa educated Nick about Staunton's views on drug dealers. He didn't like them. And although he was a moderate liberal Democrat from a congressional district trending more conservative every year, he didn't like alienating his liberal colleagues in Washington by moving tough law enforcement legislation.

"At the very least, you're going to need a Democratic cosponsor for Staunton to even consider a hearing on this bill, much less allow a vote on it."

He described his discouraging meeting with the Republican committee counsel.

Lisa rolled her eyes, "Oh, forget him. He couldn't inspire a turtle to cross the road. Let me think on it and give you a call later in the week. I'll help you where I can."

Nick walked up a crowded sidewalk along Independence Avenue, straining to make sense of his predicament. A loophole in the law was allowing drug dealers to walk out of federal courtrooms unscathed. There was a simple legislative solution, but the congressmen who cared had no power to fix it. The congressmen with the power to fix it didn't care. And, the only person he knew who might really help worked for a party whose politics wouldn't let her. A Maryland State Police cruiser pulled to the curb directly in front of him. John Staunton exited from the back, gave a soul shake to the driver and sauntered toward the Capitol Building. Nick watched him cross the road and wondered, *What actually motivates these members to legislate?*

Lisa didn't call until the following week but suggested they have a drink instead of a meeting. Lisa Castile was the all-American girl: Texas-raised, independent, and patriotic. She'd been fairly social in college at the University of Texas, but more of a loner when studying law in New England. While Harvard Law School had managed slight changes in her culturally – smoking pot and embracing cynicism – pressure to conform to an increasingly *we know best* Congressional agenda was affecting her on a more personal level. What western common sense she had left competed daily with the partisan lens defining the issues in Congress and her obligation to sharpen the majority's arguments for those debates.

They met after work in the bar of an upscale restaurant on Capitol Hill. Lisa seemed tired and flustered and ordered a scotch and water with a twist. She downed the first drink within minutes of their conversation. Nick tried to get her to focus on him as she fidgeted with her pearls, "Lisa, I really appreciate..."

She cut him off, "It's no problem. In fact, it's a welcome diversion considering the bullshit going on in my office. Well, I have good news and bad news. First, the good news. Congressman Clifton, a Georgia Democrat, has a tight race against a law and order Republican – he's looking to show that he can be tough on crime. I think he'd be a good cosponsor for your bill. Chairman Staunton likes him and would help him by moving the bill. Now, the bad news. Chairman Staunton might be inclined to help if it's Clifton's bill and Palmer just becomes one of the cosponsors."

"Are you kidding me? Not only have we done all the work on this bill, but as you said, this issue is important to Florida. It has nothing to do with Georgia or frankly, anything Congressman Clifton gives a damn about. I'm not letting this inter-party bullshit keep us from doing something worthwhile."

"Look, I'm telling you what I've learned. You asked for my help and intelligence gathering is one way I can. And, for the record, in this town, it's not like that jazz musician says, 'Don't worry about mistakes, there aren't any.' There's a mistake to be made on every corner here, Nick. It also might not show, but the Chairman is pretty uptight these days about his endless need to raise more money."

"How can Staunton be hurting for money? He's a Chairman. He holds a huge fundraiser every other week at that mansion of his in Georgetown."

Lisa finished another scotch and lit a cigarette. He bummed a cigarette and ordered himself just one more drink as he avoided noticing her very toned thigh supporting her crossed legs.

"I don't know, Nick, but it seems this fundraising business is trickier than it appears." She squinted against the smoke of her cigarette to scan the bar for who might be listening.

"I don't want to pry, but since you brought it up, what did you mean that night in front of my place when you said to Sivore something about *scam* fundraisers?"

They looked different directions at neighboring tables, "I didn't say anything of the sort."

Lisa carelessly flicked her cigarette toward a glass tray, but missed and her ashes went into Nick's drink. She laughed, "Hey, you want to get a table and something to eat?"

They were moved to a rail-side table on the upstairs level of an atrium style dining room, so they were looking onto the diners below. It was a good table, but, suddenly they were transformed from two colleagues having a drink at the bar to feeling like they were on a date. Only slightly awkward at first, Nick noticed Lisa missed a step coming up the stairs and seemed at the very least, relaxed.

Once seated, Nick lamented. "Most of these members, Lisa, they seem so disinterested."

Lisa immediately ordered a glass of wine and gave Nick her take on Congress. "All these members are different people, Nick, from different parts of the country, and different generations – and all of them are here for very different reasons. The old ones hang on too long and the new ones come in with much fanfare but eventually become either bored or politically vulnerable. Most members just go along to get along, but a handful dig in and try to make a difference. And that's where the trouble starts." She chuckled cynically.

"You'd think if they worked so hard to get here, they'd work harder at the job."

Their server placed crispy breadsticks on the table along with their menus. Lisa dug in crunching away as she continued in a seductive Texas accent, "Look, Nick, they're not bound to any code here to get anything done – except get reelected." As she continued, the breadstick emphasized her points until she got to what must have been the punch line when she inadvertently let go of it. Nick watched the half chewed dough sail over the railing onto a table below. The couple seated there stared bewildered at the ceiling. When Nick glanced back at Lisa, she was looking at him with a glazed smile and had no idea what she'd done.

Lisa ordered onion soup when the waiter walked by. But when it arrived, she proved both extremely hungry and absolutely incapable of wrestling the hot stringy cheese from the bowl onto her spoon or into her mouth. After managing only two spoonsful she gave up – melted cheese was everywhere. She searched in vain for her napkin then yanked the cloth from the basket of rolls like some great magician. The rolls ricocheted off their wine glasses and onto the floor.

She wiped her mouth, "Great soup! Should we get a bottle of wine?"

"No! I mean, I don't think so. I'm not really that thirsty."

Nick didn't really know Lisa that well. She was kind of important to his job, and he was definitely attracted to her. He was hoping the steak she ordered would sober her up. Finally their entrees arrived.

To his dismay, Lisa took only one bite of her steak, "You know whut? I'm really not dat hungry. I'm just gonna go to ther-radies' room."

He watched her lean and sway toward the restroom door and cringed like a parent watching a child's first bike ride. Nick sat down, inhaled his food, and thought, *I've got to get this woman out of here before she does some damage.* He wondered if Lisa had just had a bad day or if this was an average night for a seasoned Hill staffer. When she returned to the table, she sat down a little too hard and her teeth chattered as she landed on the chair. After politely suggesting she try eating anything on her plate, Nick gave up and signaled for the check.

He pulled out Lisa's chair. They had to maneuver through a

passage of tables and around a corner to the stairs. He wanted to hold Lisa's arm to stabilize her, but didn't want to insult her.

"After you," he held his hand out toward the exit.

It was too narrow to walk beside her, so he followed close behind. Lisa was precariously leaning with each step as her long legs and high heels became more like stilts. She brushed along the edge of one table and dragged a set of silverware to the floor. Another diner leaned away as she side-swiped his chair. Lisa was oblivious to her path of destruction, and once clear of the tables, picked up the pace.

Nick caught up as she descended the first flight of steps. His hand was below her right elbow. But in a flash, she grabbed the rail at the landing and swung around onto the bottom flight of stairs. She missed the next step and fell headfirst down the stairs. The speed of gravity and her coat camouflaged the descent making it hard to tell the degree of impact. Lisa flew off the last step and spun around feet first sliding into the host station like it was third base. Her blond hair was wrapped around one shoulder and her skirt was hiked up her thin legs as she skidded into the ankles of the maître'd.

The headwaiter and maître'd tripped over themselves to help her up, "Ma'am, I'm so sorry. Are you all right?"

Lisa straightened her blouse and threw her head back, "Well, of course, I'm all right!"

Nick shook his head, smiled, and led her out into the cool night air. He drove Lisa to her apartment, practically carried her to a couch, took off her shoes, and covered her with a blanket. He couldn't help but notice her breasts under a partially unbuttoned blouse or the full length of her legs when she turned and twisted into the couch to sleep. He turned out the lights and left.

––––––––––

The next morning while driving to work he found Lisa's appointment book in his car. He thumbed the edge pondering the ethics of rifling through it, but now unable to get her legs out of his head, he plowed through curiously looking for any interesting references. On the prior day's date, there was no star next to *Drinks with Nick*, but there was one next to a four o'clock meeting to discuss "Staunton fundraising prob..." The ink was smeared and he couldn't decipher the remaining letters. He wondered if it was fundraising *problem* or *probe*. He called the committee office and was told Ms. Castile wouldn't be in all day, so he left a message that he had her book and was thankful for her professional insights and exceptional personal advice.

Certain her curiosity would require she call regardless of her condition, he rehearsed some lines that would exaggerate her behavior. To his dismay, Lisa didn't call; but when he returned home that evening there was an envelope taped to his door with a note that read:

> Nick, I'm really embarrassed about how smashed I got last night. That's never happened before, at least as far as you know. Thanks for tending to me and getting me home. Please call on Sunday if you get a chance. My home number's on the back.

The following day, pondering his legislative predicament, Nick became frustrated over Palmer's inability to introduce a viable bill on his own. He headed out for a run to clear his head, but after carefully peeling a wet $20 parking ticket off his windshield he came across his landlord, Eugene Ity, tinkering in the garage. Ity lived only part-time in the building next door where he housed an old mint condition, 12 cylinder Jaguar XKE.

Nick often joked that he'd be glad to maintain it when he was out of town, "You know, make sure the engine gets run every now and then." The Major, not a big talker, usually returned a sideways glance as if to say, "Not in my lifetime." Nick was surprised on this morning when Ity asked how things were.

"You've been around long enough to get a feel for things – so how bad is it for Republicans up there?"

He automatically went to his diplomatic response, "Well, you know, the Democrats have been in the majority for over thirty years, so the Republicans have to pick their battles..."

The Major cut him off, "You mean you guys can't get a thing done without caving in to the majority – and even then they still screw you?"

Nick conceded, "Yeah – basically."

He then unloaded on his experiences, his efforts at amendments, the crime legislation, and the Committee Chairman's arrogance.

"Who's your Committee Chairman?"

"John Staunton."

Ity looked down and shook his head in disgust, "Good Lord, he's one of the worst in the whole place. He's our neighbor, you know."

"I know, very nice house."

"Can't afford it – not a dime. Nor the yacht he has docked in Annapolis."

"What do you mean he can't afford it?"

The Major paused as if pondering whether Nick was worthy of sharing information. "Trust me, son. I sit on enough financial boards in this town and have enough friends who own banks across this country. You're more financially sound at twenty-seven than John Staunton. I don't know how he maintains all his facades, but I can assure you there's something below board involved."

"He's got a yacht in Annapolis?"

"Entertains the lobbyists and ladies there. Understand he works hard at rendering his business associates and employees somewhat compromised through his extracurricular antics."

"How does he get away with that?"

"He also has a lot of business associates south of the border."

"Interesting."

"Look son, I don't know how politicians get their money, or get away with their other ungovernable indiscretions. You tell me how these things work. You're the political lawyer."

Nick had no response – being defined as such was a first for him.

Ity cranked up the Jag and rolled slowly down the street avoiding the potholes. Nick went for a long run and thought about what he'd just heard.

Staunton had been in Congress for twenty years. He spoke about helping the poor and railed against corporate America, but held private fundraisers raking in millions from corporations. A congressman's salary was about $85,000. Staunton had a million dollar house in Georgetown and a home in Texas, and allegedly a yacht in Annapolis. The Major sat on several bank boards and there might be a probe regarding Staunton's fundraising activities. One other matter Nick had to consider: Major Ity seemed to know many interesting facts, like Staunton's and Nick's financial status, and Nick's age – he'd never told Ity how old he was.

He decided he'd call Lisa later to make a date for Sunday, but figured he'd make it lunch. When he returned the Major was closing his garage door. Nick liked the Major and though he didn't know him well, considered him a friend. He seemed like a man who'd served his purpose in life and was reflecting upon where he'd been. Though he had no children or family other than his wife and he didn't seem lonely; Nick sensed there was a void within.

"Hey, Major, thanks for sharing your thoughts about Staunton."

Ity smiled, "Well, I know what I know. Maybe you better learn the part of politics that doesn't take place in the committee room, but has a profound effect on what does."

7

They met at two o'clock for lunch at an open air market and restaurant that held the aroma of freshly grilled food in the air. So far it was the nicest day of spring, and the setting was perfect. They laughed a lot about how the evening had transpired when they were last together. Nick teased Lisa unmercifully and embellished those parts that she couldn't remember. The once arrogant majority counsel was on the defensive.

After lunch, they walked the streets of Georgetown and strolled through a few shops. Lisa was wearing the best fitting jeans Nick had seen in a while. They walked and talked for many blocks and each time Lisa tried to offer an apology for their last encounter, he would cut her off and change the subject. The only political subject they touched on was immigration because Nick had been researching the early bill drafts and was puzzled by what he saw.

"Lisa, tell me something. Amnesty is the core of this immigration reform bill – right?"

"Basically, yeah."

"Most of these people are here because we failed to stop them at the Mexico border. Yet, there's been no determination that any of them are political refugees or escaping political persecution like we've required of Cuban immigrants and other groups in the past."

"Nick, I doubt the political asylum argument would work here. Last I checked Mexico wasn't a dictatorship or communist country."

"Right. So we're basically considering just letting them stay simply because they're here, even though they came in illegally

61

and in reality we have no idea where they're actually from."

"That's why they call it blanket amnesty. It's a humane gesture – get it?"

"Explain that to those who survived the Atlantic in homemade rafts and landed on or fifty yards short of Florida's beaches to be sent back despite pleas for political asylum. Do you think Floridians would put up with thousands of immigrants crashing its shores every week simply to be left to move up the coast into the shadows? No way. It sounds to me like whether or not you get to stay here illegally depends upon which border you choose to cross."

"Well, like I told you it's complicated. But Palmer's triggered amnesty isn't going to cut it. A statutory waiting room where Congress would hold in federal limbo the fate of all these people until that God-forsaken border is secured? I don't think so."

Around four o'clock, they stepped into The Saloun on M Street where a jazz band was playing. They ordered a beer and got a chance to simply learn about each other, where she was from, where he grew up, what music and movies they liked. Although she wouldn't admit it, Lisa was enchanted with the part of herself she saw in Nick – that part which arrived in DC years before, unprepared for the seduction of cynicism that is so Washington. As they asked and answered each other's questions, their body language changed.

The pace was slow and the music good. The bartender talked them into trying a drink he was inventing. It was a flavorful concoction with a strong base of Gosling's rum. They ordered appetizers and continued chatting about anything that came up – except politics. Nick wanted to test her on what he'd heard about her boss, but didn't know how she'd respond.

He ventured in slowly, "What was it like to interview with Staunton for your job? He's such a trip."

"Oh, I didn't really have to interview. I'd met him before.

He was a friend – well acquaintance of my father." Lisa paused, "Staunton was on the Agriculture Committee when he was in the Texas State Legislature. My dad was a rancher." She changed the subject.

After talking in some depth on several more topics, they looked up from their world of conversation. The place was packed. Their bar stools were flush together, the room smokier and the music louder. He decided against discussing Chairman Staunton's rumored activities; he didn't want to risk ruining the evening. Lisa was leaning on his knees so they could hear each other. While they listened to a Miles Davis song, he wondered whether he could kiss her later, but then said, "It's really different being here, you know…uhm…with you." *What did that mean? Did he really just say that?* But before he could recover, she leaned into him, clasped his face in her hands and laid a long kiss on his lips – the whole bar as their witness.

They stumbled out of the club around nine o'clock and headed to Nick's apartment. The alcohol was fully absorbed during the short time they'd walked to the street corner by his building. While making out and leaning hard against Nick's door, they fell into his place. He kicked the door closed. Their clothes were off in a matter of seconds and the sex lasted longer and was better than either had expected.

After a silence and drink of water, Lisa semi-panicked, "Hey, where's Mr. Winston?"

"Oh…I…let a friend of mine take him for today and… tomorrow."

"What?"

"Well, she was the next door neighbor to my friend who, you know, died, and she used to take care of him sometimes… and…she misses Winston, and is really good to him…"

"That is so sweet."

Lisa stayed the night. When he awoke early the next

morning, she was already up making coffee.

"Sleep well?" he asked.

"Best in a while which isn't saying much."

"What keeps you awake?"

"I'm gonna be late for work, can I take this cup?"

It turned out Lisa had parked right outside Nick's building before they'd even met for lunch. He watched from his window as she drove away and thought it must be nice to be a woman and actually know ahead of time when you're going to get laid.

———————

At work that morning, Nick was at his desk reliving the evening when Alexi brought him crashing back down to earth. "Sandy's flying in from Florida and wants to meet with you and me ASAP – something must be up. You don't suppose he has surveillance cameras in his house and just checked the film, do you?"

"Funny. No, probably something he heard at the citizens' town meeting."

"Right. Or at the yacht club?" she suggested with a sneer. From her perspective, there was little difference between sworn testimony and social gossip. He was often struck by how cynical Alexi seemed, but attributed it to her having cut her teeth as a reporter. This mischievous South Florida journalist contrasted in so many ways with Lisa, the Ivy League Texas lawyer that he couldn't begin to compare them. He was thankful their relationship hadn't actually crossed the Rubicon and had remained, for the most part, professional.

Congressman Palmer arrived and, after several calls, summoned Alexi and Nick to his office. As they were about to enter, Val cut in front of them from her doorway which adjoined Palmer's door. "Sorry, I just need Sandy for a minute."

Val had become aware of the friendship brewing between

Nick and Alexi and didn't approve. From an office perspective, it weakened her hand, and from an out-of-office perspective, it represented another Florida-based alliance which she envied. Val was born and raised in a fishing camp in Alaska and although she had good DC relationships, had few Florida connections or friends.

Nick just rolled his eyes and indicated he would wait outside Palmer's door. But Alexi gave a look of disgusted boredom, "Tell me when Miss Manners has concluded whatever insignificant prattle with which she's engaged," as she walked away.

When they were finally alone with Palmer, he just stared at them for a moment with a somber expression, "You two enjoy working together?" Palmer was pretty straightforward as politicians went and didn't play games with his staff.

After a pause, they nodded toward each other and then back at him as if guilty as charged.

"Good. Because I want to introduce our *'International Waters'* bill this week. I'm not waiting anymore for a Democratic cosponsor. Nick, get as many Republican cosponsors as you can and we'll plan for introduction on Thursday. Okay by you, Alexi?"

"Yeah, Thursday's good. We'll do a press release that morning and shoot for a local interview on Friday or Saturday." She offered Nick a sideways glance of relief.

"All right – you two keep me posted."

It was technically a *Customs Waters* bill, but Nick couldn't shake Palmer off the international moniker, so he let it slide. He got busy calling the staff of Republican Members of the committee. He knew most of them and had made friends with a few. He walked the bill and memo to several of the offices and talked with staff directly about it. By Thursday morning, he had seven Republican cosponsors for the bill.

He took the bill draft and signature sheet for the cosponsors to Palmer's office along with a speech he'd prepared for him to introduce the bill. While they were talking about what points to emphasize from the speech, the Congressman's scheduler told them that Congressman Clifton of Georgia was on the phone.

Nick asked, "What does he want?"

Palmer picked up the phone, "Hello, sir, what can I do for you? That's correct. I'm introducing a drug enforcement bill. Well, I'd be delighted to have you cosponsor it; you'll be one of about ten. We'll add you to the bill. Thank You!"

Congressman Palmer looked at Nick, "I assume that's all right?"

"Absolutely, we'd hoped to get a Democrat to cosponsor from the beginning."

The scheduler got their attention again to announce that Congressman Tatnall was on the phone. Tatnall was a liberal congressman from New York who chaired the subcommittee where Palmer's bill would be referred for consideration. As Palmer reached for the phone, he looked at Nick, "What's he going to want?"

Nick gave his serious lawyer look and shook his head. It was important to know how to give that look when one didn't know the answer. He'd acquired it while practicing law.

"Hello, Mr. Chairman, how are you? I'm fine, and by the way, I appreciate your remarks at the reception last week regarding our Florida efforts. Well, yes sir, I am introducing a bill today and, yes, it is a drug enforcement bill to be more specific. Well, of course, I'd be delighted to have you as a cosponsor." Palmer looked at Nick and shook his head in puzzlement, "We'll add you to the bill, then. And, thank you, sir."

"Why would Chairman Tatnall want to cosponsor your bill?"

"Makes no sense. He hasn't allowed a hearing or a vote on anything to do with practical law enforcement the whole time

I've been here. But, add his name."

Nick made some more edits and gave Palmer the final draft of his statement for the floor, and the bill with seven Republican cosponsors and two Democrats. Palmer said, "Meet me in the cloakroom off the floor around one o'clock. I'll introduce the bill."

––––––––––

Palmer missed a few words during the bill introduction, but overall it went well. Sandy was really just a down-home Welshman by nature, and not driven by Washington's power or imagery. In his previous life he'd been an architect, and initially run for city council because of frustration with the local zoning board's impact on his practice. Although he lost that campaign, Republicans noticed him and ran him for federal office the following year. Palmer won, only to learn that Congress had no authority over the Flamingo Beach zoning board.

But their credible drug bill was introduced and with some impressive supporters. Nick and Palmer had a celebratory bounce in their step as they walked back to their office, and Nick felt proud to be working for Sandy. A warm sun and early spring leaves welcomed them to cross Independence Avenue outside to the Cannon Building instead of through the dark tunnels running underneath the Capitol. Nick said, "Sandy, this is how a fair process is supposed to work – we introduce a bill, we'll have a hearing on it, debate it and vote it on the floor all in public view. I also like that they say a prayer and pledge to the flag each morning here – maybe we should try that in our courtrooms too." Palmer squinted at Nick and scrunched up his mouth into a smirk.

The next morning, Nick got a call from Ken O'Malley, a Republican counsel on the Senate Judiciary Committee. They'd met at a Supreme Court reception a few weeks before where they'd discussed the differences between House and Senate procedure. Ken was a hard-core surfer from California, but went to law school in Alabama. He now worked for the Chairman of the Senate Judiciary Committee where the Republicans were in the majority; and if one forgot that fact, he'd remind them.

"Hey, Nick, I see your guy introduced a drug enforcement bill."

"Yeah, we've been working with the U.S. Attorney's office in Florida on it for a while."

"Yeah?"

"The criminal defense bar down there has blown a pretty big loophole in an enforcement provision of the U.S. Code."

"So what are your plans for this bill? You think you'll get anywhere with it?"

"I wouldn't have until Chairman Tatnall became a cosponsor."

"He did? Wow, I missed that."

"He's listed with the others on the bill in the Congressional Record."

"So he is – interesting. You'll probably get a call from folks in the Administration on this. Just a heads up. I've got to run – I'll call you back."

Nick was convinced that this was a legislative opportunity to do something good for his country. He'd find a reason to call home and mention the bill's introduction to his parents. Within the hour, he got a call from someone in congressional affairs for the Drug Enforcement Administration. They wanted to come in and talk about the bill. He set a meeting for the following week.

Lisa called that afternoon with passes to hear Jerry Jeff Walker play at a bar in Virginia that night. Lisa was a Texas girl at heart, and although he wasn't originally from there, this guy's songs reminded her of home. She drove to Nick's place where he was changing clothes and drinking a beer.

As he was dressing and talking to Lisa through the closet door, he smelled a strong but familiar aroma. He looked out to see Lisa sitting at his kitchen counter taking a drag off a crumpled cigarette. "What the hell are you doing?"

"Just getting a little buzzed for the show."

"You can't smoke that here!"

"Oh Please – lighten up, dad."

"Lisa, I'm working to pass drug enforcement legislation in the Congress. Your committee works on drug enforcement laws – right? It's too hypocritical. You need to put that out."

"Okay – relax. I'm putting it out. I only smoke about once a year, anyway. I don't think that my smoking on occasion undermines my ability to work on legislation. Are you ready yet? Let's go."

"So collectively it's okay to enforce the law on others, but individually it's a subjective standard depending upon whom we're talking about? That's real consistent."

When Lisa didn't respond, Nick decided to let the subject slide. Ironically he had other things to discuss. On the way, he told Lisa about his day's events, the Subcommittee Chairman's cosponsorship, the Senate committee counsel call, and the DEA meeting he'd set.

"Yeah. We need to talk about that later. There's some stuff you need to know."

"Later? No, tell me now!"

"No! Right now, we're going to hear the only one who can change my perspective on the world 180 degrees. I know you're going to like him." She leaned over wearing a mischievous smile and pinched the inside of his leg.

Nick smiled back, "I guess."

The Birchmere felt like an authentic log cabin and had red-and-white checkered tablecloths. It smelled like barbecue and old saddles and served bottles of Rolling Rock beer in buckets

on ice. And she was right about the musician. He was older than
Nick expected with a ruddy complexion, deep blue eyes, and a
perfect cowboy hat. His voice was friendly and his songs relaxing
– part country, part folk. It washed away Nick's obsession with
legislation or any DEA guys.

After the show, Nick found a quick opportunity to shake
the singer's hand. He was taller than he seemed on stage, "You
make me want to move to Texas."

"It's still there!" he replied with a welcoming gesture.

Lisa raised her eyebrows looking at Nick.

Waking up late next to Lisa the following morning, Nick
scrambled to the door. She lived only a few blocks from the
Capitol so she could get up at eight o'clock and be at work
by eight-thirty. However, Nick had to drive against traffic to
Georgetown, shower and dress, and drive back to the Hill. He
didn't get to work until almost ten o'clock.

Congressman Palmer, who was an early riser, happened to
be standing at the front desk when Nick walked in looking a
little disheveled, "Get lost?"

"Uh, no, I hit a lot of traffic this morning. I think there was
an accident or something on Rock Creek Parkway." Palmer just
smiled. One of the reasons Nick liked working with Palmer was
that although he often could be a stern boss, he had a friendly
sense of humor.

Nick never got a chance to talk with Lisa about the drug
bill, so they met for lunch in the Rayburn cafeteria. He told her
all that had occurred. Lisa, seemed impatient, "Well, the only
reason Tatnall's on your bill is because he wants to have a hand
in anything that Chairman Staunton tries to do for Clifton.
Tatnall and Clifton don't exactly get along. Clifton's a good
ol' boy from Georgia, Staunton's a good old pol from Texas,
and Chairman Tatnall's an inner city liberal lawyer from New
York. My guess is your bill will likely get lots of civil liberties

arguments thrown in its path – maybe for good reason."

"So let me get this straight. One Member got on the bill to help his re-election though he couldn't care less about the issue, and the other got on just to screw with the first one?"

"That's about right."

"And in the meantime, drug dealers are having a field day on the coasts of the U.S., including in my home town. And – what are you doing?"

"Trying to avoid being blinded by your earnestness."

"You're just worried we might shut down your supplier. I'm trying to actually help the people of my home state here, Lisa. We can't just do nothing about this."

"That's touching, but it wouldn't be the first time, Nick. Look, we don't take the Hippocratic Oath here. Members of Congress swear to uphold the Constitution – remember?"

The next day, Nick met with dark-suited men from the DEA. Two had piercing eyes and asked questions. The third had distracting thick glasses and said nothing, but kept moving about the room. They were curious as to how Palmer became interested in the customs waters bill. He reviewed the history of his meetings with the U.S. Attorney's office. They asked if Palmer was working with a Senator to introduce a companion bill. When Nick replied that they were not, the mute one rolled his eyes as if to imply that Palmer and Nick were amateurs.

So he turned the tables on them, "I know that drug enforcement has been a priority of the President's. Will the Administration support our bill? It certainly would help."

The DEA suits just looked at each other and bluntly ignored his question, "Have you been working with anyone in Chairman Staunton's office on this legislation?"

For the first of many times in Washington, Nick felt the vague threat from inquiries about one's political allies, but in this instance he felt threatened both for himself and for Lisa.

He responded quickly, "No, we haven't worked with any Democratic Members. In fact, we were shocked when Subcommittee Chairman Tatnall and Congressman Clifton cosponsored the bill. So, will the Administration endorse our bill? Would it help if I had the Congressman write the White House and copy your boss to seek support?"

"We'll get back to you on that. Frankly, as I'm sure you're aware, the chances of this bill going anywhere are pretty slim. You don't really expect the majority to give you a hearing on it do you?" They thanked Nick for his time.

8

Early May 1985   Georgetown   59 Degrees Dark

That Thursday night, Nick asked Alexi to meet him for a drink in Georgetown. She was flying in from Flamingo Beach where she'd been working in the district office all week. Alexi showed up tanned and beaming like she'd emerged from a health spa. She wasn't anywhere near as serious about politics as Lisa Castile. Lisa was a substantive lawyer who thought she was making a difference; Alexi was a fun loving reporter who considered the whole process a game.

"So, how was Florida or dare I ask?"

"It was great!"

They sat in cushy oversized chairs in the bar at the Four Seasons Hotel on M Street. The low lighting and spacious seating around intermittent hard-wood floors made it seem more private than it was.

"Did you actually get any work done or just go to the beach?"

"Oh, don't be silly. I got lots of work done – at the beach! Saw your friend, Quartel, the cloture judge – love that story. He says hello, asked how you were. I lied, told him you were fine. And, what's with you, honey? You look a little rattled."

Nick explained his disappointing meeting with the DEA guys, their ambivalent reaction to Palmer's bill, and odd questions.

"That is strange. I would've assumed a Republican White House would support your bill – especially this President's Administration."

"Yeah, you'd think."

"Well, keep working on them – there's more than one way to skin a cat. I have to run."

"Have to run? Run where?"

"I have a date."

"A date? Now?"

"Yeah."

"With who?"

"None of your biz, dear. But thanks for the drink."

He'd just ordered another rum and tonic, so downed it and walked out with Alexi. They went their separate ways once outside the building; and as darkness fell he took the long way home down a less crowded than usual M Street.

While walking up a cobblestone alleyway between the colonial buildings off Wisconsin Avenue, Nick came upon a black limousine parked tight against one of the old brick walls. A door on one side of the idling car was partially open and gasoline exhaust held thick in the humid spring air. The alley was so narrow he turned almost sideways in order to try to pass. As he started, the middle door swung open, and an older man stumbled out against the wall. An Hispanic man also stepped out and stood in the light from the car's interior with his arm draped over the door.

Between the two voices, one sounded familiar. "You just keep those gateways open so our guys can work, old friend, and no chits ever need be collected – *comprendes*?"

"Loud and clear, *amigo*; don't bother yourself worryin' 'bout my end of things. Ya'll go ahead – I'll walk from here."

The Hispanic shook his head in disgust and then glanced into the dark toward the back of the car at Nick. Nick turned away and put his hands up as if to say, "Don't look at me."

The door slammed shut and the limo pulled away. The disheveled man slumped against the wall with his hands on his knees. Nick realized it was Chairman John Staunton. He didn't know whether to offer help or hide his face and walk away. Staunton hadn't noticed him so when Nick spoke, he jumped a foot in the air.

"You all right, sir?"

"Oh...just fine, son. I'm fine."

"You need a hand?" Staunton was staring into the cobblestones as if looking for something. Nick could see he was drunk. His shirttails were out, his eyes bloodshot, and he seemed exhausted.

"No. But ya know what, son? If you're inclined to help a stranger, I could use five bucks for a cab."

He was slightly offended, but very much relieved that Staunton hadn't recognized him, "Oh sure, man, here you go," as he handed him a five dollar bill. "There should be a cab at the end of the alleyway."

"Thanks, I'll find one," mumbled Staunton as he squinted toward Nick for the first time, then looked down again.

Nick returned down the alley retracing his steps, and then circled around the block to see where Staunton went. When he came around the corner, a cab pulled away. He looked in, but it was empty. As he started toward home, he saw a cleaned up Staunton coming out of a 7-Eleven with a beer in one hand and a cigarette in the other. Nick slowed his pace so he could stay behind. They walked toward P Street where they both lived. Nick kept his distance as Staunton limped along drinking his beer. Then Staunton clumsily dropped the half-empty can and after first looking toward his neighbors' homes, kicked it to the curb. Nick watched him go through the gates of his palatial house.

Nick was dumbfounded. He walked to his apartment, got some iced tea from his fridge, and sat at his desk. "Who the hell *is* this guy?" he said to no one. He was convinced he needed to talk with Lisa about her boss, and soon. The Hispanic man's stern face was etched in his mind. He looked a lot like that popular television journalist whose name he could never remember. But his hair was straighter and parted in the middle and he had dull blue eyes.

The next morning, Nick called his Senate friend, Ken O'Malley, to see if he would meet him after work to discuss his less than inspiring DEA meeting.

O'Malley gave a knowing laugh, "You mean those guys didn't leave you with a warm and fuzzy feeling about your bill?"

"Not exactly."

"I'll meet you at Bullfeathers at six o'clock."

They ordered drinks at the bar which had an old pub feel to it and smelled of stale beer. Nick started in, "So what's those guys' problem? Wouldn't you think they'd want to help a Republican Member move a drug enforcement bill?"

"Well, not exactly."

"Why?"

"Look dude, some of these career *jamokes* don't care so much about enforcement policy as they do about protecting their jobs. You think they don't have legislation they've been working on for years they'd like to see moved? A bill that has their fingerprints all over it – legislation they've not been able to get introduced much less a Democrat to cosponsor? They're probably scratching their heads raw trying to figure out how you got the Subcommittee Chairman on your bill."

"Well, so what? I don't care if they share credit for this. I'll say it was those *jamokes'* idea if they want." Nick had never heard that term before, but liked it.

Ken chuckling, "Look, that won't work; they know that's not the case. You think those guys want to owe a favor to some upstart rookie from Florida? If I were you, I'd forget the DEA. Just try to get a hearing on it, create some momentum, and watch them come around. The subcommittee will seek the Justice Department's testimony if they hold a hearing. Justice will go to DEA and ask for their input; and what do you think the politicals at the Drug Enforcement Agency are going to do, come out against your bill?"

"Good point."

He was impressed by the likely accuracy of Ken's cynical calculation. "Hey, you mind if I ask another question?"

"Ask away."

"Why would the DEA care if I was working with anyone in Chairman Staunton's office on this legislation?"

"Are you?"

"Well ... no, but why would they care?"

"I don't know man, but you do pick up some bizarre rumors in this town about Staunton *and* his staff."

"What kind of rumors?"

"Oh, you know — just about wild shit going on, parties with hookers and drugs in some bungalow he's supposed to have."

"Where?"

"I'm not sure ... somewhere in Maryland I think. Hey, I've got to run. My girlfriend and I are headed to the Eastern Shore for the weekend. You'll probably get a call from the Coast Guard folks on this too. Good luck — keep me posted."

———————

That evening, Nick and Lisa ate at Clyde's in Georgetown and saw the movie, *Witness,* starring Harrison Ford, about a boy who witnesses a crime and doesn't know who to tell. In a relatively short time Nick and Lisa had become comfortable together and some people knew they were dating. They ordered hot chocolate afterwards at an outdoor café. He was torn between the seemingly opposing concepts of nurturing their growing relationship or coming clean with what he knew about her boss.

He finally said a little too urgently, "Lisa, there's something I've wanted to talk about for a while."

Lisa, looking at her nails, smiled, "I'm listening."

Nick glanced past her to the neighboring tables, "It's about your boss – it's serious."

"Oh, this should be good. The rumors have been repeated a thousand times. I'm occasionally oblivious, Nick, but not blind. I can assure you they're exaggerated."

He proceeded to recount his discussion with Major Ity. Having rehearsed this conversation in his head many times so as not to miss any facts, he went through point by point about Staunton's finances and the alleged yacht near Annapolis. He continued into the Major's background, his involvement on the board of several banks, and his intelligence community experience.

As Lisa was absorbing these facts, he let go with his other evidence. He explained his encounter with the limousine, Staunton falling down in the alleyway, the Hispanic man, and the cryptic conversation between them. He also told about loaning him five bucks for a cab which he used to buy a beer that night. Nick described the Latino's face as familiar to him, and indicated how disrespectful he'd been toward the Chairman.

Lisa didn't say anything. For a while she only stared intensely at Nick. Then looked around, shook her head, and fidgeted in her chair.

He continued, "I didn't know how to tell you this, and for a while simply didn't want to ..."

"Are you out of your mind? You really expect me to believe this? Your friend, the Major, is an eccentric old nut – and you're listening to him? You're such a right-winger. You just buy it all hook, line and sinker, don't you? Everyone knows Staunton's got a healthy appetite for alcohol, but your attempt to turn his association with apparently wealthy foreigners into some full-blown conspiracy is ridiculous!"

"No one's blowing it up into a conspiracy. But, I think it's worth considering and acknowledging."

"What, that my boss is some kind of a crook?"

"Well, he's got some fairly odd facts surrounding his finances and has somewhat questionable conversations with foreigners about chits being owed. Are you aware of any problems regarding his finances – personal or campaign related?"

"Who are you, Sherlock-fucking-Holmes all of a sudden? Give me a break. I've heard enough of this bullshit. You think Congressman Palmer and all your little Republican Members are so squeaky clean? Are all Democrats suspect in your world and Republicans above reproach?"

"I didn't say anything like that. If you don't want to hear it, that's your right. Let's just change the subject."

"Change the subject? After those accusations about my boss? The person who's responsible for my being in Washington? Right!"

He planted his hands on the table, "Listen, if it's even partially true – then what? I'm not trying to provoke you. I'm trying to protect you."

"You know what? I need to leave. Have a nice night. And, don't call me – okay?"

Nick watched her walk away. He'd no idea what had happened.

9

June 1985   Capitol Hill   71 Degrees Raining

Nick had lost his girlfriend and probably his best friend. He hadn't spoken to Lisa since he saw her briefly at a meeting where she'd ignored him and looked the other way. He was naive not to calculate how threatening his findings might be to her. If they were true and became public, Staunton could lose his congressional seat, and Lisa would be out of a job.

His existence in Washington became painfully routine. His one room apartment even seemed empty, and if he read one more constituent letter or ate one more bland meal at the Rayburn cafeteria, he might drop dead of boredom. But he received an unexpected call from a friend in Flamingo Beach who was traveling to DC for business. His friend, Jonas, was a securities broker whom Nick had once represented in a contract dispute. Nick allowed the brokerage house to keep its commission on a large sale of stock for which a customer claimed she'd never given permission. He'd matched the firm's phone company records with the timing of the New York Stock Exchange's bid and sale of the stock, and the parties settled.

They had dinner and talked much of the night about Flamingo. They recalled how they would go for a run after work to stay in shape and then drink rum and tonics made with fresh limes picked from the neighbor's trees. The evening was a good diversion although it reminded Nick of the many friends he had in Florida and how few he felt he could count on in Washington.

A diversion of a grander scale also came his way. The Select Committee on Narcotics Enforcement was planning a congressional delegation trip or "Codel." The Chairman of the Select Committee was a liberal from New Jersey who wasn't opposed to showboating for the media. He'd caught wind of recent polls detailing how concerned Americans were becoming about illegal immigrants smuggling narcotics into the U.S. It presented an excellent excuse for a trip with good press and photo-ops depicting a Congress engaged in the war on drugs.

The Committee's itinerary would take the delegation through the southwest to hold hearings and meet with the Mexican Federales. Democrats needed one more Republican to make the trip bipartisan. Palmer was asked to fill in at the last minute. Each Representative was allowed to bring one staffer and Palmer tapped Nick for the job. While initially excited, Nick discovered the places they'd be visiting were not the Chamber of Commerce's top picks, but the dusty border towns like Nogales, Arizona and El Paso, Texas where one might be confused as to which country they were in.

He had twelve hours to pack and be at Andrews Air Force Base for departure. The plane they would be traveling in during the five day trip was previously used as Air Force One. It was a hefty white and royal blue four-engine jet with "United States of America" emblazoned in black letters down both sides of the fuselage. The first cabin where the congressmen sat had large leather chairs and couches with coffee tables, wet bars, phones, and televisions. The second cabin was more like the first-class cabin of a commercial jet but with oversized cushy seats and an extra wide center aisle. The plane was staffed by sharp Air Force personnel.

Nick staked out a window seat. As they departed toward the northwest he gazed down onto the Latin cross connecting the White House, and the Jefferson memorial, the Capitol and the Washington and Lincoln memorials. They were served eggs benedict for breakfast on fine china. A staffer older than Nick occupied the seat beside him. He was with a Congressman from New York. John or "Jonne," as he was quick to specify, told of how he'd grown up in Westchester County and gone to Yale. Nick would later learn that Jonne actually grew up in the Bronx, and though briefly attended Yale, actually graduated from New York University. Nick had heard embellished resumes many times in Washington. It was an indication to him that Jonne was both insecure and anxious to impose his over-credentialed guidance on an unsuspecting America.

The first stop was Texas where a police escort whisked them to a dilapidated building on the border near Juarez. They were briefed by the U.S. Border Patrol who explained the difficulty in tracking smugglers. It was evident that the approximately 2,000 mile border separating the U.S. from Mexico was basically open to anyone willing to cross. While careful with their language, it became obvious that the border was so undermanned they couldn't pretend to stop the flow of illegal immigrants or narcotics; and considering their limited equipment, they were barely able even to monitor the illegal activity.

The trip would prove particularly timely for Congressman Palmer who'd fought hard during his first years in Congress to increase federal funding for drug interdiction efforts. He believed that the illegal narcotics problem would improve if the government could at least stem the flood of drugs coming into the U.S. This theory had become known in policy circles as the "Supply-Side" Drug War.

However, they'd recently been briefed by representatives of a think tank in Washington who speculated that no amount of money or manpower could stop the flow of drugs so long as the seemingly open-ended demand for them existed. They argued that the only way to stop the influx of drugs was to cut demand for them within the U.S. They advocated for stronger penalties for users, drug testing and high-visibility anti-drug public service campaigns — the tools of the new so-called "Demand-Side" Drug War. Although Palmer was reluctant to give up on interdiction efforts, the facts to be uncovered on this trip would go a long way toward changing his mind.

The second leg of the trip took them to Nogales, Arizona,

another dusty town unaffected by tourist dollars. At a checkpoint on the border, they received a joint briefing by the U.S. Border Patrol and officers of the Mexican Federales. The quick take away from that briefing, despite their hopeful words, was that this area of the border was completely out of control, the United States could do nothing about it, and the Federales didn't quite see what the problem was.

After staying overnight in Tucson where they ate Mexican food and drank big margaritas, they headed to San Diego, California. A morning hearing was held at the local county building where nervous federal, state, and local agents subtly begged for help with the border. The unspoken reality of their desperation for money and manpower was only slightly less palpable than their reluctance to acknowledge its hopelessness.

Before departing for a tour along the border between San Diego and Tijuana, Palmer called Nick aside and complained, "This is unbelievable. This border situation is a disaster – not just the illegal drugs, but the millions of illegal immigrants coming in!"

"I know. But nobody wants to talk about it."

"Why aren't we talking about *it*? Left unchecked, these operations could grow into powerful criminal cartels.[3] Why isn't the media reporting on this?"

"Well, one, *it* is not very sexy, and two, *some* in Congress would just as soon let them continue to come in."

"Why? There are stringers covering this trip, why aren't they filing stories on what we're seeing here?"

"Sandy, the illegal workers help powerful constituents pick the crops – and they vote."

"What? They can't vote. They're not citizens."

"You wanna bet?"

Palmer nodded toward the reception desk, "The man over there wearing the beige windbreaker is head of the Border Patrol. I want you to walk him away from the group and arrange a private tour tonight for you and me to see what they call the soccer field where apparently many cross into California at night. And, don't let him give you any push-back. I want it tonight, and I don't want any press or other staff there. I want to hear them say what they really want to tell us."

That night after the delegation's gourmet dinner on the patio of the Del Coronado Hotel, Palmer and Nick slipped out to meet border agents in a jeep by the lobby entrance. They traveled to a remote dirt road atop a ridge looking south onto a vast desert valley. After explaining how the area was active with illegal crossings, the head agent described the sad condition of the would-be immigrants. He talked about the inhumanity of their enablers, the so-called coyotes, who promise a safe crossing and new life in the U.S. then rob them of their money and dignity at the border.

Around midnight, the agents handed Palmer and Nick infrared-heat binoculars and pointed to small huddles of people in the distance. They watched the infrared lighted huddles move surreptitiously closer to the border and then cross at different points.

Palmer asked, "Aren't you going to arrest those people?"

"No. We'll pick a few of them up further east in order to discourage others, but we really have nowhere to take them."

"What do you mean *nowhere* to take them?"

"Congressman, the holding facility in San Diego is full. It doesn't much matter; the authorities there will only detain them for a night or two, try to identify them, and then just drop them back across the border."

"That's it?"

"That's it."

"Unbelievable."

An INS truck pulled up with three young Mexican men in back. They'd been apprehended fifteen miles east. They stood beside the truck, exhausted, thirsty, and bewildered. Two of the men looked to be in their early twenties, the other about fifteen years old. The youngest had, without a doubt, the saddest big brown eyes Nick had ever seen. Palmer considered trying to ask some questions, but declined. Nick caught the boy's eye and unsuccessfully attempted a facial expression of both sympathy and reassurance. The men were returned to the truck to begin their process into a bureaucrat-driven legal system only somewhat less in control of their fate than had they made it across and tried to remain unnoticed within the fringes of an unlawful economy.

Palmer shook his head, "That's pathetic, and no way for anyone to come into this country."

The agent replied, "They have a dream, Congressman, to come here for a better life. They've borrowed money from their families or sold their homes to risk it all on this journey."

As they prepared to head back, Nick asked, "How many people do you estimate have come across through this area?"

"We estimate that in the past seventy-two hours, somewhere between twenty and thirty thousand people crossed this sixty mile stretch of border."

"WHAT?" Palmer barked. "What did you say?"

"Twenty to thirty thousand, sir."

Palmer looked at Nick, and Nick back at Palmer; they looked at the agent in disbelief.

"You can't be serious?"

"Congressman, with all due respect, if you ask me to repeat that for the record, I won't. We've heard the Justice Department is creating a task force to help us down here. Maybe it will make a difference."

The ride back was mostly silent. Sandy Palmer stared out the window, occasionally jotting down notes.

Turning into the entrance of the hotel, the agent spoke up, "I know those numbers are surprising to you sir, but you should know these smugglers are well organized. Many illegals go back across the border within weeks to deliver cash, food, or medicine to their families. But they'll usually come back across. The fact is this border is extremely porous; we have no way to know how many stay – and we have no idea who they are."

The next day, the jet headed to Mexico City where the delegation would meet with the head of the Federales, and have dinner at the U.S. Ambassador's home. As they broke through the clouds over northern Mexico, Jonne was blathering on again about some political theory. Having briefly worked as an assistant professor, he was apparently accustomed to a captive audience. Nick, ignoring him once again, looked out the window and reviewed his last few months. He'd managed to have worthwhile legislation introduced, was doing well in Palmer's office, and had developed a relationship with a woman about whom he truly cared. That woman wasn't returning his calls or acknowledging he existed, but Nick was hopeful it wasn't completely over.

Looking on the clouds below, Nick thought of Lisa and considered the possibility he could be wrong about Staunton. In his gut he felt intuitively right, but he didn't have any real proof. He respected the Major, but thought how uncircumspect he may have been about Ity's sources. So what if Staunton got drunk with Latinos in limousines? The more he thought about Lisa, the more he believed she might be right, maybe he was jumping to conclusions. Staunton did have a reputation for cards and drinking which he'd perfected while serving as a Navy Lieutenant in WW II. Nick actually liked that about him – he was kind of an old-school iconic character.

He decided to write Lisa a letter and try to mend the rift he'd caused. Finding the stationery he'd taken from his room at the hotel, he began his brilliant *mea culpa* manifesto. He thought about all the reasons he missed her – she was the sexiest, most accomplished woman he'd ever dated; and although he didn't really trust her, he was in love with her.

After a lunch of lobster Newburg, Nick went to the front cabin to chat with Palmer. Some Members were playing cards and drinking champagne. Palmer was talking with the only other Republican member on the trip at the front of the cabin. He gestured for Nick to join them. They were discussing their distrust of the Federales, and how convinced they were that the Mexican government was facilitating drug smuggling. They spoke of reports that Federales may have been involved in the disappearance of a DEA agent in Mexico, and strategized on whether to reference them in their meetings later that day.

It was raining and foggy when they landed in Mexico City. While departing the plane, Nick handed his letter to the Air Force attendant and asked it be placed in their priority mail. They were driven rapidly through the streets to an ornate government building in the middle of the city. Unfortunately, one of the members of the Select Committee, apparently due to a combination of the rich lunch and roller-coaster ride from the airport wasn't feeling well. He stepped out of the van and threw up on the front steps of the Federales' headquarters. It was an inauspicious beginning to a less than cordial visit with their southern neighbors.

The delegation was invited into a richly decorated room and served strong Mexican coffee. The Federales' uniforms were official with colorful medals and patches. Unfortunately for their hosts, the congressmen's frustrations with the briefings so far were transitioning into feelings of disrespect toward the Mexican government's efforts to stop smuggling.

The first speaker at the briefing had barely finished a sentence when the conservative California congressman interrupted him, "Why aren't you doing anything to stop the flow of drugs into the U.S. from Mexico? We've listened to your men along the border mince words and make excuses for days. We want answers."

Most were surprised by the bluntness of the question and its accusatory tone. The Mexican Captain in charge, Sanchez, was so taken aback, he asked to have the question translated to him twice – despite that he spoke perfect English.

Captain Sanchez attempted to smooth things over and start anew, "First, again, let me welcome you to our country and tell you how pleased we are that Members of the United States Congress have traveled here so that our two great countries may work together on law enforcement matters and fight against the evils of drugs and drug smuggling."

The Californian wasn't buying it. "Can you tell us sir, why your men aren't stopping smugglers coming into the U.S.? The evidence is so clear it's embarrassing."

He was interrupted by the U.S. Delegation's Chairman, "Captain Sanchez, thank you for meeting with us and for your warm welcome. Please continue with your briefing and we'll have some questions when you're finished," as he glared at his Republican colleague. The Californian just waved him off like he was wasting everyone's time.

Sanchez observed that exchange and was clearly unnerved. It seemed like someone had shut off the air-conditioning. The Captain shifted his papers on the podium and wiped his brow, "No, that is satisfactory Mr. Chairman, let's just go to your questions."

Nick nudged his Democratic colleague, "All right! This should be good."

Jonne looked back disparagingly, "Grow up."

But Nick would not hear another word of the briefing. As the captain shuffled his papers and was about to speak again, his right-hand man walked to the side of the podium and handed him a fresh set of papers with tabs on the sides. Nick noticed the lieutenant's ornate uniform then went blank when he turned forward and smiled at the delegation. There was no mistaking it. This was the same man he'd seen in the dark alleyway that night in Georgetown with Chairman Staunton – a familiar face, but with straighter hair, parted in the middle and dull blue eyes.

He was paralyzed in his seat, and stared blankly as the guy sat back down. He knew it was him, yet having been temporarily infected by Staunton's allure, was hoping against hope that it wasn't. The captain ended his statement and went to questions, but all Nick heard was a vague background noise "Drug smuggling is blah, blah, blah ... " Before he knew it, the briefing ended. There were no warm embraces; everyone just headed for the exit. He found himself standing next to Palmer as they filed out. The lieutenant was in the doorway bidding Members farewell. Palmer shook his hand and thanked him. Nick stared as he shuffled past on the opposite side.

"Hey, that guy looks just like that guy – what's his name on TV– doesn't he?" asked Palmer. "What's his name?"

Nick looked at Palmer in despair, "Yeah, he does."

"What happened, you and Congressman Moore eat the same thing for lunch? Although he drank half his lunch, you look like you're about to lose yours too. Well, just promise me you won't hurl in the van. I'm afraid we all will if one does."

Then he put his hand on Nick's shoulder, "Hey, you really don't look so good."

"I'm okay. But, can we talk later about something I learned at that briefing? It's important."

"Sure, maybe when we get to the hotel."

––––––––––

The remainder of the trip was uneventful. Nick never saw the lieutenant again and he never found the right opportunity to unload his theory on Palmer. He started at one point during cocktails at the U.S. Ambassador's home, but they were interrupted. When he began again before dinner, he realized he didn't have time to tell the whole complicated story without rushing and sounding like a nut.

Sandy's frustration with the reality on the border dominated their conversation back to Washington. He was stunned that neither Congress nor the Reagan Administration were doing anything to stop the hemorrhaging there, and believed Washington would only understand the implications if they began to impact DC directly.[4] Nick understood that sometimes the less aware of some facts people remain, the better prepared they may be to continue on with the ordinary purposes of life. But he was hopeful that at some point, major newspapers and networks would realize the country's southern border was crumbling into thin air and perhaps then the rest of America might wake up.[5]

The Congressman had learned more about funding for a Justice Department border project, and asked Nick to look into it. He believed it could be authorized by his committee through the immigration bill, but knew they would face a tough battle for the actual federal dollars in the Appropriations Committee. While Nick agreed with Palmer that failing to address the open border was a fundamental mistake and he would do whatever he could to help, neither could have predicted the degree to which the consequences of that failure would later divide America.[6]

10

Late June 1985   Georgetown   89 Degrees Hazy

Exiting a cab, he paused to retrieve two $20 tickets off his car, then lugged his suitcase up the narrow flights of a humid stairwell and settled back into his apartment. While unpacking, he checked his answering machine. There were messages from the usual suspects, Moxley, Alexi, one from his friend, Ken O'Malley, about golfing with some lobbyists, and then the one he'd hoped to hear. It was Lisa. She'd said, in a friendly but somber voice, "Nick, it's Lisa. I got your letter. That was really nice of you. You're a good letter writer, but I did want to..." The message was cut off before she'd finished.

He said to the wall, "You're kidding me. Did she hang up – did the machine break?"

After a cold beer, reviewing more un-payable bills, and guessing at potential message conclusions, he telephoned his friend, Ren, back in Florida to consult on the whole Lisa quandary. Ren, through his many experiences, was as close to an expert on women's behavior as a guy could be – which wasn't really saying much.

He reviewed the history of his relationship with Lisa to his confidante who went right to work. It was fortunate Nick caught him sipping a cocktail, which usually enhanced his abilities to offer advice. He could picture his prematurely white-haired friend, drink in hand, throwing his Scottish grin out over the Intracoastal waterway that meandered past his back porch.

Ren began, "Now that's a tough one. First, we've got to get some basics down. How'd you meet her?"

"On the Hill."

"She works there?"

"Yeah."

"And you work there?"

"Yes."

"You know the rules on that. You work with her?"

"No. No, the Hill is Congress, it's a big place. She's in a totally different office." He could hear the ice sliding as Ren took another sip from an almost empty glass.

"Now, this is important. I'm trying to establish if you'll see her or come across her anytime soon."

"Well, I could, but it's also just as likely that I won't for a while. It depends."

"Uhmmm...what were the last words she said, the last time you actually saw her?"

Nick didn't want to go into all the details about Chairman Staunton, "Well, after an argument about something, she just said: *You know what? I need to leave. Have a nice night. And don't call me.*"

"Very direct – I like her. How long ago was this little episode?"

"About three weeks."

"And what were you talking about when she got so mad – generally speaking?"

"Oh, it was just work-related stuff."

"I thought you said you don't work together?"

"Well, it's not that cut and dried. It wasn't exactly work-related."

"Taft, I'd hate to see you on a witness stand."

"Look, just tell me what you think."

"Well...women are tricky. She could have been saying, *you're a good letter writer, but I still want you to fuck off and never call me again.*"

"Great."

"Or she could have been saying, *you're a good letter writer, but I want to hear you say it to my face?"*

"Better."

"Or she could have been saying, *you write well, but I still want all my shit back . . . "*

"Wonderful."

Call-waiting clicked in. He asked Ren to hold.

"Hello."

"Nick, it's Regina. There's something I just have to tell you."

"Oh, Moxley, hey, I'm on the other line. Can I call you back?"

"Yeah. But don't forget. The oddest thing happened to me and Sir Winston today. You'll want to hear this – trust me."

"Yeah, yeah, okay. I'll call you right back." In addition to ill-preparing her to aptly argue politics, Moxley's education apparently disarmed her from stating anything succinctly – it was simply impossible to have a brief conversation with her. In truth, he wasn't sure it was fair to blame her university. Moxley's pharmacological consumption during her nearly decade long undergraduate studies could have dazed a small town for years.

He clicked the phone back to Ren. "Okay, so what's your bottom line here?"

Nick could hear his friend stirring the ice of a new cocktail. "Well . . . it's complicated. The fact that she called is a good sign. That she was willing to leave you a message is also positive. If she truly didn't want to have anything to do with you, she wouldn't have called. Chicks do that, you know. Sometimes they just walk away. But she's not really doing that."

"So . . . ?"

"So, here's my advice. Don't call her. You're in the dark on what she actually said. Last thing you want to do with a woman is presume anything. Just wait until you see her and see how she reacts. If she alludes to the phone message, look surprised and tell her your answering machine's broken. It might be broken, right?"

"Yeah, might be. Hmmm...I guess that's good advice. You usually know these things. All right, that's what I'm gonna do."

"And figure out a way to run into her. I want to hear how this turns out."

––––––––––

Thursday morning started off hot and muggy. Rush-hour traffic moved slower than usual. When Nick got to work, Barb was standing guard as always, "Good mornin', Congressman Sanderson Palmer's office, hold please." She switched lines, smiling at Nick, "Good mornin', sorry to keep you waiting, how may I help you? Oh, I don't really know what music is playing when people are on hold. I've never actually heard it myself. Well, I'm sorry for that...uh huh, I'll be sure and tell him. Well, you have a nice day now – okay?"

Alexi and Val came out from the back office. Alexi asked Nick with much enthusiasm, "So, how was your cool trip with Sandy to Mexico? Did you and Sandy down some margaritas together?" she asked with a cheeky grin.

Val gave a strained smile and hurried into her office. Alexi put her hand on Nick's arm and pulled close, then only half whispered, "Val's been in a total snit about that whole trip. She's so jealous – it's hysterical. Ever since you left, she's been trying to downplay its significance."

He rolled his eyes and smiled.

Alexi said, "Sandy's over at the Rayburn Building at a meeting of the committee Republicans, something about a shakeup on a subcommittee ratio. He wants you to meet him over there."

He looked briefly at the constituent mail stacked on his desk, then headed to the meeting. Nick moved quickly through the now-familiar underground tunnels and escalators toward

Rayburn, choosing to stay inside the well air-conditioned buildings. He had to maneuver between the mail carts and garbage bins throughout the basement of the Longworth Building as he hurried past the warm, humid air pouring in from the loading dock. When he came to the elevators in Rayburn, the doors were just closing, "Could you hold the door please?"

A hand reached out and pulled the door back. Nick slid in, "Thanks." But as he looked up, he realized it was Alec Sivore, Staunton's Chief of Staff, and next to him in the small elevator was the even taller Chairman Staunton, and behind him, backed into a corner, was Lisa.

Staunton looked at Nick, "You just made it, young man. Good thing Alec here has some manners. I'd a let the door slam shut on ya myself," as he smiled and winked.

Alec gave Nick a dismissive glance.

Nick smiled and then pushed number one on the button panel. Levels B and 2 were already lit up which he noticed since it was just Staunton and his staff in the rapidly shrinking space. He looked at his watch and then over at Lisa. She shot him a look that could have killed an elephant. Nick was taken aback, but before he could respond, the elevator opened. Staunton and Sivore stepped out. Staunton looked back at Lisa, "Alrighty then, darlin', we'll see you back at the office."

The doors closed, but before he could speak, Lisa let loose, "You bastard!"

"What?"

"I met your girlfriend yesterday."

"Who?"

"Oh please! And after I left you that ridiculously sweet message. No wonder you didn't call me back. It must have been awkward after she told you – hmmm?"

"What are you talking about?"

The elevator doors opened again and Lisa stepped out,

looking straight ahead.

"Lisa, wait! You're making a mistake. You've got this really wrong – I swear." But Lisa just kept walking forward. "Will you just talk to me for one second?"

Lisa wheeled around with her hand on her hip. "Ten seconds."

Nick stepped out. "Who'd you meet and why do you think she's my girlfriend?"

"Regina Moxley? The leggy redhead who Mr. Winston belongs to? She picked him from his litter in Middleburg and has owned him ever since? Oh, and who she sort of shares with Nick Taft because they're so close – they've known each other since their college years? 'Oh, we're sort of like brother and sister at this point, but you know how it goes when you've known someone that long!' Yeah, Mr. Winston's your dog. Man, am I gullible or what?"

Nick's failure to return Moxley's call the night before suddenly weighed on him. "Lisa, you've got this all backwards. Moxley was my cousin's college roommate in California. She occasionally visited my relatives in Florida. She isn't my girlfriend. Are you kidding me?"

Lisa started to turn away down the long crowded hallway behind her.

He caught up beside her, "Okay, listen. Sir Winston is her dog. The only reason I told you that was because you seemed to like him so much, and I ... really wanted to get to know you ... so that part was made up about his owner ... being, uh ..."

"Dead! You said she was dead."

"Yeah, I did say that."

Lisa stared at him and then with moist eyes, looked down the empty hallway in front of her.

It was the first time Lisa had outwardly shown any emotion for Nick. He was relieved at that development and wanted to tell her he loved her, but instead said, "I've really missed you."

She replied curtly, "Then why didn't you return my call? Did you even listen to my message?"

"I could only hear the first few words ... it was impossible to tell what you'd said other than you got my letter, then the message just stopped. I think ... it's broken."

"Are you an idiot?"

"What? No! I picked it up yesterday after returning from Mexico."

"Well, couldn't you have just called back to ask what I had said?"

"You can listen to the machine if you want."

"She's your *cousin's* friend?"

"Yes, she even calls me her adopted cousin."

Lisa, slightly smiling, "Well, maybe I'll have to listen to that message myself."

"Fine. When should we go?" Sliding his hand around her waist, "Now?"

"No." Lisa pushed him away. "Maybe after work – maybe."

She walked off in a businesslike manner toward her office.

11

Same Day   Capitol Hill   92 Degrees Sticky

Upon arriving at the meeting, Nick's mood was brighter than it had been in weeks. The meeting, called by the ranking Republican was to announce the departure of a senior member and fill the now empty ranking slot on one of the subcommittees. Congressman Grybek, a conservative from Pennsylvania, had succeeded in his bid to become a member of the highly sought after Ways & Means Committee where the country's tax policies originate. Consequently, he had to give up his seat on the Judiciary Committee. Congressman Palmer was next highest in seniority which allowed him to become the ranking Republican on the Subcommittee on the Constitution if he so desired.

In Congress, as in any other political body, it only makes sense to accept a senior position if it comes with some power and leverage. Palmer decided to take the position and along with it, the right to have his own counsel on the committee. Nick couldn't wait to tell his dad of his promotion. However, to actually accomplish that job change, Palmer was asked to consult with the Chief Minority Counsel, the long-serving and notorious, Denny Folgier.

Folgier was a tough conservative who'd fought the Democrats tooth and nail his entire career. He was smart, politically savvy, and hardened by years of being in the minority. Denny had scraped forever just so Republicans could simply offer amendments, only to lose every time in the Democrat-dominated Congress. Such experiences have a way of sharpening one's senses of distrust and dislike as well as honing one's skills at analysis and process. He guarded his committee staff closely, and didn't take kindly to giving up a counsel slot to just anyone much less some kid whose boss simply happened to rise in seniority one day.

Fortunately, Nick had a few things going for him. One, Folgier liked Palmer. Two, the counsel whose place he might be taking was already thinking of leaving. And three, Nick and Folgier had already worked together on one of Palmer's amendments and had gotten along okay.

Palmer told him to wait in the ante room while he met with the full committee ranking Member and Folgier to discuss his ascendancy to the subcommittee ranking slot. Palmer had a worn-out look when he emerged from the meeting.

"Denny Folgier wants to meet with you after lunch to discuss your potential counsel position."

"What do you mean discuss? Is it like an interview?"

"Yes, consider it an interview."

As they walked back to the Cannon Building, he congratulated Palmer on his new title. Palmer said he thought it could be a good opportunity and reiterated that he'd like to have his own counsel there to work with him. "Folgier can be kind of tough. Be sure to let him know you've practiced law and been in a courtroom."

"Do you think he wants me working over there?"

"I don't know. He seemed a little out of sorts about the whole thing."

"Oh, wonderful."

"Don't worry. You'll do fine. You realize if you're able to work for the committee, Folgier will be your boss and you'll be on their payroll."

"Right," he said as if he understood. But in reality, he'd no idea of the changes ahead for him or how central to his future this move would be.

"We'll still be working together, but you'll answer directly to the Republican ranking Member and indirectly to Chairman John Staunton, who controls the budget."

"But, I'll be a Republican counsel."

"Yes. But this majority controls every committee and all the money, and they have since 1955!"

Nick had never been to the committee's minority office in the basement of the Rayburn Building but found it with no trouble. The assistants to the minority counsels all sat at open desks in the front office. When he introduced himself, all three smiled in a vaguely indifferent manner. As Folgier opened his office door and asked him to step in, the assistant whose desk was closest caught Nick's eye and gave a wary look with a raised eyebrow.

Folgier's office had an apolitical feel to it compared to most Nick had seen. He had none of the usual photos on the walls of him shaking hands with various politicians. Instead there were lots of papers and federal statute books everywhere along with countless bound reports and hearing records.

Folgier was tall and fit, and though hard to detect, lacked vision in one eye and hearing in one ear due to service as a Marine in Vietnam. He was very friendly and frank in explaining his version of what had occurred on the committee from a procedural perspective. Except in his version, Denny Folgier and his boss, the ranking Republican, both conservative New Hampshirites, had full authority to accept or reject Nick as a minority counsel. After completing his version of things, he began the interview.

"Your resume says you attended Wentwirth University. What *is* that?"

"It's a school...in the South. A pretty good one, actually."

"Is its law school accredited?"

"Yeah," Nick said, beginning to realize what he was up against. "It's been around for about a hundred years."

"So, what's your legal experience?"

Nick explained his work as a litigator for his previous Florida firm, hoping Folgier hadn't done much homework on that front.

"Is it true your previous firm no longer exists?"

"Well, it split up soon after I left. Several of the partners started the Flamingo Beach office of the huge New York firm, Primrose, Greener, and ..."

Folgier cut him off, "I know. The firm which is now facing bankruptcy and a criminal investigation? I hope you weren't too closely tied in with your former partners. Half of them may end up in jail."

Nick knew the investigation of the nationwide firm had begun but didn't believe anybody would go to jail. "Well, it seems like kind of a mess now. I wasn't a partner."

"I'm aware of that."

Before the next question could be asked, Nick jumped in talking about the lobbying he'd done and his law practice. He talked about his first state legislative victory in Tallahassee where he'd represented one of the relatively few real farmers left in Palm Beach County, and how he'd killed legislation that would have regulated him out of business. He was proud that he helped prevent his client's land from becoming another condo-lined golf course.

Denny Folgier listened attentively to the story and then said flatly, "We don't really deal much with farm-related issues on the Judiciary Committee, Nick. I'm sure Farmer Jones' concerns may be of some interest to Members of the Agriculture Committee. But here, we're primarily concerned with constitutional and antitrust issues, and as I think you're aware, issues surrounding immigration and criminal procedure."

"Yes, I know that. I just thought you'd be interested to know that I'd actually practiced law, been in a courtroom, and dealt with the legislative process before."

"Okay, thanks for that. Look Taft, Palmer is a really respected Member and one of my counsels is leaving to go back to the private sector. You might be a good addition. I assume you want to move up from a personal office to a committee counsel position?"

"Absolutely."

"Since I already talked at length with Palmer about you, I don't suppose I really need to call his staff director for a reference," Folgier asked with an anticipatory grin.

"...Probably not."

Folgier gave a knowing smile, "You and Sandy work out when you want to start. Nick, a lot of people think politics is just a game. It's not – not on this committee. I've got an interesting constitutional issue you're going to be working on that may end up on the front page."

Nick walked back to the Cannon building feeling three feet off the ground. He'd made up with his girlfriend, and now he was going to be a counsel on the infamous Judiciary Committee. He couldn't wait to see Lisa's face when she found out he'd become one of her counterparts.

––––––––––

Before he could give Palmer the good news, Palmer informed him that he'd already spoken with the ranking Republican. He congratulated Nick and told him he was expected in Chairman Staunton's office for an interview at four o'clock that afternoon.

"Chairman Staunton? You mean I...have to interview with...him? But, Folgier told me my salary would come from the Republicans' budget."

"That's right. And the Republicans' budget comes from Chairman Staunton. It's his policy that he interview all counsels,

Democrat or Republican."

His upbeat mood sank to his stomach. The new position was a great opportunity, but he was worried about Staunton for two reasons. First, he was convinced more than ever the Chairman was corrupt and, second, he was not certain that Staunton hadn't recognized him in the alleyway that night. He'd seen Staunton a few times since then, but the Chairman had no reason to notice Nick in those circumstances. On top of that, Nick knew Staunton's Chief of Staff, Sivore, didn't like him. He'd discovered that Nick and Lisa were dating.

John Staunton's office was decorated just as one might guess any powerful Texas politician's would be. There were photos of expansive Texas landscapes on one wall. Another wall held a set of polished Texas longhorns along with the Lone Star Flag. After his second year in Congress, Staunton wanted a shot at a U.S. Senate seat, but the Texas Democratic Party, acknowledging his early record of squeaking out victories by so few votes, publicly denied him its support.

Nick studied an old photo of the chairman accepting some honor from the University of Texas Board of Regents as he shook hands with former President Lyndon Johnson. Nick was stunned by how much younger and happier Staunton looked. Another plaque on the wall was an award to Staunton by the Terrell County, Texas Bar Association for extraordinary *pro bono* work on behalf of indigent clients. Nick suspected there was a lot more to that story.

The door to the office opened and Alec Sivore came out smirking, "Sorry to keep you waiting. The Chairman will see you now."

"Thanks," he said as he followed Sivore into Staunton's office. Staunton was seated at his desk looking over some papers with a half-smoked cigar in hand. His full head of thinning hair looked whiter than Nick remembered it.

"Come on in, young man," the congressman said with a thick Texas accent.

"Hello, Mr. Chairman, nice to see you."

Staunton pointed to a glass case behind him, "Best collection of cigars in Washington. You smoke a cigar, Nick?"

"No sir. Thank you though."

"How 'bout your daddy – he smoke 'em?"

"Well yes, he does."

"Here's a very nice Cuban for your dad. Have a seat over here."

The short chair he sat Nick in was just inches from Staunton's so he was pinned between him and his desk. "Ya know my Chief of Staff, Alec?"

"Yes sir, we've met."

"Well, good." Staunton leaned back in his chair with a curious look on his face, "Ya know, son, you look familiar to me – how do I know you?"

Nick tried to swallow. "Well, sir, I work for the Congress... the Congressman, I mean Congressman Palmer. I cover his Judiciary issues. You've seen me at several of the, uhm... Nick's mind went completely blank... "committee hearings and markups."

"Hmmm... that's probably it then. Don't you like ol' Sandy? Why do you want to leave his office? He's a good guy."

Nick tried to sit up straighter in the small chair, "Well, yes he's a great guy, but this seemed like a career opportunity. You know, to move up."

"Had you been lookin' to move up from Palmer's office before this came along?"

Nick was caught off guard by the question, "Well... not much. I had talked with some friends in the Administration about maybe going over there at some point, you know, but..."

Staunton cut him off, "You meeen the Reagan/Buuush

Administration?"

"Yes sir."

Staunton looked down at his desk shaking his head, "Mm-mm. Good Lord, son. Ya know...I don't dislike Ronald Reagan or George Buuush. I just think they're stupid – know what I mean?"

"Well...I guess."

Staunton smiled and chewed on his cigar. Nick looked over at Sivore who sat on the couch wearing a Cheshire Cat grin.

"So, how'd you like working with Palmer?"

Nick sat back, "It's all right. Although you do have to go through a lot of layers of people to get a final answer on anything – the chief of staff, the district office folks, then to the Congressman. It's a little frustrating, but..."

The chairman cut him off again, "Well, I'll tell you what son, you don't got to go through a lot of layers of people 'round here to get an answer. Cause I'll tell you right now, Taaefft – fuck youuu! Staunton laughed and looked over at Sivore, who was snickering. "Ya got that?"

"Yeah."

"Okay, then. Now you're gonna like it up here on the committee. We work on lots of interesting stuff." Staunton opened a drawer to his desk and handed Nick a plastic Judiciary Committee keychain. "Congratulations, you're a Minority Counsel."

12

August 1985   Capitol Hill   91 Degrees Hot

Nick never told Palmer or Denny Folgier about his bizarre interview with the chairman; and he never gave his father the cigar. He was to start his new job during the August recess when things were a little slower. He arrived at the minority office with a couple boxes of legal books and his faded print of the Declaration of Independence. The minority clerk, Hannah, showed him to his new digs. Compared to his current desk, it was spacious with high ceilings, lots of file cabinets, and a very large window. A temporary partition separated Nick's space from his new office-mate, Wesley Barksdale III, who seemed uninspired at the idea of a new office mate.

He fixed his area up in minutes; legal books here, small TV there for watching the House floor, the faded writing on the wall, and he was done. A quick introduction to his office-mate, Wes – who was about fifty, and looked sleepy – and he was ready to work.

Denny Folgier called Nick in and eyed him warily, "You have much experience with arguments surrounding the separation of powers doctrine?"

Nick first attempted his serious lawyer look, but then just admitted, "Uh, no."

"Well, you're about to. The independent counsel statute, passed by Congress after President Richard Nixon resigned, is a law based upon the rationale that cutting the Justice Department out of investigations involving the White House is the best way to ensure an ethical investigation. You familiar with this history or were you still in kindergarten?"

"I'm familiar with it."

"It's bullshit."

"Yeah."

"If a President's Administration is so corrupt that its Justice Department can't be trusted to carry out a legitimate investigation, then that President should be impeached. It's up to the voters of this country to determine whether they want a President or his appointees to stay in power, not up to some nitwit prosecutor appointed under some cockamamie convoluted statute. That's why they call it a government of the people, by the people!"

"I'm with you on that."

"Well, good – you're supposed to be!"

"Right."

"So, the majority loves this law because they can use it to appoint an independent counsel to investigate any presidential appointee at any time for just about any reason. And, they've used this mechanism, let me say abused it, on President Reagan countless times. No less than eight such investigations are ongoing right now."

Folgier looked out his office window toward the traffic on Independence Avenue, then sharply back at Nick and continued. "And the best thing for the liberals is the political damage they seek is done the minute an independent counsel is appointed. It's the suspicion that is raised and the debilitating news coverage that does the damage. The factual conclusions of the investigation years later are irrelevant."

"I agree."

"You heard much about the Iran-Contra Affair?"

"No."

"Well, you're going to. And this committee and you will see it teed up through the reauthorization of the independent counsel statute."

Nick was excited to be working on such an important constitutional issue. It would be good practice for the real battle looming on immigration reform. Since the Watergate scandal forced President Nixon to resign, the appointment of special prosecutors or independent counsels to investigate alleged wrongdoing by a political appointee in a President's Administration, though historically rare, almost always created a political firestorm, scandal, and headlines.[7]

Folgier told Nick, "I don't want you getting bogged down in the external politics surrounding this issue. Just stick to the language of the legislation and the current statute, and pay close attention to any actual legal analysis the majority staff in fact *do*; and to what Democratic Members in fact *say*. That will lead you to the weakness of their arguments and to the real reason they want to strengthen this ridiculous law."

Over time Nick grew to admire Folgier's political instincts and his willingness to fight the good fight, despite the overwhelming odds against him. He was also intrigued by the wealth of new resources and information available to him as a committee counsel. The minority counsel's office alone received dozens of research publications – legal, policy, and agency specific documents – it inspired him to broaden his knowledge of the government and public policy debate. Occasionally he would take them home to look over, but would usually fall asleep trying to read them.

One random agency publication he was looking through while eating lunch at his desk on a late afternoon caught his attention. It was the monthly publication of the Federal Election Commission (FEC) which published the registrations and activities of federal campaigns and political action committees (PACs). Pursuant to federal election law, corporations are not allowed to give money directly from their treasuries to federal candidates, so PACs were created to allow company employees to contribute money to a fund which then may be used to contribute to a candidate. Among the things Nick noticed was that the FEC report listed the campaigns that had violated election regulations. Nick's radar went up.

He asked his new assistant for back issues of the publication and found the one published during the month he first had drinks with Lisa. After a little searching, he found what he was looking for. And to his surprise, it was right there in a chart for anyone to see. Item 4 (b) under Disciplinary Actions: *The campaign of U.S. Congressman John Staunton, 42nd Congressional District of Texas, has been assessed a fine of $500.00 for incomplete or inaccurate reporting of funds and will undergo an audit by the Commission.*

The report didn't offer much further detail beyond who on Staunton's campaign had been notified of the fine. It was Alec Sivore, designated as a campaign advisor. Nick didn't know what authority the FEC had but knew it was an independent agency whose commissioners were appointed by the President. He wondered if the FEC had any investigative staff, and was curious as to how thoroughly they might investigate a campaign like Staunton's.

Lisa showed up at his office unannounced and interrupted his reading. She'd brought him a leather-bound volume of the House Rules as a congratulatory present for his promotion. Nick's first couple of weeks on the committee had been such a whirlwind, he and Lisa had barely seen each other. They were going to remedy that – being Friday night, they were headed to Georgetown for martinis and dinner.

What little time they'd spent back together was the best of their relationship. They admitted how much they'd missed each other. Their lowered defenses allowed Nick to see the softer side of her, and the make-up sex doubled their physical attraction. The only stubborn chink in the armor reappeared when Lisa complimented Nick's maturity in apologizing for his previous corruption theory about Chairman Staunton. He hadn't yet mustered the nerve to tell her what he'd seen in Mexico to confirm his suspicions after writing that effective, but acquiescent letter.

A fun night at their favorite haunts seduced them into staying out too late. University students, back for the fall semester made the bars livelier and the music louder. Things were good between them and Lisa seemed happy for Nick in his new position. But, along with the usuals like, "So, you're really going to become a right-winger now," she'd jokingly added, "you're actually going to have to start watching your P's and Q's... and that inquisitive little mind of yours, too." She'd pushed him a little too hard when she said it, and their attendant laughter allowed the admonition to pass. But it caught in the back of his mind like a fish hook.

13

September 1985   Capitol Hill   60 Degrees Clear

Congress reconvened in September. Lobbyists and Members were trying to accomplish in the next two months what they hadn't all year. Campaigns were heating up for the next year's midterm elections and everyone was busy. Lisa complained about the pace of work and the fact her chief of staff, Alec Sivore, was suddenly never around. He always conveniently would claim there was some campaign-related work to do out of the office when things got hectic. After sitting in as committee counsel on several meetings, Nick was beginning to feel at home in his new job. Hearings on reauthorizing the independent counsel statute would begin in a couple of weeks, and he was ready.

On Monday of the third week back, Nick was leaving his office to meet with Palmer on how to properly beg the majority to allow a hearing on their *Customs Waters* bill when his phone started to incessantly ring. He ignored it because he was already late, but his assistant caught him before he could get out the door and told him Lisa was holding on line two and sounded upset. He stepped back into his office and picked up the phone, "Hey, what's going on?"

"Oh, Nick – it's horrible." Lisa was sobbing. "Alec was mugged on the street in front of his house last night. They shot him!"

He could hardly make out what she was saying. He knew that Sivore lived on the Hill a couple of blocks from the Capitol and that most of the neighborhoods outside of three to four blocks were fairly crime-ridden.

"Lisa, take a deep breath. Let me meet you somewhere. I'll come by your office."

"Okay. I can't believe this. I can't even think."

He hurried to the Judiciary majority office. When he walked in, Chairman Staunton had his arm around Lisa trying to console her and other staffers. Since Nick had seldom been to their office, under the circumstances, he felt like an intruder. But Lisa rushed over and walked him to the foyer. The others and Staunton looked his way but acknowledged nothing in their faces. Nick and Lisa stepped out into the hallway.

"Alec is dead."

"What?"

"The Chairman met with the DC Police and the Capitol Police this morning. I heard him yelling at them in his office."

Nick was stunned and vaguely distracted. "You said he was mugged. Did they rob him or his house or steal his car?" he asked, pulling her toward him.

"I don't know," Lisa mumbled. "He was shot five times in the chest and head. His car key was broken off in the door lock – half was in his hand. He may have lived a while after being shot. Our office manager, Judd Traynor is going to be the one involved with the investigation."

"I guess that makes sense."

"Yeah, he knows everything about everyone, maybe a little too much. I want to think some of this through. Can I stay at your place tonight?"

"You can stay all week if you want. You know that."

––––––––––

It was an unusually cold and bitter fall day for those attending Alec Sivore's funeral at Saint Joseph's on the Senate side of the Capitol. Present at the service were his family, friends, congressional staff, and members of Congress. Most people talked about how shocked they were despite Washington's ranking as the murder capitol of the country. The *Washington*

Herald reported the tragedy with few details but quoted Chairman Staunton talking about how unfortunate it was that such incidents were taking place more frequently. There were rumors about a police lead but no specifics were available.

When Nick and Lisa were leaving the church, they came across Ken O'Malley. Mascara lined the side of Lisa's cheeks and she was withdrawn like Nick had never seen her.

"Ken, how are you? It's been awhile."

Ken introduced them to the man he was with, "This is Tom Countryman. He's with the Department of Justice. Nick works for Congressman Palmer, and this is Lisa Castile, who works for Chairman Staunton."

"I'm very sorry about your colleague."

"Thank you." Lisa said softly.

The group walked down the sidewalk toward the Capitol. After an awkward silence, Nick asked, "Tom, does the Justice Department have jurisdiction over a crime like this?"

"Sometimes, if we're asked to get involved, but usually the DC Police or the U.S. Attorney for the District of Columbia will take the lead, depending upon the circumstances. On occasion we'll be asked to come in if a federally elected official is implicated."

"Under these circumstances, you'd think they'd want any available investigative body involved."

"You know how it goes with turf issues and such. We'll see how it plays out."

"Right."

Ken broke in, "We're headed to The Monocle for a bite – we'll catch up later."

––––––––––

The next morning Nick was focused on the impending hearings to reauthorize the independent counsel statute. This was the first set of hearings for which he was the lead minority counsel. He was looking forward to being in the counsel chair and comparing firsthand the process between a legal hearing and a Congressional hearing.

He spent hours editing his memorandum to Republican committee members which was an attempt in seven pages to explain the history of the statute, the policy arguments for and against it, and who the witnesses were and why. The recent media frenzy around President Reagan over allegations involving a weapons for hostages exchange between Iran and the Contras fighting for control of Nicaragua focused new attention on the statute. Calls for an independent counsel to investigate the newly coined "Iran-Contra Affair" began to surface.

Nick's suspicions that Alec Sivore's death was not a run-of-the-mill DC mugging weighed heavily on him, but he couldn't afford the distraction. Lisa's distraught state of mind over the tragedy coupled with her inescapable connection to Staunton forbade him from sharing his thoughts with her. The more he considered the consequences if his suspicions were right, the more he kept it to himself.

The first hearing in the counsel's chair went fairly well. He was disappointed to learn that his members had little say regarding anything except when it was their brief turn to ask questions of the witnesses. He also discovered that while technically the majority could allow the minority to invite one witness, it was really more like a courtesy extended when they felt like it. Republicans actually had no right to call a witness for a majority scheduled hearing. Nick kept a highlighted copy of his memo at the ready along with several prepared questions. Palmer, who was now the ranking Republican, sat next to the Subcommittee Chairman on the dais, and Nick sat right next to Palmer. The four other minority members were on Nick's left in order of seniority.

Palmer commended his memorandum and asked about the witnesses. When it was his turn to ask his allotted five minutes worth of questions, he asked the ones Nick had prepared. When the witness's answers were incomplete, Nick whispered follow-up questions to Palmer.

As the hearing progressed, Nick wished more Members would ask questions; however most of them looked fairly bored. Finally a congressman sitting in the last chair waved him over. Nick brought his notes with him to reference if needed.

Crouching down beside the older Congressman, "Yes sir?"

"Nick, can you tell me, who is that long-legged woman in the front row in the red skirt?"

Slow to grasp the depth of the inquiry, Nick looked at the attractive brunette for a second, "No sir ... I don't know her. Do you want me to find out?"

"No, no, that's all right. Thanks anyway."

He returned to his chair, reluctant to accept the lack of interest his Members displayed in the constitutional debate unfolding before them. The highlight of the day was the testimony of two former U.S. Attorneys General who'd overseen the implementation of the statute. They testified against reauthorization because the law was often used solely for political purposes. What made their advocacy compelling was it was bipartisan: one was a former Republican Attorney General, the other, a Democrat. Despite their stark recommendation, the majority and the press characterized the hearing as a good first step in reauthorizing a law which was proving more critical everyday as allegations against the Reagan Administration unfolded.

Dinner that evening with Lisa to celebrate Nick's first hearing had a melancholic tone. Lisa was struggling with Alec's death and her guilt for the way she'd treated him. She'd become depressed at how unfair life in big cities like Washington could be and the fact that decent people were murdered for no reason. Nick lacked the will to tell her what he thought was actually behind Sivore's demise.

He asked, "Have they determined yet what the murderers wanted from Alec?"

"I haven't heard any details."

"When will we know what happened?"

"I don't know, what's the difference?" She looked angrily at Nick. "Alec is dead."

"Lisa, you just said how horrible it was that his death was so random. Don't you want to know why? And if it wasn't so random, what was it ultimately about?"

"I'm not sure I want to know."

During lunch the next day, Nick got back to his search to see if there was anything more to learn on Chairman Staunton's campaign activities. He began researching the previous Federal Election Commission publication where he'd left off some weeks earlier. There was no mention of the Staunton for Congress Campaign in the next few publications. However, Nick was learning more about election law and political action committees as he read of other proceedings.

He learned about the Commission's authority to investigate, and he read about late filings by campaigns, and amended filings, as well as what the penalties were for noncompliance. He eventually came upon what he'd suspected he might find.

The publication from a couple of weeks back reported that the Staunton for Congress Campaign was being fined again and audited for having filed a Late Disclosure of Amended Campaign Receipts. What the campaign had previously reported as contributions from the Texas Delrio Corporation Political Action Committee and its executives, totaling $30,000, in fact totaled $120,000.

Nick knew from what he'd read that corporate PACs were allowed to give $10,000 per election cycle to a candidate's campaign – $5,000 for the primary and $5,000 for the general election. Individuals were limited to $1,000 per primary and general for a total of $2,000. While it might have been feasible for the Delrio group to have given a total of $30,000 ($10,000 from its corporate PAC and $20,000 total from ten different executives), it was unrealistic for it to have legally given $120,000. The publication also revealed that the Delrio Corporation had proffered as a defense that three affiliated PACs from subsidiary corporations had each donated separately. He frantically searched for the most recent publication in the office file cabinets.

Unbeknownst to Nick, Folgier was an advisor to the reelection campaign of his boss, the ranking Republican. The door to Folgier's office was slightly ajar when Nick knocked and the door creaked open.

"Hey, Nick. What's up?"

"I was just looking for the latest FEC report and Hannah mentioned you might have it."

"Yeah." Denny lifted his hands to show he was in fact reading the report.

"Oh, that's okay. I'll take a look when you're done."

"I'm finished for now," as he handed it over. "Are you interested in campaign law, Nick?"

"No, not really."

"Then why are you looking at that boring publication? I was pretty sure the only people who read those were election geeks or PAC lawyers."

When Folgier handed the volume over, he did so with the pages opened to the place where he'd been reading. Before Nick answered, he glanced down at the open report and on the left page he could see Staunton's name.

"Well, I do find it somewhat interesting in general, and in particular, the news about certain campaigns."

Folgier smiled, "So do I, Nick – so do I."

He began poring over information on the Chairman's campaign and was pleased by what he discovered. The audit of the Staunton for Congress Campaign had been expanded into a formal Commission investigation. The amended campaign receipts filing had been amended again up to $210,000. What previously had been listed as three affiliated PACs of the Delrio Corporation had increased to five. Something else Nick hadn't noticed before, the Delrio Corporation's address: 200 Meror Street, Normandy, Texas. According to a map, it was in Maverick County and right on the border.

14

Early October 1985   Georgetown   55 Degrees Sunny

Nick left work early on a Friday afternoon. Moxley had deposited Sir Winston at his apartment on her way out of town. Nick leashed him for a walk in the neighborhood. They'd developed a routine which took them immediately to the big tree in front of his building to sniff around a while and then across the street to mingle with the other neighborhood dogs. One of those dog owners was a flirtatious DC socialite with whom Nick enjoyed bantering. Although her dog, Gunter, was a Rottweiler with a nasty attitude who constantly eyed Winston as dinner, Winston always bravely stood his ground.

On this afternoon, however, as Winston was furiously sniffing, Major Ity exited from a champagne Mercedes Benz that had pulled in front of the building. The female driver yelled hello to Nick – it was Mrs. Gentmore of Middleburg.

"How are you, Nick?"

"No complaints, I guess."

"Glad to hear it. Take care, Eugene." She drove away.

"Major, I didn't know you knew her."

"Oh, I know a lot of old folks around here. How on earth do you know her?"

"I met her at a party at her house when I first moved here. She's a big liberal."

"Is that right?" The Major went into his narrow but neatly organized garage and started his Jag. Thick blue smoke from the seldom-run engine filled the air.

Nick needed help and knew that Ity had serious connections, but was reluctant to push the limits of his landlord-tenant relationship. He stuttered over the sound of the engine, "Hey,

Major, can we talk some time again about... Congressman Staunton?"

"Sure, what's on your mind?"

"I've...learned a lot about the guy since we last spoke."

Ity looked at Nick for a few seconds. "Why don't you get in? We'll take a drive."

"Well, I've got Sir Winston..."

"It's okay. He's the only guy who can fit in this excuse for a backseat anyway."

Ity drove slowly down the narrow streets. The interior smelled of old leather and the shock absorbers creaked. But, the engine hummed like the finely tuned machine it was. After they crossed Key Bridge into Virginia, the Major turned onto George Washington Parkway and opened her up heading north along the Potomac River. Winston, who sat on the panel just behind them where his head was level with theirs, looked back and forth at them during the drive as if following their conversation.

As they drove, he told Ity about the night he came across Staunton in the alleyway with the Mexican. He described his congressional trip to Mexico and of seeing the same guy in a Federales uniform. He explained to Ity how he was learning about Staunton's unusual campaign activities and of the FEC audit. Then he told what he knew about Alec Sivore's murder that hadn't been reported in the paper.

Ity pulled the Jag to the roadside at an overlook of the river. They got out and let Winston sniff around. After a few minutes, he spoke. "Nick, do you have any reason to think that John Staunton knows what you know?"

"No sir, I don't think so."

"You know anyone at the Justice Department?"

"Not really. I've met Tom Countryman there who seemed like a good guy."

"Tom Countryman? Know him well. He's head of the Public

Integrity Section at the department. One of the few people I trust in this town. Could be a very good person for you to get to know."

"What does the Public Integrity Section do?"

"It oversees investigations of federally-elected officials."

"Oh."

"You're dealing with a powerful man, Nick. Be mindful, son, everyone has a blind spot."

The ride back into Georgetown was quiet. It was a beautiful October day, and the leaves were still turning under a distant fall sun. During a long silence, Nick was tempted to ask Ity questions about his family and earlier life. But, as if he knew a personal question was coming, the major spoke up and the moment passed. When he closed his garage door, Ity promised to do some further checking into the Staunton situation.

15

Late October 1985   Washington, DC   57 Degrees Clearing

The majority abruptly shut Congress down for the year in October. With no pressing legislation and sufficient groundwork laid to jab at the Administration through Christmas, the session was gaveled closed. The media had enough fodder to chip away at President Reagan and if more was needed, a field hearing could easily be convened. Nick soon learned the upside of adjournment. With no committee hearings scheduled and without power to plan any upcoming agenda, he had time on his hands.

One of Nick's law school friends was also involved in politics. Bud Marskey, who worked for a state representative in Texas, was a tobacco-chewing, story-telling Texan who liked to ride motorcycles. During their law school years, they'd occasionally ridden dirt bikes in the mountains of north Georgia where Nick's grandparents had acres of farmland. The barn there had a pair of old Yamaha 250s that Nick kept maintained just for riding the overgrown logging trails – it was a good break from the rigors of school. Bud had frequently offered to return the hospitality by taking Nick motorcycling in the Texas Hill country.

Veterans Day weekend in early November looked convenient for a trip west. Praying that his Visa card had just enough room left on it, he charged a round trip airline ticket. Bud met Nick at the Austin airport in his pickup and, after a cold beer, gave a tour of the State Capitol which he took pride in pointing out was taller than the U.S. Capitol. He bragged that Texas was the only state that was actually an independent country before joining the Union. He carried on about that giving Texas certain unique secessionist rights, but wasn't very specific.

After a dinner of the biggest ribs Nick had ever consumed at a wood and stone-walled restaurant, Bud introduced him to the Mexican cook, Abel, whom he boasted was one of the best chefs in the state. He mentioned that he trusted him more than anyone he knew, and that he never missed a Sunday church service.

They discussed their different work experiences since graduating from school. His friend was enjoying learning the legislative process at the state level. Austin was more friendly and laid-back than DC, especially with regard to political partisanship. Bud explained how, despite the fact that Democrats had controlled both the State House and Senate there for over a hundred years, the Republicans and Democrats got along well. In fact, Republicans there voted every year to elect the Democrat Speaker of the Texas House.

"You mean Republicans here don't even vote for their own guy for Speaker of the House?"

"Look, they know, due to the count, they're gonna lose anyway, so rather than alienate the Speaker, they just vote for him. Most of the time, they don't even run a Republican for Speaker."

Nick thought the Republicans in Washington had rolled over but this was a new low for the party of which he'd become so invested. He argued that should the Republicans by some miracle ever take the state legislature, that such bipartisan spirit might disappear. Bud disagreed and emphasized that they all *went along to get along* in Texas where ugly partisanship just didn't cut it. They shook on a twenty dollar bet that if the shoe went on the other foot, there would be a different side to Bud's friendly counterparts.

He told Bud about how bitterly partisan Washington was, and described how a Democratic majority had ruled Congress with an iron fist for over thirty years. Bud, like most Americans, had no idea how polarized things were in DC and counted his

123

blessings it was not so in his state. As they were leaving the restaurant, Abel walked them to the parking lot and reminded Bud he could pay him next time for the bet he'd lost on the previous Dallas Cowboys' game. Bud accused Abel of taking advantage of him.

Early the next morning, Nick was surprised to discover that his friend had graduated from dirt bikes to powerful street bikes. Bud planned to take them on a long ride into the Texas countryside. The bikes, a new Honda 750 Interceptor and a slightly older Honda CX 500, were sleek and fast with low centers of gravity. Nick had little experience with street bikes — he was strictly a woods rider. He admonished his old friend, "It's one thing to deal with trees and dirt, it's altogether something else to deal with cars and pavement!"

"Aw, nonsense," Bud replied, spitting tobacco juice, "Taft, you know how to ride, it's the same thing as a dirt bike, just heavier and faster! We'll be cruisin' in the country anyway. There aren't hardly any cars to worry 'bout."

"Well . . ."

"Well, nothin'. Here's a helmet — now fire that thing up."

Bud explained that they could go in any direction. The scenery would be different depending upon their choice, but there would be a good barbecue or taco stand on the roadside regardless of which way they chose. Nick had done his homework before leaving Washington; he was there to do more than visit his friend.

"How about toward Mexico?"

"Southwest it is. Follow me."

Although he was nervous on the big bike maneuvering through traffic, once out on the interstate, its weight and power began to feel comfortable; and, Bud was right, they soon left the traffic behind. The sunbaked highway moved quickly out of their way and the scenery of the Hill Country provided a liberating landscape. The further from civilization they got, the more they cranked up the speed.

Within a few hours they'd traveled over 170 miles. Bud pulled over by a roadside hut that served tacos, tamales, and cold beer. They sat at a wood table under the only shade tree for miles. After lunch, gnawing on toothpicks and chasing ants off the table, Nick began to unload the story of his extracurricular activities in Washington. Bud was surprised at the depth and detail of Nick's story.

"Holy shit, Taft. Yur in a world of trouble. Why you tellin' *me* all this?"

"Because the Delrio Corporation is headquartered outside of Normandy, Texas – about fifty miles southwest of here."

"And what exactly you intend to do there?"

"I just want to visit the address, see if it's a real business." Nick knew Bud liked adventure and wouldn't balk at the likelihood of a little mischief.

"Well, then let's check 'er out." He put on his helmet.

Normandy, Texas was not a booming metropolis. Buildings were dusty and dilapidated, and the streets were faded and potholed. The few people in sight wore tired, expressionless faces. Their high-tech bikes were the most functional things the town had seen in a while. They pulled over to check the address. A weathered woman pointed them down a road toward the outskirts of town.

The lone building on Mero Street looked vacant; it had a concrete front office attached to a large metal warehouse. Nick knocked on the front door. A look in the windows showed a couple of desks, phones, and chairs, but no people. They walked around the back of the building. There was a large steel door and a stairwell to a smaller wooden door one floor up. They climbed the stairs and looked in the window. The big warehouse was mostly empty except for a pickup truck, a jeep, some boxes, and a long fuel tanker truck with an illegible logo on its side.

Nick and Bud looked in, then at each other, then back inside again.

"What do you make of that?"

"I don't know, man. It's an odd mix a shit for sure."

There were no gas pumps in sight, no products, no machinery, no agriculture equipment, and none of the usual business equipment, fax machines or copiers.

"You say this company contributed $210,000 to Staunton's campaign?"

"Yeah, this company and its five affiliated corporations."

"Hmmm...you might be onto somethin' there, Taft. Doesn't really add up, does it?"

"Nope."

"Well, what do you wanna do?"

"See what's in those boxes."

"How you gonna master that?"

"By getting this door open."

"You 'member anything from law school, Taft? That's breaking and entering – I'm not doin' that."

"Then how about you just move our bikes around to the back of the building? I'll be the criminal."

Bud gave a long stare, "Washington's rarified air is messing with your head, son."

"Just give me a couple a minutes."

The Texan walked back down the stairs, "Knock yourself out!"

It didn't take much effort to jimmy the dry-rotted door open. Nick climbed down the interior stairs and began looking through boxes. To his surprise, they contained nothing but clothes – blue jeans, T-shirts, thick jackets, baseball caps and sneakers. Nick looked in other containers which turned out to be coolers with twin compartments in an upper and lower chamber. He had thought for sure he'd find something more sinister than that.

His bewilderment inspired him to check out the tanker

truck. The driver's cabin showed nothing unusual, just maps of the area, Texas and Mexico. He climbed up top and struggled to open the small tanker top hatch; he was clueless as to what type of fuel it might be hauling. Once open, he peered inside. It was empty. And, not just empty, but perfectly clean and dry with no smell of gasoline, diesel, or fuel of any kind. It was too dark to see inside it.

Bud opened the door at the top of the stairway, "Taft, what the hell you doin'? Let's get outta here!"

"Hey, Bud, I need some light. You got a flashlight or anything?"

"How about I just flip the wall switch here, detective." Bud flipped the switches and fluorescent lights across the ceiling lit up.

He looked back down into the fuel tank, and then pulled back. Along the bottom of the tanker was a makeshift wooden floor. Along both sides were wooden benches. Large plastic jugs were scattered around and what looked like old shirts, jackets and baseball caps were on the floor and benches.

"I'll be damned."

"Taft, we got to go – I'm serious. Two cars are comin'."

Nick scrambled off the truck, slammed his knee into a handrail on his way down, ran up the stairs and pulled the door shut. He hobbled down the outside stairs. Bud handed him his helmet and they took off as fast as they could. A few miles down the road, they pulled over.

Nick, looking back behind them asked, "You think we lost 'em?"

"Who?"

"The two cars!"

"Weren't any cars, I just wanted to get back on the road."

"You idiot, almost got myself killed getting out of there!"

"Hey look, it was just a matter of time before somebody did see us. The place creeped me out and I felt like we were being watched. I got a sixth sense about those things, you know."

"Right, Marskey. Shit, my chest's beating so fast – I about had a heart attack."

"Oh, relax, there's no one 'round for miles. Well, what'd you find out, Sherlock?"

Nick told Bud of his discoveries in the warehouse.

"Sounds like a smugglin' operation to me."

"Drugs?"

"Drugs, people and whatever else."

"People? You mean illegal immigrants?"

"Yep – it's pretty big money. The cook, Abel, who you met last night, was a product of an operation like that."

"Illegal immigrants have that much money?"

"Enough of them at five hundred bucks a head can get up there. Big business – the smuggling, false documents, drugs and protection – and it's gettin' bigger."

"Up there where you can afford to write checks worth $210,000 to one politician?"

"Maybe, maybe not. But there does seem to be a lot of cash going back and forth."[8]

They gassed up their bikes in Normandy and rode back to Austin as the sun was fading in the west. The blue, orange, and yellow sky blanketed the west Texas prairie like a rainbow. When they were back and finished wiping down the motorcycles, Nick thanked his friend for the ride, "Hey, Bud, I didn't really mean to drag you into all this mess."

"I'm not dragged into anything, Taft. I work for Representative Burwell. I've got no beef with Staunton. We've made enough enemies of our own. As far as I'm concerned, we never had that conversation, and I've never been to Normandy, Texas."

16

December 1985   Capitol Hill   33 Degrees Blustery

Thanksgiving and Christmas came and went quickly. There were several prominent holiday parties in the Capitol and around town; everyone seemed friendly and full of good cheer. Nick and Lisa dressed the part and attended a few receptions together including the Judiciary Committee party where Chairman Staunton played Santa Claus. Members and staff seemed to all get along and no one mentioned politics or the other unpleasantries of the past year. Staunton's thin frame didn't quite carry off the Santa image, but his red nose from imbibing helped him look and play the jolly character well.

Nick visited his family in Florida for the week, and they saw Palmer at a local restaurant one night having dinner with his wife and children. Sandy told Nick's parents how much he enjoyed having him on the staff and that he was becoming a good legislative lawyer. Lisa spent the holidays in Texas on her grandparents' small ranch outside of San Antonio.

Fishing with friends one day and on the beach the next made his vacation. The ocean waters seemed restorative, far from the machinations of Washington. He never shared the darker aspects of his Washington experience with his family, and only once hinted to his dad of Staunton's corruption. Not a fan of politicians, his father responded, "Nothing you need do about that son." Dr. Taft once challenged the American Medical Association and its seemingly unethical president on a position it adopted contrary to the interests of his practice. He and the majority of votes he'd garnered suspiciously lost in the end, and he'd never let it go.

Christmas Day provided the usual mêlée of presents and

wrapping paper. Nick took a break to visit Maleva at her home across town, and they exchanged Christmas cards. She needed some legal advice but didn't want to discuss it then – she said she'd call him soon. He told her to call any time.

Nick's traditional family dinner was a little different this year because his grandmother overdosed the plum pudding with too much rum. When his dad tried to flambé it, the dried hollies caught fire. Everyone grabbed their water glass to douse the flames. Although dessert continued, the all-hands fire drill accelerated the usual tryptophan impact of their turkey banquet, and within an hour, everyone under thirty was out cold in front of the television.

The holidays would end too soon. Nick, who'd talked to Lisa many times by phone, wished he could've spent New Year's Eve with her. But he knew they needed a break from things they'd learned together and from the fear of things not yet revealed. On New Year's Day, after watching football games with his family, and nursing a champagne hangover, he repacked his dirty laundry for a flight back to Washington.

17

January 1986   Capitol Hill   24 Degrees Gray

The Hill didn't come back to life during most of January except for the President's State of the Union Address. The media had worked itself into a frenzy about whether Reagan would reference any of the scandals it had been spinning up. As Nick read and watched, he wondered how many outside of Washington bought into their constant manipulation. His visits to Florida were a reality check for him. He found that even when he talked politics, nobody really listened – the Dolphins were in the playoffs and the ocean was flat, perfect for fishing. The real issues of life were played out in the everyday world, not in the strained conspiracies of Washington.

By February of 1986, the government process was churning again. The legislative branch got off to a slow start, but the executive branch never really shut down except for Christmas and New Year's Day. So, for most of December and January those government folks, including the Federal Election Commission, were still chugging along. When the January FEC publication arrived at the Judiciary offices, the reading was fascinating. The agency had referred part of its investigation of the Staunton Campaign to the Department of Justice on evidence that the Delrio PAC was associated with a mere shell of non-existent corporate entities.

He took the article in to Folgier, "How is it the *Washington Herald* has not reported this? If I wasn't aware of this obscure publication, I'd have no idea that John Staunton was being investigated by the Justice Department for campaign fraud."

"To them, it's not newsworthy, Nick. Staunton's one of their good ol' boys, so they figure this must be about some election law snafu."

"Snafu? The guy's being investigated by the Department of Justice and the FEC! How the hell's that not newsworthy?"

"Networks and papers decide what's worth reporting, Nick, and that position gives them enormous power."

"Power to do what?"

"It happens every day, my friend."

"The President is alleged to be doing a dozen different frivolous things a month and it's blistering front page news each morning and the lead story on every nightly news broadcast. But the Chairman of the House Judiciary Committee, who oversees our criminal justice system, is being formally investigated for lying to stay in office and it's not worthy of one story?"

"Hey, it's a free country, Nick. If they have no political interest in a storyline, they don't write – kind of like your immigration issue."

"No – it's more than that."

Folgier sagged in his chair as if the fight had long gone out of him on that front, "Yeah, it's called protect politicians who give you scoop and sometimes it is called laziness. Believe me kid, I understand. But our first amendment allows them to choose their priorities and they ain't yours – okay?"

Nick was discouraged by Washington again. One party had controlled Congress for over thirty years, and the so-called journalists, who were supposed to challenge and keep those in power in check, instead were in bed with them. Should Republicans ever regain the majority in Congress would the media treat them with equal deference? Was it just easier to scratch the back of the party in power?

The hypocrisy gave him a kick of determination to uncover Staunton's lies, deceit, and possible complicity in murder. He called his friend, Ken O'Malley, in the Senate to see if he and Tom Countryman of the Justice Department could meet.

Aware that Nick would be buying lunch, O'Malley made reservations at an expensive restaurant in downtown Washington. Countryman proved to be a no-nonsense guy. When Nick asked questions about the jurisdiction of the Public Integrity Section, Tom didn't bat an eye. But when questions veered toward the Alec Sivore investigation, Countryman shut him down.

"Taft, with all due respect, I can't discuss an ongoing investigation."

"I thought you guys weren't involved in that case."

"We weren't, but we are now."

"I thought the Main Justice Department didn't have primary jurisdiction to investigate the Sivore case?"

"Somebody from Congress specifically requested we get involved."

"Who?"

"I don't recall."

"I presume it wasn't John Staunton."

"Based on the level of cooperation we received from his office, that's a safe assumption."

"Son of a bitch. I knew it!"

O'Malley, taking a bite of braised lamb, "You knew what?"

"I'm telling both of you – this guy Staunton is dirty – and there's something fishy about Sivore's death too."

Countryman and O'Malley looked at each other and simultaneously took a sip of their waters.

"Look Taft, Ken says you're a straight shooter, but I can't really talk about this case unless I'm authorized to do so. Why are you so interested anyway?"

"I knew Alec Sivore, and I've run into Staunton under less than favorable circumstances."

"Circumstances?"

"Yeah, circumstances."

"Nick, sorry I can't be more forthcoming."

Countryman had tangled with the likes of Staunton before, albeit on a smaller scale at the U.S. Attorney's Office in New York. That culprit had slipped Countryman's noose embarrassing the young prosecutor for failing to lay the proper ground work for what should have been an easy indictment.

"Look, it's not like Staunton doesn't hold some leverage over us. As you know, his committee oversees our department."

"Of course," Nick said a little too cynically.

After lunch, Ken walked a few blocks with Nick, "Hey, try not to let this town get to you. Step back every now and then and look at the bigger picture."

"I know. I shouldn't have been so impatient with Tom. He seems like a good guy."

"Don't worry; he'll get over it. Did I hear that you and Lisa Castile are together?"

"Well, kind of."

Ken smiled. "She's sharp. Be careful though. I hear she was a champion calf roper in her younger days, and some at Harvard would say she has more than a few sides to her." He flagged a cab and was gone.

––––––––––

Coincidentally, Lisa Castile was at a lunch of her own just up the block from Ken and Nick. Lisa's roommate from her freshman year at the University of Texas worked in the public relations office at the Kennedy Center. They were once close friends, and although only saw each other occasionally in recent years, always enjoyed catching-up. They usually gossiped about everything Texas and Washington, including the men in their lives. Without mentioning his name or occupation, Lisa described her relationship with Nick in more detail than she'd intended.

"Sounds like you have him right where you want him."

Lisa, hesitantly, "I ... I guess I kind of do ... yeah."

"You like him though. I can tell."

"Yeah, I do. He's different. I almost trust him."

"How old is he?"

Lisa, laughing, "He's four and a half years younger than me, and doesn't have a clue."

"Nice work. Does he know about your *real* Washington connections?"

"No, not really."

"Well, men don't need to know everything, do they? Most times the more they know, the worse they get. Know what I mean?"

"I do."

The leadership decided to bring two key bills to the floor that winter – reauthorization of the independent counsel statute, and immigration reform. Nick did nothing for days but prepare for the committee markup of the independent counsel legislation. He hoped it would be a good primer for the upcoming fight on immigration. He and Folgier worked together on some technical amendments including one to allow targets of investigations to be reimbursed for attorney's fees. These amendments were well-intentioned, but they lacked *punch*. Nick wanted something to make the law's supporters realize its potential for abuse.

He'd been so busy with Folgier he'd barely had time to keep Palmer abreast of what he was doing. However, the House would be voting until midnight that evening, and Palmer invited Nick to join him for a late dinner in the Capitol Building. The Members' Dining Room had a regal feel to it due to its location and who happened to be dining there at any given moment.

The room itself was not remarkable, but noticeably austere with white table cloths, bland walls and a worn royal blue carpet. Nevertheless, he straightened his tie and brushed off his jacket before entering the tall entrance doorway. Palmer was seated at a corner table and looked tired.

"Sandy, how are you?"

"I'm fine. Have a seat. What do you say we get a drink?"

"Fine by me."

Palmer sipped down a Dewar's and soda, and the conversation loosened up. "Can you believe I've been voting in this body for three years now and have never won a vote?"

"Yeah, I can – it's a joke. They run this place like a gulag to ensure neither you nor anyone in our party ever wins. Losing is like a disease around here."

"No – most diseases are curable."

He sympathized with Palmer's despair; he was experiencing it himself. No matter how hard one worked, the way the majority stacked the deck, Republicans had little choice but to abide their enduring power.

"They're an arrogant bunch, Sandy."

About then an older Alabama Republican who was a member of Palmer's subcommittee stopped by their table. He'd had a few drinks, "You know what, Sandy? In this town sometimes you got to call a skunk a dawg and a dawg a skunk – that's what I'm telling you. See y'all on the floor tomorrow." He kept moving.

"I'm sure that was good advice, but I've no idea what it meant."

Palmer got back to the subject. "Take this independent counsel statute for example. Their assumption is that due to the relationship between the President and the Attorney General, the Justice Department is going to act unethically every time they're asked to investigate the Administration. That's absurd. There's no evidence to support it. Isn't that the same thing as saying the Justice Department shouldn't be trusted to investigate a Member of Congress who has legislative responsibility over the Justice Department? Shouldn't we appoint an Independent Counsel to investigate us because of a potential conflict of interest?"

Nick's eyes about bugged out of his head. "Yeah! As a matter of fact, it is the same thing; and we should be able to appoint a counsel for that reason. Sandy, you're brilliant!"

"Yeah?"

"You've just articulated our killer amendment for this bill. The majority is arguing the Attorney General can't be trusted to investigate the president because the president appointed him and has influence over him. Therefore, they claim there's an inherent conflict of interest. But like you just said, the authority of the chairman of our committee who oversees the Attorney General's budget creates the same conflict."

"Go on."

"If you were the Attorney General, would you want to investigate the Chairman of the House Judiciary Committee knowing he could call you in front of his committee anytime he wants and blister you for how you're spending the department's resources?"

"No, I wouldn't. That sounds like an inherent conflict of interest."

"Sandy, you should offer an amendment to the independent counsel bill to include Members of Congress as people who may be investigated! Then we'd find out what they really think of having a prosecutor with unlimited funds and power going after potential wrongdoing – when the potential wrongdoer is them."

"Good idea. Why don't you and Folgier try to hammer something out?"

On his way out of the dining room an older gentleman he'd never seen before inquired if he was getting settled in all right on the committee staff. It struck Nick as bizarre that total strangers would ask such questions in Washington. When back at his office, he quickly described to Folgier the idea to cover Members of Congress under the independent counsel statute. They drafted the fairly simple amendment language, then key arguments for and against it. While driving home along the Potomac, Nick recalled he may have met the curious older gentleman in a brief meeting with Palmer during his second month in Washington. Nick thought he might be a lobbyist for the yacht-building industry.

Arriving home after midnight, Nick was tired, but optimistic that he had a real chance at winning a vote in the committee. He believed this amendment would probably make Staunton angry and hopefully squirm a bit. He would call several staff to Republican Members of the committee first thing in the morning and seek their support for Palmer's language.

Nick had learned many political lessons since working in Congress, some were more painful than others. On the morning of the committee markup, Folgier called him into his office to inform him that Chairman Staunton had met with the ranking Republican and discussed Palmer's amendment. They'd agreed the issue presented some interesting constitutional questions, but needed more time to be vetted before being voted on. They'd also agreed that Palmer would offer the amendment, debate it, and then withdraw it per an understanding that the Chairman would work with him on it between markup and House floor consideration of the bill.

"Are you nuts? Denny, the element of surprise is the only thing we have going for us! These guys who are so anxious to appoint a single-focused prosecutor to go after executive branch officials will have to show their hypocrisy by voting to keep themselves out of the same target zone. If Palmer offers the amendment, makes our arguments, and then withdraws it before a vote, we've just given them between now and the House floor vote to figure out how to defeat us. This is outrageous. Who's agreed to this?"

"My boss! Who happens to be your boss, the full committee ranking Republican on this committee! Understand? And your job is to tell Sandy that's the deal."

"Denny, you know what a good opportunity this is."

"Look, I don't have a choice here. I don't think my boss likes this amendment any more than Staunton does. He might vote *no* too." Folgier looked down and then out his office window but not back at Nick. The relationship of Nick and the frequently surly Folgier often benefitted not by what was said between them but by what was not.

——————

Palmer offered his amendment at the markup as ordered, and Democrats were critical across the board. None bothered to mention that the independent counsel law, which they were anxious to reauthorize, was facing no less than three constitutional challenges in the U.S. court system. Those challenges were to be heard by the Supreme Court in the coming months. But the gist of the legal challenges being made by the President against that law seemed irrelevant to those who simply assumed the Constitution would protect them under similar circumstances.

The only thing that struck Nick at the preordained markup was Chairman Staunton staring at him as he whispered in Palmer's ear during debate on the amendment. He thought for a second that Staunton was looking past him, but when he sat back on one of the benches behind the dais, Staunton continued to stare. Nick glanced down at his notes and at a counsel sitting to his left in order to avoid eye contact. He listened to the debate for a minute and figured he was probably letting his imagination get the best of him.

However, when he reluctantly looked back toward Staunton who was talking with one of his counsels, he pointed his long crooked finger at Nick and curled it back toward him. Nick slowly got up and maneuvered his way over the knees of fellow staff members.

When he got next to him, Staunton said, "This your stuff?"

"What?"

"This your stuff, Taft?"

"Well, yeah. It's mine and Sandy's."

"You ever read up on the Constitution, son – the balance of power?"

"I have."

"Better read it again – this ain't gonna fly."

The Chairman got distracted by another Member and turned away. Nick stood there unsure of whether he'd been dismissed.

Staunton turned back, "Son, you want to affect this process, do it in ways that work – not in ways it won't."

"Huh?"

"I'll help you get an amendment passed if it makes any sense." Staunton winked.

Nick nodded, he couldn't think of a response.

The markup ended. The minority got rolled on all their amendments and the bill was voted out of committee. Palmer withdrew his proposed language as instructed and no vote was taken on it. Not much debate occurred, but enough to tip their hand and allow them to be slaughtered like lambs at a later date.[9] Nick didn't try to explain what had just happened to his fellow staffers; he just looked down at the floor.

———————

His discouragement with the committee charade on the independent counsel bill distracted Nick enough to take the rest of the day off. He was frustrated, but knew the amendment to cover Members had struck a nerve. He started to bundle up for a run under a cold winter sun but first reluctantly made a phone call he could no longer avoid.

"Dad, hey, we never got to finish our conversation from last week…

"The country's still safe?"

"Oh yeah…you know. Hey, I'm…a little uhm…well, my Visa bill is overwhelming me lately."

"I see."

"I finally had to buy a winter coat, not for looks, for warmth. You know how cold it is up here? And, I had to fix my car – again." Nick didn't want to divulge that some industrious Georgetown students or professional car thieves over the past months had gradually absconded with both his outside rearview mirrors, his right front headlight assembly, back left brake light assembly, and almost successfully removed his entire front bumper.

"You mean your BMW sedan?"

"Well, it is, you know, old."

"Nick, what do I have to do to make you understand? You made the choice to change careers. If you're not making enough, then quit spending or do something else for a living."

"Yeah, well, I'm doing some really good work here."

"Like what?"

"Like…exposing the hypocrisy of the majority party, and… helping fight a corrupt Congressman…and…"

"Really?"

"It's about defending our borders, Dad."

"Our borders? You've joined the infantry? Just don't end up in an army field hospital."

"Immigration reform? It's a very complicated issue."

"I'm sure it is, son. And, I can appreciate your wanting to have meaning in your work despite that it doesn't pay. But taking on unethical politicians is not a career — it's a waste of time. You'll regret it in the end."

"Well...I could use some help."

"Maybe a short-term reprieve from the harsh reality you've encountered can be arranged."

After a fatiguing run, Nick was only five minutes late to meet his landlord for dinner at his club in Georgetown. The Major, it turned out, had done some snooping of his own. After they got through the niceties, Ity explained that they were at one of the oldest private clubs in Washington. It had dark wood-paneled walls, lush hunter green carpet, and waiters wearing black tie tuxedos. The people dining there appeared focused on their own worlds and disinterested in those around them.

"Nick, your instincts about Staunton are on target. He may be in cahoots with a Mexican cartel that is as dirty as the day is long. They're suspected of being involved in drug smuggling. The Delrio Corporation is just one of their many shell companies."

"What about Staunton. What's his role?"

"It is suspected, among other things, that it's to keep that stretch of border unpatrolled and ensure no new laws increase security on the border."

"Son of a bitch!"

"I would tend to agree with that characterization."

"No. That son of a bitch is the one leading the charge in the House to make sure we don't secure the border in the immigration bill! He holds all the cards — he's the chairman of the committee with primary jurisdiction over the legislation."

"And, he doesn't just hold and play those cards in the

committee. He holds them on others after he entertains them on his yacht: other Members, lobbyists, and the money people. He does so in a way to ensure he has them on his side."

Nick's hand dropped, accidentally flipping his fork off the table out onto the plush carpet. "How do you mean?"

The Major slightly lifted his hand toward the wait staff, "There's apparently a party on the third Thursday of most months. There are strippers, hookers, and plenty of other unethical activities to go around."

"How does he get away with that? How is it that no one knows about this?"

Ity withheld his answer as the waiter replaced Nick's fork, "Washington's leverage on the human element is powerful. They dock the sixty-foot yacht at a deserted wooden pier somewhere south of Annapolis. It's down at the end of a lone dirt road."

"I've got to find that pier."

"And do what? Get yourself killed?"

"No. I just want to see him in action."

"I don't recommend it. What's your obsession here, son? The Justice Department is about to get all over this provocateur. It's going to take some time because he is, after all, the Chairman of the committee that oversees the department. So, they have to go under the radar for a while. There's a new effort afoot to focus resources on that border – only a pilot project for now, but if it gets funded, it may help immensely. Trust me, I know people there. They'll bring him down eventually."

Seemingly inattentive, Nick rearranged his fork after running it alongside his water glass and stared at it, "Maybe I can help."

Ity bluntly put the fork back in its place. "Don't do anything precipitous, Nick. And watch where you tread. I would guess these people have security. They can find you."

18

Late February 1986   Virginia   42 Degrees

The next morning, Nick got a call from Congressman Palmer who asked if he'd stay at his house for the next few days while the Congressman and his wife were out of the country. Nick had watched the house before so gladly accepted but Palmer explained that this time his teenage boys would be there. He emphasized they were good kids and would mostly be in school, but Sandy wanted an adult around '*just in case*'.

At Palmer's request, he headed to their home that Saturday afternoon for a review of the house rules in the presence of his sons, but didn't need to stay there until the following evening. The boys, 14 and 16, one, a whiz in math and the other not quite a whiz in anything just yet, didn't exactly resemble their angelic photos on the Congressman's desk but they filled out the family picture with the dog and handsome house. It reminded Nick of home – a place that of late seemed far away.

He had to scrap his weekend trip to Annapolis to search for Staunton's deserted marina. Instead, he accepted an invite from a lobbyist, Lesur Horsrong, to attend a private party in Georgetown. Known as "Big Les" to his friends, Horsrong was unique in Washington circles – once a Senate aide, he was part French and part American Indian. Although recently married, he used any excuse to get out of the house. No doubt he'd told his wife that chaperoning Nick was important to his lobbying business. Nick, of course, was aware that his status as a rookie where the majority held a seventy seat edge was practically useless to "Big Les."

After a fairly dull party, the best looking women all headed to *Nathan's* in Georgetown for champagne. Les insisted on buying

Nick a few drinks. The bar was packed, the music great, and the women drunk. His chubby host was in a fervent political discussion with two women whom Nick suspected were pros. Nick danced with a blond woman from the French Embassy with a model's legs and extremely short dress but lost her in the crowd after being harangued into vodka shots with the sultry debaters. Fending off any more drinks or cigarettes, he stumbled up the cobblestone streets to his apartment and telephoned Lisa who immediately hung up on him.

Waking up just before noon, he looked out at a rainy and cold winter day. Nick opted for a hot shower and short walk to a place the locals called the PLO Café. They served good breakfasts, but were an odd bunch. No one could figure out where they were from or their language. They wore black smocks and funny shoes. After eggs, toast, and coffee, he was functioning again. He bought a copy of the upstart conservative newspaper, one of the few willing to present viewpoints not covered by the establishment media, and went home to recuperate.

When he arrived at Palmer's home that evening, his hangover was only slightly improved. Upon opening the front door, he was dumbfounded. The house was mostly dark and completely silent. He called out the boys' names, but there was no response. First looking around the main floor, he followed the stairs down into the large basement den. An occasional odd sound like a muffled thump or click and thump echoed in the distance. The basement was dark except for one soft lamp, and smelled lightly of smoke due to a smoldering log in the fireplace. He thought he saw or heard something hit one of the windows.

Nick slowly opened the sliding glass door to the back patio. As he stepped into the only dim light shining from a third floor window, he heard the sound again and was suddenly struck on his right temple. The sting shocked him. He yelled out and fell to the ground. Thick fluid oozed down the side of his head and his vision blurred in one eye.

"Oh shit! Mr. Taft? Nick? Is that you?" It was the older Palmer boy, Lee, holding a gun in his hand. "I'm so sorry!"

"Lee, what the hell are you doing?"

"Oh, geez. It's a paintball war."

The younger boy gave Nick some wet paper towels, "We didn't know that was you!"

As he was able to look around, Nick realized they were dressed in black and well camouflaged against the night. He could also make out various colored splotches of paint on the side of the house and on some of the shrubs and trees. As he stood and scanned the dark landscape, he noticed several other boys coming out of the surrounding yard.

"Paintball is a blast. But it helps to have goggles and camo gear. We're really sorry."

"I'll be fine."

"Come back in the house. We've got something that will clean that paint up, just don't get it near your eyes!"

"It's in my eye!"

"Yeah. Shouldn't do any permanent damage – I don't think."

After cleaning up and sharing a cola with the boys in the kitchen, Nick was feeling better. He doused his eye with some Visine they found.

Lee asked, somewhat shyly, "You're a lawyer for my dad – right? I'm thinking of going to law school."

Nick struggled to think of a polite way to strongly recommend against it without revealing too much.

"Hey, do you want to join us in a paintball war? We've got extra guns and camo clothes."

"Well..."

"Oh, come on, it's just a game – dad's really good at it!"

"Well, maybe for one round. Okay, teach me the basics."

Lee, who had floppy black hair and childlike dimples, instructed Nick on loading and firing the gun. He also gave him a matching flat black shirt and pants to wear to camouflage against the darkness and advised Nick to stick close to him.

They slinked around the large back yard. Lee taught Nick to lean into the big oaks or the corner of the house just enough so his silhouette would become part of the background. They operated in teams, two boys with the same color paint made up one team. After an hour of shooting and being pummeled by stinging paint balls, Nick called it a night. Between laughter about the better shots, they hosed and scrubbed down the side of the house where errant paintballs had landed. With more apologies for taking him by surprise, the friends left and the boys headed to bed.

Although his head was throbbing, he felt great; the intensity of the game was a good stress reliever. He went to his room upstairs and chuckled at how bad he looked. His eye was swollen and dark blue paint covered his eyelid, eyebrow, and side of his face. One of the boys knocked on his door to inform him they'd be off to school by six-thirty, and offered up soap that was good for removing paint. But Nick was so tired he just fell asleep.

The Congressman was due back from England that Wednesday night. When Nick swung by the house to collect his things, the boys insisted he take some paintball guns and camo gear and emphasized they had lots of extras. He obliged while they talked more about the locations the paint wars were played. "Let me know if you go out with your dad some time – we'll take you on."

He returned to the solitude of his apartment in Georgetown and regrouped. Considering the weaponry involved, Nick had survived his brief stay with Palmer's family mostly intact. Although he and the boys had bonded, their retriever, Basil, would likely never forgive him. In his hurry to work that harried Monday morning, he'd forgotten to let her back in the house. When the boys got home from school, the old retriever greeted them in the driveway with half the colors of the paintball rainbow frozen to her coat.

19

Early March 1986   Capitol Hill   47 Degrees Dark Skies

At the committee staff meeting the next morning, Denny Folgier announced that the Administrative Office of the U.S. Courts was hosting an issues briefing that Thursday and Friday at the Governor Calvert House in Annapolis, Maryland. Folgier mentioned that several majority counsels would be attending and asked if anyone on the minority staff was interested.

Nick's hand shot up, and he practically shouted, "I'd love to go."

"Okay, glad to hear it. Anybody else?"

The room was silent. Nick raced back to his office after the meeting to call Lisa. After some hesitation on her part, he convinced her to sign up for the briefing and accompany him to Annapolis. He'd think of something when he got there.

———————

The historic Governor Calvert House situated across from the Maryland State Capitol was in a word – old. It had a sweet musty smell and the floors creaked no matter where you stepped, but some of the rooms had been restored and the interior woodwork was beautiful. The reauthorization of the independent counsel statute was among the subjects included in the briefing. Nick came prepared and asked many questions of the panel. Lisa would later describe his questions as obnoxious, but she wasn't handling that issue and didn't know it well enough to argue the substance.

When the briefing was over, staffers asked if he and Lisa could join them for drinks. Nick declined before Lisa responded and offered an excuse that they had other plans. He'd conjured up a story to tell her about looking at some Chesapeake Bay real estate for a potential investment idea with some friends. Acknowledging how expensive the market was near Annapolis, he'd said it was slightly off the beaten path south of town. The Major had learned that the suspect pier was likely one of two abandoned ones within approximately five miles from the State Capitol.

Since Nick wasn't sure which road would lead to the right place, he figured his foil of searching for some property, the location of which was uncertain, might provide cover. What he hadn't figured out yet was the transitional conversation from, *Well, I guess this isn't the property, but why don't we go explore the yacht at the end of that deserted pier and see if your boss is there hanging with some hookers?*

The afternoon sun was beginning to fade as they traveled south of town. Nick was trying to read the cryptic directions he'd scribbled from Ity's instructions. Lisa asked him why he hadn't mentioned the real estate venture before.

Making it up as he drove, "Well, it's kind of a long shot, mostly just talk at this point, but since we were going to be here and it's decent weather, I figured what the hell. Let's just see if we can find it. Good deals on waterfront property aren't easy to find, you know."

Lisa was momentarily impressed, "Okay."

Nick was never great at directions. His closest friends would often have him choose which direction to go when lost, then go the opposite way. As it turned out, the first road he turned down was to someone's private residence and they stood on the front porch glowering as he and Lisa did a lap around the driveway. The second road had more *No Trespassing* signs than a hardware store. After passing several of those warnings, Lisa laughed and suggested they turn around, "Pretty soon we're going to come to that sign from the Wizard of Oz's witch's forest that says *I'd turn back if I were you!"*

Lisa noticed his seldom-used expensive camera with the biggest *Nikon* telephoto lens attached, "What are you planning to do? Take photos of the bare trees to show your co-investors?"

Nick turned up the radio and mumbled, "Thank goodness for *March Madness*."

"Shouldn't we be looking for a *For Sale* sign?"

Nick was frustrated and beginning to reach. "According to my directions, one of those first three roads had to be on target – maybe it's the one with the *No Trespassing* signs. The owner is apparently a quirky guy. Maybe that's why there's no *For Sale* sign."

When they got past all the posted signs, the road split. Nothing in the directions indicated a split or which way to go. Nick chose the road to the left which took them through the woods to another dead-end. They got out and admired the soft curves of spring. The sun was still shining, but dusk was soon upon them. Lisa broke the silence complaining she would have brought a jacket had she known they were embarking on a field trip.

Nick, a split second ahead of her, pulled out two heavy black camo shirts from the trunk. "Compliments of the Palmer boys," he referenced the night of the paint ball games.

Lisa noticed the water through the trees to their left, there were few leaves on the trees and the evergreens scattered about were easy to see through. "That looks like a big dock through there. Let's check it out."

Nick nervously grabbed his camera while Lisa explored the landscape.

The ground crunched as they walked across once frozen twigs, grass, and acorns. As they approached a clearing, they noticed several cars parked at the entrance to the pier. A lone yacht was docked at the end of the long pier with its interior lights on and a muffled audio system playing "Hotel California."

Lisa looked at the yacht, then to Nick, then at one of the cars, "What *is* this?"

"It looks like a dock and a boat to me. I just don't know if this is the right property."

"Nick, that Bronco is our office manager's car!"

"What are you talking about?" He stayed focused on the water.

"The car right behind you! It has a Congressional tag. And, that yacht's probably the one everyone talks about with all the so-called parties."

"Are you sure that's his car?"

"Nobody else has a green Bronco with congressional plates from Texas's 42nd District unless there was a special election yesterday that I happened to miss."

"Well, what do we do now?"

"I don't know. What did *you* have in mind?"

"I had nothing in mind. We can keep driving if you want."

Lisa was spinning her pearls back and forth in front of her throat. "No. No, let's take a look. All the bullshit I've heard for so long about this – I want to see for myself."

Nick let go a long sigh.

"But, Nick, I don't think we want to be seen here. And, whatever we see stays between us, understand? I'm not going to take down my own boss. And, give me that camera!"

"I understand," he said handing over the camera.

Nightfall began closing in as they stepped onto the pier. The construction looked fairly solid, but with each careful step the squeaky planks became less stable. The yacht was moored at the far right end of a big T dock. The bow was pointing away from the pier making it seem like anyone on board would be looking the other way. There were no lights on the dock, but the yacht's dim bow and stern lights glowed. The brighter interior lights were all on and most of the window curtains were only partially drawn.

It was half tide which allowed them to look down from the dock into the well-lit living quarters and galley. The difference between the inside and outside temperatures created a condensation frame around each window. Despite the impediments, the first partial view revealed a svelte young woman with tight jeans and an open blouse leaning in close to a dark-haired man with his back to the window. On a brightly lit table there were several bottles of premium liquor, a sugar bowl half filled, and several lines of white powder laid out on a mirror.

The next window framed Staunton's familiar face, but with an unfamiliar expression. He had one hand on the shoulder of the dark-haired man, as though he was stiff-arming him in a football game. His other arm was on the bare back of a young brunette woman wearing only bikini bottoms. Most tired congressmen want a dark bar and a drink or a smoke, and to be left the fuck alone after hours – but not Staunton, he couldn't stand to be alone.

Nick was trying every angle to see who else was inside. After a few minutes of attempting to identify other silhouetted characters, the cold and potential downside to their mission was getting to Lisa, "Hey, let's go. I'm freezing and can't see jack-shit."

"Okay. But, since we're already out here, let's just take one more peek from the bow looking back. There's a big window facing forward from the galley quarters."

"All right, but let's make it quick."

They began to walk cautiously toward the bow of the yacht, the stern door from the interior flew open and two people stepped out onto the fishing deck. Nick leaned up against a piling and guided Lisa with his hand in behind him. One of the voices was unmistakable, "Darlin', you're going to be the death of me, I swear."

The other was of a female in her early thirties, sexy and flirtatious, "Oh, please, a big guy like you. I'm sure you can handle yourself in just about any situation. Should we do another bump honey?"

"You go ahead. I'll just keep sipping my champagne."

"Oh, come on, do another bump with me, we'll be up all night – how's that sound?"

"Shelly-girl, you're gonna do me in."

Nick and Lisa stayed behind the post looking toward the voices. It was Staunton all right – in a dark wool suit with his tie and hair askew. The woman was thin with shoulder length straight blond hair; she was wearing a blouse and short jean skirt. They kept going in and out of view on the back deck. Nick and Lisa could hear the sound of snorting and sniffling.

"Mmmm...it makes my whole head tingle!"

"You know it kinda makes my tongue numb."

"That best be temporary, you're going to need it later, Mr. Chairman."

She kissed Staunton, "Hey baby, it's cold. Let's go back inside."

"It feels kind a nice to me."

"Yeah, but you're not wearing a skirt with no undies."

They closed the door as they stepped inside. Lisa glanced at Nick with a half-smile, but revealed a face of disappointment.

Nick was struggling to see back inside. At that moment, a hand came across the window directly in front of them wiping condensation away and a face looked out straight at them. Nick and Lisa froze. Both tried to lean in behind the dolphin post. It was the head of the U.S. Capitol Police; the man Lisa had seen Staunton argue with the morning after Alec Sivore's murder. He stared directly at them but it was obvious he couldn't see them. The stark contrast between the bright interior and the dark night protected them from being seen.

"Who was that?" Nick asked.

Lisa said nothing.

"Lisa, who was that guy?"

Lisa shook her head, "Let's just go, Nick."

As they walked slowly and carefully away from the yacht and down the pier, Lisa kept looking at Nick as if waiting for him to say something. After several steps down the pier, they saw a car pulling up with its headlights on. They noticed another car parked and someone already on the pier halfway between them and the shore.

Lisa put her hand on Nick's shoulder. "Shit!"

"What the hell? Who's that?"

"Don't know."

A man moved quickly down the dock and yelled toward them, "Hey, what are you doing here?"

Nick looked around, but there was nowhere to go.

He was on them quickly, "Hey, Mis…"

But before Nick could speak a word, Lisa clocked the guy across the jaw with Nick's camera and he slumped to the edge of the dock. He was stunned and trying to regroup.

"Lisa, what the fu…"

But, Lisa was in full backswing again using the camera lens as a shaft and the body as a club head. With a quick pivot she struck the man hard in the neck and jaw. But this time, he saw her coming. Though too slow to deflect the blow, he managed to awkwardly throw his elbow under her shoulder, hook it around her back, and drag her off the dock with him.

Nick could see men getting out of the car that had pulled to the edge of the pier. They were under the trees, so he couldn't see them well, but he wasn't waiting for them. He wrapped himself around a dock post and slid into the cold water. Lisa

155

caught a two-by-four on her way down and was standing on a knee-deep crossbeam under the dock. The unknown man was floating between two dock posts. He was out cold.

Nick jumped onto the thick beam with Lisa, "Help me hold him."

"What?"

"Grab his other arm."

Nick, stunned by Lisa's aggressiveness, stood on a slippery wooden beam trying to catch his breath. The tide was pulling the man away. Nick took a wallet and gun from the guy's jacket.

When he looked up again the man was out of reach, "Lisa, grab him!"

The prevailing tide was not in their favor, and it pulled him out into the open.

"Oh shit."

In a whisper, he yelled, "Lisa, what the hell was that?"

"I don't know," she said quietly, staring at the floating man.

The man quickly drifted away, but with open eyes facing toward the dark sky. They watched him glide like a leaf past the bow toward a nearby point where their car was parked. They heard footsteps coming down the pier from the shore.

Nick took Lisa's arm, "Get out of this water. Climb up here."

He climbed from an angled support beam to a crossbar under the dock above the water. Lisa followed behind. He pulled her close and put an arm around her as they balanced on a beam just under the dock's surface. They sat perfectly still looking up at the underside of the pier.

As footsteps came closer, they heard conversation, "What the hell happened to Dougee?"

Someone walked quickly to the yacht and banged on a door. The music stopped – the night was suddenly silent. The only thing Nick could hear was water dripping off their shoes as it hit the bay's surface below, and the sound of dogs barking somewhere in the distance.

The footsteps got closer. "Dougee, where are you?"

More people above them still, on all ends of the pier. There was a conversation near the yacht, then footsteps coming back their way.

"They ain't seen Dougee at the boat."

"Then what the hell's goin on, what happened to him?"

"Don't know, boss."

"We think we heard a splash, right?"

"Yeah."

"He fall in the water?"

"He could've."

"Get some flashlights, and start looking between here and the boat."

Nick listened again as people moved quickly toward the yacht. Fortunately, it was a dark night, no moonlight covered the water. Nick and Lisa were tucked as far up under the dock as they could get. The powerful flashlight beams went into the water, along the side of the yacht, and up and down the pier and shoreline.

"A guy don't just walk down a dock and disappear! Dougee ain't some magician and he knows how to swim if he did fall in. Something ain't right. Keep looking. I'm gettin' the chairman outta here."

––––––––––

Nick and Lisa looked at each other as the thugs walked inches above them. She closed her eyes and squeezed his hand. After a dozen flashlights lit up the dock's surface over their heads, they heard loud conversation from the direction of the yacht.

"Sir, all I'm saying is, under the circumstances, it's best your guests move on. Let us search for our missing man knowing that you're out of harm's way."

"For God's sake, man. Will you get us where we're goin' then? I don't want any of these people inconvenienced – understood?"

The footsteps overhead seemed to go on forever: security men, party attendees, and yacht staff all departed. Lisa was shivering hard, Nick rubbed her arms and legs. After several cars left, they could hear a few voices still talking.

"Go over that boat with a fine-toothed comb one more time. And, no, if we don't find him, we don't call nobody. This boat doesn't exist, understand? We'll let his girlfriend file a missing person's report maybe in a week. You saw nothing."

Nick's watch read 7:15. They'd been under the dock for a half hour. He was sore from sitting on the cold wood. Lisa seemed comatose, but was still breathing. By 7:30, the search was done. All the lights on the yacht were off. Car doors slammed and cars pulled away.

He helped Lisa climb down from under the dock and then up onto the pier. Unfortunately, they had to get partially wet again in order to get dry. Lisa groaned as she entered the icy water. Nick helped her back on her feet once on top of the dock.

"Let's get the hell out of here."

"What should I do with these?" Lisa held up the dead man's gun and wallet.

"Throw them in the bay for God's sake – wait!" He grabbed the gun and wiped the handle and barrel from end to end with his shirt before throwing it into the dark water.

"What are you doing?" Lisa asked.

"Getting rid of our fingerprints in case someone finds it."

Nick had seen this done on TV so many times he figured it must be effective. Lisa just shook her head. They stumbled through the brush. Lisa noticed some lights from a house beyond a stand of trees on the nearby point. Once in the car, he turned on the heater and drove out of the woods.

"Lisa, where'd that come from? You just knocked a guy senseless and wrestled him into the Chesapeake Bay!"

"Do you think he's dead? I thought he was breathing – and I think he blinked."

"Do I think he's dead? Are you kidding me? He's fish food by now!"

———————

If either had frostbite, the hot shower in the hotel returned their respective body temperatures to normal. The heat in the room was on high, they got under the covers.

"I'm scared," Lisa whispered into the silence. "We obviously can't go to the police. Do you think anyone knows we were there?"

Nick kissed her forehead, "I don't know how they could."

"I know we need to talk this whole thing through – just not now, okay?"

At some point that night they fell into a seemingly deep sleep, but were exhausted when they awoke.

Blowing off Friday morning's lecture at the historic house was an easy decision. They stayed in their room, ate breakfast, and then headed back to Washington. During the drive, Lisa said she wanted to hear everything Nick had been trying to tell her.

He told her all he'd experienced, from the down and out alleyway scene in Georgetown, to the Mexican Federale, to the warehouse in Texas. He finished with his doubts about Alec Sivore's death. Lisa seemed matter-of-fact about it all.

"So, what do you think?"

"What do I think? I killed a man. And, if they find him, what am I supposed to do? I've never been so scared. But, you have to promise me something. You have to swear to me you'll do nothing about this nor speak a word about last night until we talk again."

Hearing the conviction in her voice, he agreed. Their anxiety generated an undefined friction between them. He dropped Lisa at her apartment late Friday afternoon. It was a discomforting good-bye.

20

March 1986   Capitol Hill   45 Degrees Partly Sunny

Monday morning came fast. The House Leadership decided to bring the independent counsel reauthorization bill to the floor that week. The Judiciary Committee majority delivered the committee report on the bill and gave the minority five days to add their opinions before filing it.[10] The Republicans were allowed to file views on issues with which they disagreed in the report. The majority staff, with four times as many lawyers, had used the past month to draft their ninety pages. Denny and Nick had little time to write views and have them approved by their members.

Nick had five days to convince Palmer to offer his amendment to allow Members of Congress to be investigated by independent counsels. Palmer was not enthusiastic about offering it. He knew any element of surprise was gone due to his withdrawing it at the previous committee meeting. The majority had the past five weeks to prepare to defeat the amendment. Nick sympathized with Palmer's concerns but was convinced the amendment would still highlight the hypocrisy of the majority and might draw some media attention. From a sixty-thousand foot level, the issue was about "what's good for the goose is good for the gander."

He and Folgier worked hard on drafting. Their minority views were finalized, signed by five Republicans, and ready to be filed with the House just in time to become a part of the committee report. Palmer reluctantly decided to offer the so-called "covered persons" amendment on the floor, and to seek permission to do so at the Rules Committee. Unfortunately, the national media didn't find too much to write about the amendment in a positive light – most supported the Democrats' position.[11]

Nick waited until the last minute to file their minority views. With his limited resources, he couldn't match the heft of the majority's report, but had a few surprises he thought might make them blink. The next day in the cramped Rules Committee room where Palmer sought the right to offer his amendment on the floor, Staunton sat across the narrow aisle from Nick reading the words he'd written. He saw Staunton turn to the back of the views where Nick had attached the Department of Justice's *amicus* brief filed in the federal court of appeals case which challenged the constitutionality of the independent counsel statute. The brief was well-researched and countered every constitutional argument the majority had made in support of the law.

Staunton asked questions of the counsel sitting next to him, and to Nick's surprise, as she answered, she pointed across the Chairman's chest directly at him. He would've liked to have averted his gaze, but it was too late. Staunton's flint blue eyes caught him head on. He looked at Nick for a few seconds, then back down at the report. But this time he didn't shake his head as if dismissing a nuisance; he glared back at Nick and flung the report on the floor. Palmer finished his remarks and got up to leave. Nick stood to follow him out, but then bent down and picked Staunton's copy off the floor and handed it to him.

Later that week, the legislation was debated on the House floor. Nick spent most of the previous night finalizing arguments and statements for Palmer to make on every aspect of the issue. Early the next morning he met with the Republican Leadership floor staff to seek their counsel. These guys knew their way down a political suicide run – losing was a way of life for them. Palmer offered his amendment to cover Members of Congress under the statute and made credible arguments in its favor along with a handful of other Republicans. The amendment was handily defeated on a party-line vote.[12]

The majority argued the President and his appointees were the only political figures worthy of an independent prosecutor. They boasted about the effectiveness of the law and denounced claims it was used as a political tool. They appeared distressed by arguments that the prosecutor enabled by the statute was too powerful, too expensive, or abused his power. Staunton was the last to speak. He speculated that a political witch hunt would ensue if Congressmen were covered under the law, and he ridiculed the Republicans for offering the amendment for purely political purposes.

Palmer and Nick took their defeat in stride. Every amendment they'd ever offered had been rejected on a party line vote anyway. This day was no different. To Nick it was a victory though, because to the people outside of Congress, who were actually taking note, it was one more example of the hypocrisy of the majority party.[13]

The remainder of the week went by quickly. Nick noticed Lisa was nowhere to be seen in the halls or committee meetings. When he tried to reach her midweek, she didn't return his calls. He wanted to respect her wish to be alone, but was worried about her. When they finally got together that Saturday for lunch, she looked as pale as a mug shot.

He referenced the reality of the previous weekend, "I've not heard anything on the news, have you?"

"No, but the Capitol Police Chief has been in and out of the Chairman's office a dozen times in the past few days." Lisa looked around nervously as if they shouldn't be seen together.

"Look, I'll be honest, I can't quit thinking about what happened on the dock that night either."

She balked, "I can't really talk about it." She started to tear up, but then refocused and asked one question, "Was that the property you were looking for, Nick?"

When he stuttered, she ended the conversation, "Right!" They didn't see each other or talk again the remainder of the weekend.

With too much time on his hands, Nick began to question Lisa's loyalties again, which bothered him on so many fronts. It was a place he didn't want to go. For a distraction he considered collecting all his unpaid parking tickets and actually showing his face at the DC DMV to negotiate a bulk payoff. He'd recently discovered the embedded BMW emblem was missing from the hood of his car and figured whoever was constructing an alternative vehicle with pieces, in part from his, must be about finished. Maybe it would be worth making his car legal again.

Instead he went for a long run and replayed the previous Thursday over in his mind. What was it the security thug had said just before Lisa clobbered him? "Hey, what are you two doing here? Hey, Mis..." then, slam, lights out. Was he about to ask, "Hey, Miss Castile what are you doing here?" He questioned why Lisa had a change of heart about checking on Staunton when she saw Traynor's car that night? Was it right for her to be running from what she'd done? Was he a complete hypocrite for helping her run from a potential manslaughter charge? The differences between right and wrong as to his feelings for Lisa were relegating his take on reality to suspect at best.

21

April 1986 Capitol Hill 55 Degrees Clearing

In addition to being the information center for much actual news, Capitol Hill was also *rumor central* twenty-four hours a day. Good jobs with big-name firms didn't come around every day and one seeking them had to be circumspect. Anyone in Congress who'd been substantially involved in any meaningful legislation had made enemies. There was a loser on every vote and one never knew where that loser might surface.

When Nick walked through his outer office the next Monday morning, his assistant repeated the latest Hill gossip, "I heard about Lisa's new job. Tell her congrats for me!"

He was speechless, which was fortunate as it was better that he seem unsurprised than appear out of the loop. Lisa called before Nick could get to his desk, "I'm sorry. I had to get it done – signed, sealed, and delivered."

"What did you *get done*?"

"I had to get out from under Staunton. This business with thugs and dead men – it's too much for me! I've been negotiating for the past two weeks; I just signed a contract with Maloney & Whitaker. You've heard of it, the biggest law firm in Texas."

"Maloney & Whitaker? Yeah, I know a third-year associate there who finally just saw the inside of a courtroom – he got called for jury duty. When do you move?"

"Well, get this, I signed up to go back to Texas to do litigation or office practice, I didn't care which; and they were all fine with that. But two days after I signed the contract, they called and want me mainly in the firm's Washington office to practice law and to lobby. They've concluded that my experience and knowledge of Congress will make me a more valuable asset here. And guess who they want me to lobby?"

"You can't be serious!"

"But what was I supposed to do, say no? They think it's great that Chairman Staunton and I have such a good relationship."

"I see. So, when do you start?"

"In about four weeks, but I'm taking a week off. I figured I'd go home to Texas. Will you come with me? We both could use a break."

———————

Lisa's relatives' place was apparently only about an hour's drive from Austin. Nick's lingering doubts about Lisa's loyalties made him reluctant to become any further intertwined with her, but he figured the trip might give him an opportunity to visit Bud Marskey again while in Texas so he called him to check in.

"Good timing, Taft. I was actually just about to call you."

"Why?"

"Guess who I got a call from just this morning?"

"Who?"

"The Maverick County Sheriff's Office in Normandy."

"Why?"

"It appears the Delrio Corporation has a penchant for security cameras. And one of them has a fuzzy shot of a motorcycle parked near a door during a time frame when there was an apparent break-in at their building in Normandy."

"You're so full of shit."

"Wish I were, my friend."

"What?!"

"Yep. Apparently the company has a low-tech, low-speed security camera and they only check the video every now and then. It seems they rarely use the building we visited. They just discovered a potential break-in about a month ago. When they checked their surveillance footage, they couldn't make out much inside the building, except for a few brief moments when the lights were turned on!"

"Oh, fuck!"

"They think they can make out a person climbin' down from a tanker in their warehouse, but cannot make out a face. The footage is apparently not of very good quality. However, the outside camera with the benefit of daylight caught a glimpse of two motorcycles ridin' away from the building at what appears from the time-lapsed footage to be at a high rate of speed. No shit on that one – we were haulin' ass! Fortunately, the make of the motorcycles can't be seen on the video and there are no identifying particulars except one."

"What's that?"

"The camera caught about two thirds of the license tag on one of the bikes. It happened to be the one you were ridin'."

"They can't prove anything with that. Right?"

"No, Perry Mason, they can't. But it didn't stop them from speculating about the other digits and inquiring as to any trips I might have made last fall to Normandy."

"What did you say?"

"What do you think? I said, 'Oh, yeah, I remember now. I loaned that bike to my unbelievably stupid friend, Nick Taft, on that day. And as I recall, he was headed for the Mexico border ...'"

"That's not funny, Marskey. You've no idea what kind of weird bullshit I've been through on that front lately."

"You're right. It's not funny. And, for the record, I don't want to know any more about your goings-on."

"Fair enough. But, what did you tell them?"

"I told 'em I didn't know what they were talkin' about. And that I've never been to Normandy and happened to be workin' on that particular day. I may have mentioned that I work for

State Representative Burwell. I don't think they'll be callin' back. Unless of course, they take that footage to someone who knows how to clarify it and they recognize you or the rest of my license tag – at which point I give 'em what little information I actually know about you like your name, address, phone number and apparent IQ level."

———————

Her grandparents' ranch was a half hour northwest of San Antonio. It was small by Texas standards but big in Nick's eyes. It had wooden fences that seemed to go on forever corralling cows and horses. A lazy lake fell away from the backside of the ranch into sunlight from the west. The house, a blend of wood and stone with inviting worn leather furniture, had a tall beamed ceiling. The oak dining table looked like it had been there for centuries and two stone fireplaces were as big as any Nick had ever seen.

Lisa wore a quiet smile while she drove a crippled Jeep past barns and outbuildings as they headed down to the lake. Nick noticed a longhorn steer standing by the shoreline and wondered if one day its horns might end up on somebody's wall. Other than the lake, the place was dusty and dry. A few large-limbed shade trees stood here and there, but most of the grounds succumbed to a hot sun throughout the day.

They had dinner with her grandparents who, while gracious hosts, were not big talkers. When they nervously asked how things were in Washington, and Lisa anxiously replied that all was fine, the inquiry was over. They opened up only when talking about Lisa's younger days as a calf roper and all-around cowgirl. Nick had seen little of that side of the Harvard graduate, but hoped to get a snapshot of it while in Texas.

Barely a word was spoken of Lisa's parents who'd divorced years ago. Nick learned while there that her mother passed away during Lisa's first year of law school and that her father, whom she seldom mentioned, had failed at ranching and moved on years before. The only kind thing she'd ever said about him was he'd really gone the extra mile through a connection at the University of Texas Board of Regents to help her get an almost full-ride scholarship to Harvard. He'd once owned the largest ranch between San Antonio and Austin, but went bankrupt when Lisa was in elementary school. Her parents separated when their land was auctioned off, and he thereafter very seldom visited.

Lisa and her mother later went to live on her grandparents' smaller spread where she spent her adolescent years. Their place was the only home Lisa would ever acknowledge from her youth. Nick noticed that Lisa seemed almost like a different person in Texas, she was more down-to-earth. Her grandparents were obviously proud, but worried about how thin she appeared. They encouraged her to eat more steak at dinner, more roast beef at lunch and more sausage with her eggs at breakfast. They'd even offered beef brownies for dessert one night.

After sunning on the floating dock one day, they headed to Austin to see Bud Marskey. During the drive, he recounted to Lisa his adventure with Bud at the Delrio building and of the Normandy police department's recent phone call inquiring about the motorcycles. She seemed to be taking it all in, but about half way there, Lisa pulled to the roadside and stood quietly looking across a large stretch of farm land. She explained it was her father's old ranch – and she intended to buy it back. Nick estimated it to be worth millions and pondered how she would ever afford that.

They met at a restaurant near the university campus where Bud and Lisa had both attended college. After introductions, some reminiscing on their UT glory days, and Bud's expression of shock that Nick actually had a girlfriend, they got down to the unfortunate business at hand. A Maverick County Sheriff's deputy had just paid an unannounced visit to Marskey's apartment.

The deputy had asked the same questions as before, checked out the motorcycles and took some notes. Bud asked what it was all about and if anything of value had been stolen from the building. The officer reported that over $50,000 in cash had been stolen. Bud emphasized how he'd had to swallow hard not to call bullshit on that, but kept his cool. He told Bud the security film had been turned over to an independent lab to enhance the quality and sharpness.

Nick and Lisa shared everything they'd experienced to date, except about the dead security thug. They decided to keep that one just between them. Bud was sympathetic, "These people are obviously crooks and thieves, and dangerous. I don't know how much I can afford to get involved Nick, but their lies may now be implicating me. I'll help you where I can."

"Thanks, Bud. You don't know how much that means to us. How well do you think they can clarify that film? And what if they do it to the point of showing my face or the tag on your bike? How long might that take?"

"Now, hang on a second there, Taft. Don't go gettin' all paranoid on us all of a sudden. Let's just think this thing through."

They spent hours considering potential outcomes: if they could identify Nick; if they could identify Bud's bikes; if they could identify anything. They then calculated their defensive odds, and pondered potential offensive moves. They covered a lot of ground. Before leaving the next day, they promised to stay in touch and cover for each other. Nick and Lisa drove back to San Antonio. Lisa gave her grandparents a tight hug and they boarded a plane to Washington.

22

Late May 1986   Capitol Hill   77 Degrees Cloudy

No one was around when he arrived at his office the following Monday. He checked his voicemail. Tom Countryman indicated he needed to talk about an investigation they'd been brought into near Annapolis. Nick hoped this was the Justice Department's investigation of Chairman Staunton to which the Major had referred. He suddenly had an appetite and walked to the cafeteria for a real breakfast before returning the call. On his way, a guy he'd never met yelled a big hello and began chatting him up like an old acquaintance. He asked how Nick's apartment was, and if he'd been able to get his car fixed. Later while eating, he realized the guy was a lobbyist he'd met with for one minute on an antitrust bill during his first week on the committee.

To his surprise, when he returned, Tom Countryman was standing in the doorway to Denny Folgier's office talking as if they were best friends. "Hey Nick, do you know Tom Countryman? He and I go way back."

"We've met before. Nice to see you again."

Countryman looked at Nick, "I'm glad you're here. I wanted to touch base with you about one of the issues you're working on. Do you have time for a quick cup of coffee?"

Nick walked back down to the cafeteria, but this time with no appetite and making awkward small talk with Countryman. They bought their coffees and sat behind a square pillar in a far corner.

"Tom, I'm really curious as to why you'd want to talk with me about an investigation near Annapolis? Of course I'd be glad to help if I can. You know I once worked at a State's Attorneys office and know something about investigat..."

Countryman interrupted, "You better hear me out first, Nick."

"Sure."

"A little old couple, the Aikens, and their two hounds have lived forever on the Chesapeake Bay south of Annapolis. They are a stubborn, survivalist, Scottish duo. They wouldn't sell to the government when we bought out all adjacent landowners to create a wildlife sanctuary several years ago. So they remain on this little spit of property surrounded by acres of pristine federal land. But legally speaking, they are treated as if they are on federal real estate – that's why the Justice Department got pulled in."

"Okay."

"Early one evening a few weeks ago, their dogs barked endlessly while tracking something floating on the shoreline. The Aikens investigated and fished a man out of the Chesapeake Bay. He had a fractured jaw apparently caused by a blunt force trauma and was practically frozen."

Nick, sitting back in his chair, "What does this have to do with me?"

"Well, considering how short a time we estimated this man was actually in the water, and having checked the tides and currents for the night they found him, we believe he may have fallen from a nearby pier. Upon searching under that pier at low tide, our investigators discovered a handgun and a Nikon camera with a large telephoto lens. Nick, we ran the product numbers on the fairly unique camera lens. It was sold in Georgetown last year – to you."

His legal training told him not to say another word.

Countryman continued, "Listen, I want to help you, but you need to help me."

"Tom, do I need a lawyer?" Everything was implicating him

– even his own words.

"Hang on. It turns out the man they fished out of the bay isn't dead. But, in addition to the severe blow to his jaw which is now wired shut, he was suffering from hypothermia. The old survivalists took good care of him and warmed his body temperature back to normal. They may have kept him longer but discovered he had amnesia and couldn't even tell them his name. So they took him to the local hospital. That's when we were called by the state police. The doctors say his jaw will heal, and that his amnesia, common with hypothermia, will likely be temporary."

Nick was silent.

"Is there anything you can tell me about this?"

"Look Tom … I don't know what to say."

"You're going to have to do a little better than that, Taft!"

The kitchen staff bussed a nearby table.

"Okay. Did your investigators see the yacht or find out who it belongs to?"

Countryman, with his hands out, palms up, "What yacht?"

"The sixty-foot fishing yacht docked at the end of that pier! Are your men blind?"

"Nick, there's no yacht or boat of any kind docked there. So you *were* there?"

"No yacht or boat of any kind?" Nick whispered as much to himself as to Countryman.

"What's that?"

He leaned in, "Tom, I can tell you things about that pier that might be of extreme interest to you."

"Well, go on."

"First, we have to talk about my situation. What can you do for me? I probably should have a lawyer. But knowing that the *security goon* isn't dead, I'm not sure exactly what crimes may have been committed."

173

"Look, I can be your friend here or I can sink you now. You want to lose your law license here – and in Florida? *Security goon?*"

"Yeah. It's a long story. I can help you out with his name though – it's Dougee."

"Go on."

He recounted his observations of the yacht and pier that night in great detail, and it did get Countryman's attention. He emphasized only one other point, that the first person in Staunton's office after Alec Sivore's death was also on the yacht – the U.S. Capitol Police Chief.

"If all this is accurate, it's very damning information. Anyone else who can corroborate this?"

"Uh...no."

"...All right. What's the name of this yacht?"

"Name? I never saw one. But it was a Hatteras."

"A phantom sixty-foot yacht with no name? Shouldn't be hard to find."

"Look, these weren't the most optimal circumstances to record information! I honestly don't remember seeing one anywhere."

"You say these parties take place on the third Thursday of every month?"

"That's what I was told."

"We'll check into it. Nick, I can't stop the department's investigation of the man pulled from the bay or their interest in your whereabouts then, but I might be able to buy you a little time."

Between spells of paranoia, Nick spent his hours imitating a congressional counsel which helped preserve his job and sanity. His obsessions alternated between how soon the security video in Texas could be clarified to when Dougee in Maryland might regain his memory. But he would have to ignore those distractions. The majority was on a roll again – this time focused on opening the U.S.-Mexico border to any semi-healthy pedestrian.

The leadership scheduled their immigration reform bill for a floor vote.[14] They hoped to have the House bill passed and conferenced with the Senate-approved bill, and send it to the President's desk for signature before Congress adjourned that fall. Nick was anxious for Palmer to offer his previous amendment to delay amnesty for illegal immigrants until the US-Mexico border was secure.

A final draft of the committee report on the immigration bill was provided to the minority late on a Wednesday afternoon. The bill was scheduled to be on the floor the following week. Folgier and Nick had a few days to draft dissenting views to the 220 page report and prepare their Members for a floor debate. Unfortunately, all Members would be back in their home districts over the weekend, and wouldn't return to Washington until late the following Monday. Nick and Folgier worked into Friday night on the Republicans' views.

The majority's language in the committee report was stunning. The bill was creating a sanctuary throughout the U.S. for all immigrants who'd come into the country illegally.[15] Forget the thousands who'd filed papers to enter legally and who'd been waiting for years pursuant to U.S. law. The majority would pass a new law allowing the millions who came in illegally to stay and become citizens. The more Nick read of the committee report interpreting the bill's provisions, the more incredulous he became.

"This is absurd. We're actually going to let all those who came in illegally become citizens simply because they're here?"

Folgier sighed, "Look, their position is that it's our fault for not adequately guarding the border and allowing these folks to get in here to begin with. By that logic, since we missed them at the border, we should now protect them."[16]

"That's insane! Why don't we reward those who obeyed the law and punish those who broke it?"

"I don't know. But, wouldn't you try to sneak into this country if you were them?"

"Maybe. But that wouldn't make it legal. We're rationalizing this by blaming ourselves? But no provision in here actually *requires* we secure that border going forward. So this process could simply repeat itself in twenty years?"[17]

"Perhaps."

"Denny, in my time here, I've discovered the more I learn about any issue, the less black and white it becomes. I get that, but the fundamentals of some issues are hard to ignore. We allow some in due to political persecution, we send others back in part for a lack of it; but under this bill, anyone who makes it across the Rio Grande River can stay regardless of where they're from. It's so indiscriminate. Why would Congress do this?"

"I don't know, kid. But, many of these people are just visa-overstays who have had jobs or small businesses and have paid taxes. There are no simple answers. Let's just get these written."

The following Tuesday, Nick submitted Palmer's and Sedgwick's views for the committee report. He faxed a copy to Palmer in the district office, and the Congressman had signed off. They weren't anywhere close to the 220 pages of legalese in the majority's report, but Nick thought they laid the foundation for an amnesty-related amendment on the House floor.[18] When Palmer arrived back from Florida, he spent time with Nick and Alexi reviewing the triggered amnesty amendment which had previously failed in committee on a mostly party-line vote.

Palmer hesitated, "You really think it's worth our time to offer this in the full House? We got slaughtered in committee and that was with a Democratic cosponsor."

He knew Palmer was tired of going it alone on amendments and getting trounced. Nick had waited to play this card, "Well, that's just it, Representative Sedgwick, a respected Democrat and good debater who cosponsored the amendment in committee, is willing to offer it with you again. It will delay amnesty until a commission has determined the border is secure; some call it triggered amnesty. It's in the Senate-passed version of immigration reform."

"Staunton and the majority will still defeat it on the floor."

Palmer didn't know all the intricacies of immigration law, or the many sordid details of illegal immigration. A congressman in Washington could go a long way speaking passionately about many issues generally, but it was easy to get tripped up in the weeds of a highly emotional debate. Staunton, on the other hand, while no expert on history, knew a lot about immigration – he was brought up around it in his border town school in El Cenzio, Texas. He also knew about it because of kids he'd grown up with, it was pursuant to U.S. law that most of them were north of the Rio Grande. Staunton could argue immigration issues all day, and his personal stake in illegal trafficking was a very motivating tool in the midst of a generally ill-informed debate.

"Maybe, Sandy. But, this amendment has begun to get some play. Alexi should get a press release out – it's a good issue. There's a silent majority out there who care about our borders."

Alexi sighed, "No, that's a waste of time. *Nobody* cares about immigration reform."

"Well, it never hurts to try now does it?" Nick said looking to Palmer.

"Nick, Alexi has her finger on the pulse of the media. If she says it won't get ink, it won't."

Nick, squinting at Alexi, "Finger on the pulse?"

"No, I have a pulse."

Palmer stood, "Okay, you two. I'll offer it, but let's not worry about the press angle."

Nick spoke quickly, "You have to testify at the Rules Committee hearing tomorrow to get permission to offer the amendment. Congressman Sedgwick will testify in favor of it with you."

––––––––––

One of the things Nick liked about working in Congress was he learned something new about politics and the process every day – it was also one of the things he disliked.

Palmer and Sedgwick testified together before the Rules Committee about their triggered amnesty amendment. Staunton was standing in the back of the room.

As they walked out after the hearing was over, Staunton gave Palmer a big smile, "Nice work, Sandy." Most politicians are only as loyal to a cause as their electoral base will allow – Staunton was clearly an exception to the rule.

"What's he grinning about?" Palmer asked as they walked

the colorful encaustic tiles of the Capitol Building. "Didn't he vote against that amendment in committee?"

"Yes sir, he did."

"Then what's with the look and compliment?"

Nick gave his best puzzled serious lawyer look, "I don't know." Dead guilty is what Staunton looked to Nick – and like someone who needed an oxygen bottle.

—————————

As usual, Staunton was smiling because he knew everything before anyone else. That evening, the rule to govern debate on the immigration bill was made public. Many controversial amendments were made in order. The previously-defeated Judiciary Committee amendment requested by Palmer and Sedgwick was not among them. The Rules Committee had denied them the right to even offer the amendment on the floor.[19] Nick and Palmer were once again disgusted by the process and the arrogance of the majority party. The House Leadership, uncertain they had the votes to defeat the amendment, but aware the Republican-controlled Senate had included similar language in their bill, chose to preclude any vote on the issue in the U.S. House of Representatives.[20]

"Sandy, this is an important issue. They can't just quash debate on it altogether. That's un-American – should be political malpractice!"

"I'm afraid they can, Nick. They wrote the rules. But it doesn't mean what the majority party is doing pursuant to *their* rules is what's best for the majority of Americans."

Sedgwick sought time to debate the resolution issued by the Rules Committee. Once given permission, they took the floor and articulated the stark realities of the open border and illegal immigration to an otherwise predisposed and indifferent House chamber.[21]

When they were finished, Palmer looked at Nick and chuckled, "What are you going to do? You can't make 'em listen. But mark my words, this thorn tree will bear thorns. One day they'll see we were right – and that these numbers are truly staggering."[22]

The Alabaman on Sandy's subcommittee walked by and grumbled that even a dawg knows the difference between being tripped over or kicked. Palmer smiled and told Nick he was going back to his office. He'd had enough of the majority's games for one day. The congressman's words faded as Nick noticed Staunton's gaunt face looking his way from a few rows back.

Nick stayed on the floor to help with questions that Republican members might have. It proved to be a long day of debate and confused discussions about temporary workers and resident aliens. After Palmer departed, Nick was near the center aisle of the House which divided his party's side of the chamber from the Democrats'. When his conversation with a counsel ended, he looked up to see Chairman Staunton smirking from a few feet away. He looked at Nick and shook his head, then seemed to enjoy a private joke while marinating in his own craven arrogance.

Nick wanted to walk right up and say "Fuck you, you corrupt old bastard." Instead, he retreated to his party's side of the aisle. How had he thought democracy would work – flawlessly? His disappointment was more an idealistic mistake than a learned one. Late that afternoon, after several heartfelt but historically questionable speeches about all Americans being immigrants (implying illegal), the bill was approved by the House.[23] Congress's propensity to recast history for its political purposes could befuddle even the keenest of minds.

There was a going-away party for a staffer to a Florida Senator at Bullfeathers that night. Running late as usual, Nick hurried back to his office and dropped off his files containing his unused arguments regarding the so-called triggered amnesty amendment. As he set down his papers, he pondered whether it was worse to lose to the majority due to just another lopsided vote or from being denied the opportunity altogether.

He hurried down the long halls of the Rayburn Building to exit through the parking garage. The elevator doors opened and to his dismay, there stood two older congressmen and Chairman Staunton.

"Well, son, what are you waitin' for?"

Nick stepped in. He pushed the button for the bottom garage floor level G1; one other button was already lit up. On level G3, the other two Congressmen exited the elevator. Nick stared straight ahead as the doors slowly closed.

"Just what are you up to, son?"

"Excuse me?"

"I said, what the hell you think yur doin'?"

"Just doing my job, sir."

"Does your job include messin' with me?"

Nick could tell Staunton had consumed a few cocktails. "Messing with you, sir?"

"Son, I may be elected, but I'm not stupid."

Considering the look on Staunton's face, Nick was uncertain as to which "messin' with him" he meant. "Sir, it was just an attempt to offer an amendment. It's all we can do in the minority, you know – offer amendments. You guys win every time anyway."

"Is that so?"

"Yes sir."

Staunton leaned back into the elevator railing to balance himself, "Well, if that's your answer, then let me ask you somethin'."

"Okay."

"So you're against amnesty for all those poor folks here, as you say, illegally. What is it you want, the federal government to go knocking down people's doors and snatchin' them from their homes, schools, and places of work? So we can drag 'em back across the border – after we let them in here in the first place? Is that what you and your little Republican friends want America to do?"

"No!"

"Then what?" Staunton snorted.

"We want to control our frigging border! So we don't allow another twenty million in illegally – then blame ourselves for it all over again. Look, I'm not against any one of these people, or against them becoming citizens."

And, as an equal might do, Nick continued, "Why don't we really raise the legal immigration levels from South and Central American countries to help them come here legally? Open the gates if you think we can absorb them. But don't pretend we can by leaving the border open, then stamp them illegal once they're here. Under your rules they deserve an entrapment defense. Why pass half a law that facilitates illegal trafficking, and encourages more to come in and live here in fear? It's not like they're living the American Dream – they're afraid to!"

"You want us to build a Berlin Wall?"

"No, more like a Hadrian's Wall. If that border was certified by our government to be secure, there'd be no valid accusations against any group of people being here illegally. They'd either be citizens, or on a path to citizenship, and free to live their lives as they choose. Let's do more than just what feels good in the short term, but what's most humane in the long run."

Unduly bordering on insolence, Nick stood arguing with the Chairman of his committee, and a man he was otherwise pushing the limits with. But he wanted an answer, too. Unfortunately, the elevator doors opened. Nick stretched his palm-up toward the door in respect to the Chairman. Staunton's jaw tightened. He stood perfectly still requiring Nick to repeatedly hold the automatic doors from closing. Nick looked at the door, then back to Staunton, and then permanently back at the door.

Staunton stepped out, "Don't fuck with me, son, you're way out of your league here."

The doors closed.

Nick continued to the party where he tried to be upbeat with his Capitol Hill cronies, but was preoccupied by his interaction with Staunton. The barkeep offered his usual beer. He ordered a Coke instead and thought about his deteriorating circumstances. The bartender asked if he was all right. Nick replied that he was just tired.

In reality, he was beyond tired – and consumed by the events taking place around him. He missed his hometown, his family and friends. He'd grown weary of the art of politics and the place to which it had led him. He was beginning to question if he had any skills in it at all. When he thought of his odds against Staunton, the question had become not about whether he could win, but by how much he would lose. At that party, he was around good colleagues, but their political banter was like strange conversations passing him by. He simply had nothing to say.

Everyone was having a beer and relaxing; he was probably the one who should've been drinking. He left Bullfeathers and walked in a misty rain up First Street to the Cannon Building. It was only seven-thirty, and Congress was still in session. He decided to stop by Congressman Palmer's office to see some friendly faces. Alexi was on the phone at her desk reading through headlines – she waved him off with a look of disdain. Palmer's attempt at offering the triggered amnesty amendment had required she answer some fairly patronizing press calls on a concept she thought was stupid to begin with and, of course, it was all Nick's fault.

Nick stuck his head in Palmer's office. He and his wife were preparing for a weekend trip back to Florida.

"Hey, Nick. We're trying to get out of here. What's up?"

"Oh, just the usual."

Many times he'd wanted to tell Palmer everything. But hearing the whole story, he didn't suspect the Congressman would say, "Well, let's see, you're my counsel, but you're guilty of breaking and entering in Texas, you're an accomplice to assault in Maryland, you're about to become the subject of a Justice Department investigation, and you think the chairman of my committee's a murderer. Right then. Keep up the good work."

He took the long way back to his office hoping for any distraction.

23

Keeping reality at bay was no longer an option the following Monday when Tom Countryman called. "Nick, the man who was rescued from the water is still in the hospital in Annapolis. However, his memory is coming around."

"Well, what has he said?"

"It's not what he's saying that worries me so much as who he's talking to."

"And who might that be?"

"Yesterday, a couple of men no one recognized came to visit. They apparently didn't look like family or friends – or friendly. We're tracking them."

"What has the man told you so far?"

"He now remembers being on the dock and being hit by somebody. He thinks it was a woman. Can you tell me anything about a woman there?"

"Uh... did he say what she looked like or anything like that?"

"No. Why?"

"Like I told you, there were several women there – hookers or strippers I presume. Did he tell you about the yacht and all the people on board including Staunton, his office manager, and the Capitol Police Chief? Did he tell you that he was working security for them?"

"He can't seem to remember why he was there and has no recollection of a yacht or party."

"How convenient. So, he just claims memory loss for why he was on a dark, deserted pier on a cold winter night, but is quite able to remember details like who hit him so hard it knocked him unconscious? That's bullshit! You're going to let him get away with that?"

"I've let you get away with not admitting you were on that dock. Like I told you Nick, this is not entirely a Public Integrity investigation – not yet anyway. As I also said, if you could help us fill in some holes here, it might become my investigation. You must share with me all the information you have on any other person who could have struck this man."

––––––––––

Knowing the stress Lisa was under in her new job, Nick held off on telling her about his conversation with Countryman from the week before. However, the details of his most recent conversation forced Nick to come clean.

They met for dinner at Rumors a couple blocks from her K Street office. She was working on a new client project and had to go back afterwards. Lisa spoke a little too enthusiastically about how well a fundraiser was coming together that she was co-hosting with her firm for Staunton. She boasted that they'd raised more money so far than any single event put on for the Chairman all year.

Puzzled by her apparent zeal at raising even a dime for her former boss, "Why are you happy about that?"

"Like him or not, he's chairman of the House Judiciary Committee, Nick. It's part of what I do for him – for my firm I mean."

"I find that absolutely incredible, Lisa. You can cover as well as anyone I know in this town. Why don't you just pretend to raise money for that son of a bitch – but just not succeed so well at it?" A vague question mark was beginning to take shape in the back of Nick's mind regarding Lisa's new job.

"Don't you think it might seem a little suspicious if I wasn't trying to help?" Lisa emphasized a cynical twist on the word help.

Once she had sampled her dinner, Nick decided to let it go, and instead began to relay Countryman's information: first, the voice message, then the conversation over coffee, and finally the latest phone call. His attempt to be chronologically accurate didn't facilitate getting the whole story out in a timely fashion.

Lisa interrupted after he recounted Countryman's first voicemail, "Oh, shit. Nick, how did they connect you to the dock? Did somebody see us?"

"Lisa, calm down. Let me finish."

He went on to explain the calculations of the currents that night and the investigators' discovery under the pier at low tide.

"Oh, my God, I completely forgot about your camera. This is all my fault."

"It's not your fault. We'd be dead if you hadn't done what you did."

"But now we're toast anyway. We could be going to jail!"

"Lisa, wait. Dougee's not dead."

"Who the hell's Dougee?"

"The security thug you clobbered. Don't you remember they were calling out his name – Dougee, Dougee?"

"Oh … yeah. What a weird thing to remember."

"The point is he's not dead. You're not a murderer. You killed no one."

He went on to recount the rest of the story. Lisa began to calm down after he painted a little brighter picture, and actually took a bite of food.

"So the best news you have to offer is he can't remember anything?"

"Yeah – sort of."

"What do you mean, *sort of ?*"

"Well, the doctors say his memory will likely come back. And it kind of already is."

"Nick, what are you not telling me? This is serious, level

with me."

"Okay, okay. He claims now he has no recollection of why he was on the pier: no yacht, no Staunton, no party. However, he does think he remembers that he was hit across the head ... by a woman."

"Oh shit, that's not good."

"Lisa, think about it. With all he's been through, and it was pitch-dark. You hit him so hard and he was into that water so fast. No way he'll remember what you look like."

"Dougee will remember, Nick. He looked right into my eyes."

Lisa stared at the floor clutching her pearls, "What are we going to do?"

She'd declined a glass of wine earlier as she needed to get back to the office, but changed her mind and ordered a double scotch and water with a twist. A clear conscience would have been a better salve, but a stiff drink would have to do for the moment.

24

August couldn't have arrived sooner. With Congress in recess for a month, people scattered in every direction. Members went back to their districts to campaign for the coming November elections. Some staff went on planned vacations while others volunteered on House or Senate campaigns. Several went to work on new challengers' campaigns in hopes of getting a better job in the next Congress.

What recess meant for Nick and Lisa was that Staunton would be out of Washington. Whether the Chairman was back in Texas or on a congressional boondoggle somewhere, they didn't care – as long as he was gone. Nick didn't have any big plans except for trying to stay out of jail in Texas – and Maryland. Lisa was too new at her firm to have earned much vacation time yet. It looked like a hot and humid Washington August for them. But as long as they could keep their heads down, and off of any thugs' radar screens, they could keep breathing.

Friday morning of the first recess week brought an invitation to play golf with some lobbyists. It came through Nick's Senate friend, Ken O'Malley. Two guys with one of the few Republican firms created when President Reagan came to power invited them to an upscale country club in Virginia. Nick had played on occasion in Florida although he hadn't since moving to Washington. But he owned decent golf equipment and shoes and could at least swing a club.

Ken and Nick drove to the posh course together, but stopped for donuts and coffee and were late arriving. There was no time to hit any practice shots on the driving range. Their hosts looked the spitting image of successful Washington lobbyists: creased cuffed slacks, perfect fitting golf shirts, polished traditional golf shoes and the latest in golf club technology. Ken apologized for being late, which was quickly forgiven. They went directly to the blue tees of the first hole and the hosts teed off – two beautiful drives far down the middle of the fairway. Nick was slightly intimidated. Ken went next, took a few practice swings, and then hit a shot that started left before slicing back toward the right side of the fairway to land in the middle just short of the others.

Nick stepped up, took a practice swing, and then swung as hard as he could. The ball shot off the toe of his club diagonally – a line drive into the middle of a nearby oak tree, then ricocheted back at them. Everyone ducked. The ball hit his hosts' cart, then bounced and trickled down the cart path onto the ladies' tee. He was mortified.

"Wow. Sorry. Should I hit another one?"

"Sure, go ahead," the hosts reluctantly obliged.

This time everyone stood behind their carts. He tried to relax, slowed his swing, and hit a shot that sailed a foot above the ground landing sixty yards down the fairway. It wasn't pretty but he was thrilled the ball had simply traveled in the right direction.

Ken half whispered, "Man, what the hell was that? I thought you played golf?"

"I do. It's just been a while."

They rode in the cart together. Nick hit a lucky 4-iron shot to the front of the green and managed to get down in five. The others all got a par with fours. Before he drove off the next tee, Ken strongly advised him to keep his head down.

"I'll watch the ball. You just keep your head down through your entire swing. And follow through completely – follow through is everything."

He did as he was told and really connected with the ball, but never saw where it went. As they wheeled down the cart path, Ken told Nick of new changes in his career. He was leaving the Senate to be a political appointee in President Reagan's Justice Department. Nick found this to be welcome news. He needed all the friends he could get at Justice. Ken also indirectly complimented Lisa for her relatively new job at the powerful Texas law firm, and hinted that one doesn't get a position like that unless someone powerful like Staunton makes it happen. Nick's mind plunged into a fog. But, before he could ask any questions, Ken suddenly stopped the cart.

"Ken, what are you doing?"

"Letting you hit your ball."

"I hit the hell out of that ball. It's got to be somewhere up by the green."

"You hit the hell out of the ball but popped it straight up. Didn't you see it?"

"No! You told me to keep my head down. I didn't see shit."

Ken murmured, "I can see this is going to be a long day."

Nick's game settled down after a few more holes to the point where his hosts were warming up to him. After a hot dog at the turn past the ninth hole, Nick was feeling more confident. He began talking politics with his hosts who were, after all, the experts. Their conversations came and went in spurts between tee boxes and greens, but he'd at least broken the ice. They'd just returned from a trip out west where they raised some initial money for a future U.S. Senate candidate in Montana. The only question Nick wanted the experts to answer was whether Chairman Staunton's FEC problems might cause him to lose his seat.

The eventual answer was harsh, "You're dreaming, kid. Staunton has one of the safest seats in the House. And we don't really want him to lose – he throws the best parties on the Eastern Shore." They chuckled and nodded at each other.

"Really?" Nick admired his party's lobbyists for their success, but there was a sneaky arrogance to them that was a little unnerving.

"I wouldn't expect him to be taken down anytime soon."

"Certainly not by the media," Nick blurted. "They won't seek answers from his party."

After Nick sank a lucky 12-foot putt on the approaching green, one of the hosts asked him, "What is it that you would have exposed about these politicians, Nick?"

"I don't know, but whatever it is, it should be exposed equally of both parties."

"Sometimes you have to look at the bigger picture, Nick. How long you been on the Hill? Maybe you're ready to make some real money again – back in the private sector?"

While waiting to tee off on the 16th hole, one of the lobbyists mentioned he'd been on his back porch the day before with his economist pondering the upcoming elections. Nick was impressed.

He said to Ken after they were back riding in the cart again, "These guys must make a fortune. That guy's got his own economist? I mean, most people have a lawyer, and maybe an accountant, but an economist – damn."

"You realize, of course, you're a moron."

"What?"

"*The Economist*? It's a magazine."

On the last two holes, Nick kept his head down and concentrated solely on his game. Afterwards, Ken explained his new job as a Deputy Assistant Attorney General where he'd be working on several projects including trying to salvage funding for a new prosecutorial task force that was to focus on border-related criminal activity. Tom Countryman had helped him get the appointment. Nick hadn't told Ken of his troubles with Chairman Staunton or his henchmen, but figured he might need to do so in fairly short order.

The Department of Justice investigation of the Delrio Corporation had made slow but significant progress throughout the summer. The person who signed the checks for the Delrio Corporation PAC was Rudy Jimenez, the treasurer of the company. The investigators discovered the corporation's PAC followed virtually none of the FEC's regulations concerning the collection or disbursement of funds.

Furthermore, the company had only eight employees. They were either security personnel or drivers. All the money that went into the PAC account came from checks written by just three people: Rudy Jimenez, Hector DeVallies, the company's president, and Anna Jimenez, Rudy's sister and the secretary of the corporation. All officers of the Delrio PAC were U.S. citizens, and the company was incorporated under Texas law. The only officials to which the PAC had ever contributed money were Congressman John Staunton and the Governors of Maryland and Texas.

The break in the case came when investigators discovered that Rudy and Anna worked closely with a colleague who was not a U.S. citizen. His name, coincidentally, was Juan Jimenez, and he was a Mexican citizen. The preliminary inquiry into the background of Juan uncovered the fact that he had never paid any taxes in the United States despite having been paid with Delrio Corporation checks. That discovery led to a broader investigation of the tax consequences of the Delrio PAC's activities and, unfortunately for John Staunton, opened up a whole new flank of illegal activity.

It turned out the Delrio Corporation also hadn't paid any taxes to the U.S. government and that several of the checks written to the John Staunton for Congress Campaign were missing a few important words – the "for Congress Campaign" part. All of these so-called PAC indiscretions wouldn't amount to much in terms of penalties. The FEC would simply shut down the Delrio PAC and once again fine the Staunton campaign. However, the fact that John Staunton was accepting money directly from a corporation in any sums, much less the substantial sums he got from the Delrio Corporation, was enough for the Department of Justice to refer the case to the Public Integrity Section of the department headed by Tom Countryman.

Nick was at his office desk wearing blue jeans and doing what staff often do during recess – cleaning out his files and cubbyholes and planning a long lunch at Bullfeathers when his assistant said Tom Countryman was on the phone. Although he wasn't in the mood for more bad news or its accompanying stress, he took the call.

"Nick, if I've seemed to doubt your veracity, I apologize."

"What's happened?"

Countryman went on to tell Nick about their discoveries and that the case had been transferred to his division to investigate John Staunton.

"That's great news. How can I help?"

"By staying out of any more trouble and keeping your head up. Secondly, if you want my help, you need to come clean about anything else you've got your fingers in."

Suspecting Countryman knew more than he was revealing, he reluctantly told him about his trip to Texas, his law school friend, and their motorcycle venture to Normandy. He explained how he'd come across the corporation's name in the FEC filings and had read about the commission's investigation.

"Damn-devil, Taft. What in the hell were you planning to prove by breaking into their building?"

"I wasn't planning to prove anything. I was planning to find out what I discovered."

"Which was?"

"That it's a smuggling operation! Not just drugs – illegal immigrants."

"Nick, you better come downtown and talk. I'll make the arrangements."

––––––––––

The Justice Department's grounds soaked up a drizzling rain when Nick arrived at ten o'clock on a Thursday morning. He was surrounded by dreary gray walls. The Justice building's interior was drab with high ceilings and not a stitch of sunlight. If their goal was to convey depressing, it was working. Countryman introduced Nick to a man who worked with the Immigration and Naturalization Service (INS). Nick told the story of what he'd discovered in Texas. The man asked several obvious questions. Did he actually see any people? Did he talk to anyone who'd illegally crossed the border? Did he see anyone being transported? Nick answered *no* to all.

Countryman thanked the man for his time. He then asked Nick to join him for a cup of coffee down the street. They walked a few blocks to a diner on Pennsylvania Avenue where they sat in a corner booth.

Nick tried briefly to explain to Tom all his efforts on the immigration reform bill and the triggered amnesty amendment, but Tom cut him off, "I'm well aware of your efforts on the committee, Nick."

Nick found that news surprising and somehow reassuring. "Oh – okay."

"So what did you think of the INS inquiry?"

"I don't think I was very helpful."

Countryman chuckled. "Lare, come join us?"

A man sitting on a stool at the counter reading a paper turned around. He walked to the booth and sat down next to Tom.

"Nick, this is Larry Louman, he's a private consultant to the department."

"Nice to meet you."

"Likewise, kid."

"Lare knows more about what's going on down at the border than just about anyone. Nick, tell him what you saw in Texas."

Nick repeated his story about Normandy Texas and the warehouse there. Louman listened intently then asked questions about any clothing seen there and about the coolers Nick had found. He asked if he'd seen any heavy jackets lying around, and Nick confirmed he had. Countryman asked Lare to tell Nick what he knew about human smuggling.

Lare explained there were many ways to sneak across the U.S. border. He reported that much of organized human smuggling is closely tied to drug smuggling. The so-called coyotes will travel to the poor towns of Mexico and promise people a much better life in America where they can have a good job and make a lot of money. They're only promised this new life if they will cross the border per their instructions.

"The ones who have a little money will pay the coyotes to set a route for them. The smuggler organizes the pickup locations in the U.S. and has someone in Mexico get them to the border. The illegals may be offered warmer clothes or jackets en route to fend off the cold desert nights – they will have cocaine or heroin stitched into their insulation." Lare continued, "The facilitator may also be paid on the U.S. side by a future employer in need of workers. The smugglers make money from the aliens, some from the future employer, and a lot from the illegal drug importation. The illegal alien is simply used as a commodity."

Lare described further, "The few with ample funds, say $5,000, will get good documents, and will have a smooth ride into the U.S. They will simply drive to the customs checkpoints at the border. Their papers will belong to an actual U.S. citizen who will loan them for a fee to the middle man. The picture on the passport will look very similar to the individual using the documents. Once across the border, the smuggler will take the papers back and the immigrants are on their own."

"The operation you describe sounds like alien and drug smuggling. The tanker truck is probably used as a transport, and the building you describe is a drop house. Vehicles like that tanker are customized with air-intake systems and a hatch to allow people, and just enough air, in. The discarded jackets were probably once lined with drugs. But the coolers you mention sound more like something you'd find on a boat-based operation. The Administration's fight against the drug trade in Florida has pushed the importers up the coast toward Georgia and north, but I don't think west into the Gulf yet."

"Why do they hold them at this building?" Nick asked.

"Why do you think? They have to wait to confirm the other half of the money. They secure the first half before they start. There is usually a phone call to secure the second half."

"And if they get the money?"

"Then they'll let them go. The new immigrants will often try to get as far away from the border as possible. There is less threat they will get picked up further away and sometimes better employment odds."

"What if they don't get the second half?"

"Then they drop them off near the border where gangs patrol. The gangs will beat and rape them and steal anything of value, then split their take with the smugglers."

"That's pretty sick."

"It's a sad scenario all around, Nick. It's like reverse kidnapping – paying to be held captive until you're freed to hide in the shadows of an illegal economy. And any public policy that does anything but discourage these crossings is not humane. It is overwhelmingly inhumane."

"Where do the ones who make it usually end up?"

"If they're lucky they'll get beyond the border towns of Arizona or Texas up to Northern California, Chicago, or around here, the Washington, DC area. They'll end up in construction, agriculture, restaurants, or maid services somewhere."[24]

Countryman thanked Louman for his time, then he and Nick walked back to the Justice Department. He reminded him there was probably a great deal of money involved and that they were up against a sophisticated crew; and the likelihood of violence was quite high.

Eugene Ity had been at his house in Martha's Vineyard most of the summer. Nick was anxious to tell him all that had transpired and seek his always steady counsel. So he was thrilled to see the Jaguar parked in the Major's driveway when he arrived home that evening. He knocked on his landlord's door with a bottle of wine.

Ity looked tired and sounded discouraged. But a cool glass of Chardonnay seemed to perk him up. Nick unloaded everything he'd learned through the summer, and about Countryman's involvement as well of that of the Department of Justice. He told of the yacht and the security thug, about the Delrio Corporation in Texas, and the Jimenez brothers. Ity listened for a long time without speaking.

After an awkward silence, he began, "Nick, John Staunton isn't the best public servant, and he doesn't deserve the voters' confidence. But he's not your real culprit. The actors here are the ones who hold the money over him. Staunton has huge financial debt. His perceived lifestyle is an integral part of his perceived power. For far too many in Washington, perception is everything. Staunton can't lose that power. If he does, the Jimenezes will destroy him. He must continue as their puppet or be without the things that create his illusion. His future is written in stone."

"Let's not get carried away, Major. The guy knows right from wrong. He could change..."

"No, Nick, it'd be easier for him to change the past. If it weren't for his political position he'd be circling the drain right now. I also don't think Staunton murdered Alec Sivore. I think the Jimenezes did. He was the one overseeing the Chairman's money. I suspect he figured out how much leverage the Jimenezes had on Staunton and the connection to the Federales long before you did."

"Yeah, but Sivore was..."

"Do you know what Sivore did before joining Staunton's staff? He was in the U.S. Navy, graduated at the top of his class at the Academy in Annapolis – was a straight A student. He then worked as an accountant at one of the big-eight firms."

"I didn't know that."

"I'll bet the Jimenezes did."

25

September 1986   Capitol Hill   72 Degrees Sunny

August recess ended in September. Although the 1986 midterm elections were still two months away, without much real business pending, they were becoming *the* topic of conversation. The committees had to hold a few hearings to make it look like Congress was working, but the only legislation that actually needed to be passed were lingering federal spending bills.

The downside for Nick and Lisa was that Staunton would be back in town. They remained in the dark as to how much Staunton and his henchmen knew. While there was no news on the Delrio Corporation's security video, they did know a little more about the status of Dougee's memory. According to undercover work by Countryman's investigators, Dougee's security cohorts visited him one day with a box of photographs. The thugs had talked with the Scottish couple on the bay, and discovered they'd seen a car near their home the night Dougee drifted ashore – the car had a congressional parking sticker on its bumper.

Determined to learn whom from Congress, other than the chairman and his office administrator, was around that night, they brought some pictures for Dougee to look at. They had official photos of Texas Republican congressmen and their staff that Staunton suspected for years had been out to bring him down. Dougee, whose jaw and few mental faculties had not fully recovered, squinted hard at every photo, but disappointedly shook his head each time. After several attempts and Dougee's insistence that he wanted to help – which came out as "Auw . . . ont to hep", they gave up and put the photos back.

Among the group in the box was the annual Judiciary

Committee photograph which included all Members and the entire committee staff. They had no reason to show it to Dougee because there were no other Texans in the picture. But Dougee saw it from the corner of his eye and began staring. Lisa and Nick were in the photo each on opposite ends of the dais standing with their respective Democratic or Republican colleagues. Chairman Staunton was in the middle of the picture and Members were to his left or right depending upon their party affiliation.

In addition to Dougee's motor skills, his memory remained slow due to his camera-induced coma and very cold float trip. After staring, he swiped his nose with a knuckle, then pointed a chubby finger toward the committee photo and gurgled, "Wuks famiwer." His colleagues, trying to be encouraging, picked up the photo, "Yes, Dougee, that's the Chairman, you know him."

Dougee reacted badly, he yelled out, "Naaaww ... naaw ... da it ... da it!"

No one could understand him. The nurse patted his head and increased his sedative drip. He floated back off to sleep with his eyes half open. The chief security thug looked the photo over curiously and secured it in his coat pocket.

———————

With Tom Countryman in charge, prosecutors were finally coming down on Staunton and his nefarious operations. Details of the investigation were surfacing in the public record and the Chairman's campaign opponent mentioned them at every opportunity. The local media acknowledged it, but were reluctant to highlight the information.

Nick realized the likelihood of the twenty-two year veteran losing his seat was almost nonexistent yet he couldn't help but dream of how his life might change if Staunton were defeated. Those dreams were doused by reality when he looked up

Staunton's most recent electoral percentages in his district. He'd won by 72% in the last election and 68% two years before that. The next best fantasy was for Staunton to lose his chairmanship, but the Democrats would have to lose the House for that to occur. As things stood, Staunton could be chairman of the committee for as far as the eye could see and would continue to amass more power along the way.

———————

When Palmer called Nick the first Friday back in session, he'd said an opening had occurred on the powerful Appropriations Committee. The population and polical clout of Florida had grown tremendously in the 70s and 80s, and the opening was ripe for a Floridian. Sandy was not a senior Republican in the Florida delegation, but those senior to him liked their committee positions and weren't interested. Palmer liked the current assignments he had, but a seat on Appropriations where decisions were made on how and where to spend federal dollars was enticing. It would also give him some input on potential funding for the Justice Department's border task force.

Sandy confided in Nick he was going to take the open seat. One drawback was, due to the fact it was a primary committee, he'd have to give up his seat on all other committees to take it. Nick was happy for Palmer and agreed it was the right move for him, but was worried he'd be left unprotected on the Judiciary Committee. He believed his work there was solid and that he and Denny Folgier got along, but without Palmer as a ranking member, he wouldn't be guaranteed a job.

The Congressman was two steps ahead of him as usual. "Look Nick, I'm aware my moving off the committee may leave you in a bind. But, I want you to know you're welcome to join me and work on appropriations issues."

He knew what Palmer was offering was for him to return

to his personal office because he would be too junior on Appropriations to have his own counsel there. His *Hobson's Choice* was not attractive; go back to Palmer's personal office to work under the politically entrenched Val, and answer constituent mail again, or stay on the committee unprotected and roll the dice with Staunton.

He immediately went to Denny Folgier. "This is not great timing, Nick. After the elections in a couple of months there's sure to be some shifting around of Members and staff on this committee – it happens every election year."

"Yeah, I understand."

"I'll tell you what, I can protect you through November. There's no need to make any changes now. Let's see how things shake out in the midterm elections."

"Thanks Denny." His appreciation for the temporary cover was heartfelt, but so was his newfound sense of exposure.

"Hey, you don't have to run this by Chairman Staunton do you?"

Folgier smiled a big smile, "No, we don't have to do that."

––––––––––

The end of recess also brought Staunton's office administrator back to town. Judd Traynor, the investigator Staunton met during his run-in with the law in college, didn't have any legislative duties, but he knew where everything was and what everyone did. He prided himself on picking up on the subtleties of conversations between Members, Members and staff, and staff and staff. With no real substantive responsibilities, he could roam the halls during the day and attend every cocktail reception at night. He heard all the gossip on all people, including where they were from, how much they were being paid – and the proverbial who was sleeping with whom.

When Staunton's chief security goon belatedly gave him the

latest report from Dougee, he listened intently. When told that Dougee didn't recognize any of the Texas members or staff, he nodded and took it in stride. But when told of the recovering thug's overreaction to the annual committee photograph, Traynor's eyes and ears perked up. He scanned the photo like a laser, pausing on every face. With a slight smile, he began nodding his head. He complimented the thug for his work, dismissed him, and picked up the phone to call his boss.

26

Early October 1986 Washington, DC 55 Degrees Clear

The final act of the year was all that mattered and it was less than four weeks away: Election Day. Power is everything to a politician – without it he's not a politician, just another bullshitter. One could lose many votes during the year, but not on Election Day.

Nick was spending more time at Lisa's place near Capitol Hill. She was a new and struggling private-sector lobbyist. He was her eyes and ears in Congress. They talked a lot during the day, but usually only saw each other at night. Things were generally pretty slow, and Nick was able to catch up on some stale phone messages, including one from Maleva from weeks ago about some legal advice she'd mentioned a long time back.

"Maleva, it's Nick. How are you?"

"Oh ... Nick. It's so good to hear your voice." She sounded older and more tired than Nick could remember.

"Everything all right with you?" he asked.

"Oh, yeah, oh yeah. I guess so. The summer heat just broke here – so it's a little bit better, you know."

"So, what's this legal advice you've been meaning to ask me about? You know I'm happy to help."

"Thank you, Nick. I know you will. Well, I've never told you – you know about my struggles in my early days. And, I don't really want to burden you with it, Nick."

"Come on, Maleva. I'm here."

"Well, I never thought this would be a problem or ever come up until I visited home last year just before Christmas.

"By home you mean?"

"Guatemala – you know where I'm from."

"Right. Okay."

"Well. I've had no problems before, but when I was coming back through customs that time, they questioned me about my green card."

"Yeah?"

"Well. It's been expired for years you know."

"I wasn't aware of that. You mean revoked?"

"Yeah. And the U.S. Customs man, he said they needed to question me further, and they were goin' to take my papers — and all this..."

"Uh huh."

"But, so... there was all this commotion right about then over by the luggage carousel at customs and some police dog was barking and kids were screaming. And, this man he ran over to see what was happening."

"And, so my oldest grandson, you know, Carlito? He says come on grandma – let's go. So, we just left and caught a taxi to my cousins' in Miami."

"I see."

"And I didn't think it was too big a deal, you know, 'cause I've lived here for thirty years. I'm an American if there ever was one, right? But, I left my papers with that man."

"Uh huh."

"So, anyway, I got this letter in the mail about six weeks ago saying I'm in the U.S. illegally, and that I am subject to a deportation proceeding."

"Oh, wow. Maleva. This is not good. Why didn't you tell me all this sooner?"

"I wanted to, but you're never here anymore, Nick. I've been waiting for you to visit your family. You're the only one I've told about this."

"Maleva, we need to get you an immigration lawyer."

"Nick, you know I can't afford no lawyer."

"I'll pay for it, Maleva. Let me get on this and get back to you. I'll call you soon."

That afternoon, Nick, preoccupied with how to help the dearest woman he'd ever known, was painfully aware of the hypocrisy her circumstance presented. Maleva taught him how to eat, walk, talk and laugh – how much more can you owe someone? She did that all while taking care of five of her own kids and a dozen grandchildren. He knew he could help her; he just had to figure out how best to do that.

In order to think, he took a break from his office and went to check on his apartment in Georgetown. He kept so much stuff at Lisa's he occasionally needed to go home and regroup. The building entry door was unlocked which helped him carry in an arm full of dirty clothes from his car. When he reached the top of the stairs, he saw that his apartment door was not locked either – in fact, it was ajar. He pushed the door open. His place was a disaster. Books and papers were thrown everywhere, and chairs and tables were upside down. His desk contents were dumped on the floor. If he'd been thinking clearly, he would have left and immediately called the police. But, he couldn't help but walk in and look.

After sifting through some things, he called Tom Countryman, "Nick, I probably don't need to tell you not to touch anything. I'll have some people there in twenty minutes – and don't make any more calls from this phone until we've checked it."

Countryman and his team were there quickly. They took photos and began dusting for fingerprints. They asked Nick to recount his steps and things he'd touched. Hours later, after they'd catalogued his whole apartment, he was asked to go through each item he owned again and figure out what was missing. He had no idea. Nick also couldn't tell them when the break-in occurred. He hadn't been there in days. The most perplexing thing was he couldn't identify anything that was missing.

Countryman told him to keep searching, "Taft, I think you know this was no random break-in. They were here for a reason and were looking for something specific. We must determine what it was, if they found it, and why they wanted it!"

Countryman gave him his home phone number and told him to call if he discovered what was stolen. Once he was allowed to straighten his place back up, he called Lisa. He told her what had happened. She said she would be there in five minutes as she wanted to see the scene for herself.

When Lisa walked in she turned away and started to cry, "Nick, this is bad."

Still cleaning up and thinking he'd done a pretty good job, "Well it looked a lot worse a couple of hours ago."

"No, Nick, this is Staunton's people. They don't play by the same rules."

"Lisa, I haven't played by the same rules with anybody since I got to this town. But, I don't think there's anything missing. I've been through all my stuff over and over again, my checkbook, my papers, my books. There's nothing missing."

"This is freaking me out. I've got to get out of here."

They went down the street to a small Greek sidewalk café. They sat outside and talked for a while again about their predicament. Sometimes it seemed like it was all they talked about. Nick took an opportunity to change the subject and told Lisa all about Maleva's legal problems. She gave him the name of one of the best immigration attorneys in the country – he had offices in DC. They paid the bill and walked back to his apartment. The phone was ringing.

"Hello."

"Nick, it's Regina."

"Oh, hey, Moxley. I've got a lot of bullshit going on at the moment. Can I call you back?"

"No! No, you can't. I really need a phone number from you – it will only take two seconds. Dr. Hyatt's number in Virginia

– I know you have it."

"Okay, give me a second. Shit – that's it!"

"What?"

"Moxley, I have to call you back."

Lisa, looking confused, "What?"

"My address book! With all my phone numbers. That's what's missing."

He went through all his things again to make sure. It was definitely missing. It was nine o'clock when he called Countryman's home. He left a message saying he believed he knew what was missing. Nick and Lisa waited until eleven o'clock. Lisa convinced him she couldn't sleep there. So they went back to her place and decided Countryman could leave a message back.

The next morning, Saturday, Nick went home early to see if Countryman had called. But when he pushed the button on his answering machine there were no messages; and the machine didn't beep twice like it usually would. He opened the lid. The recording tape was gone.

He called Countryman at home again. Tom picked up on the first ring, "Nick, I tried calling you back last night, but got no answer."

"Sorry Tom. But, not only is my address book missing, so is the tape from my answering machine."

"How did my men miss that?"

"I don't know. I usually erase my messages unless they have phone numbers on them that I wouldn't readily remember."

"Like whose number?"

"University friends from out of town or, uhm … like my friend Bud from Texas."

"Check in with your friend from Texas. Let's talk first thing Monday morning unless we need to sooner. We may be behind the curve."

Nick left a message on Bud Marskey's answering machine at his home that Saturday afternoon. He refrained from going into a lot of detail, but encouraged him to call as soon as he could.

Monday morning arrived quickly and there was no word from the Texan. He called State Representative Burwell's office at 11:00 a.m. Washington time which was 10:00 a.m. Texas time. "Hi, I'm Nick Taft, a law school friend of Bud Marskey's. I've left him a few messages, but haven't heard back from him. Is he around?"

"Mr. Taft, Bud's not in yet this morning."

"Do you know where I can reach him? It's quite important."

"I'm sure he'll be in within the next half hour or so. I'll have him call you."

Nick spent the rest of his day looking busy, but didn't get much done. There wasn't a lot to do anyway except read the Hill papers to see which candidates were up or down in the polls.

Upon trying Marskey's office late that afternoon he was surprised to discover they were already gone for the day. It was only four o'clock Texas time and the office was closed.

He talked to the same receptionist first thing the next morning and explained how he'd been trying to get a hold of Bud for three days.

"Yes Mr. Taft, I understand what you're saying. It appears that Bud is somewhat missing."

"What?"

"Well, he hasn't shown up for two days. We presumed he'd gone hunting with friends in west Texas as he sometimes does this time of year. But he usually tells one of us or at least checks in. We haven't heard a word from him since last Friday."

He immediately called Tom Countryman, "Tom, Bud Marskey's missing! His office in the State Capitol just told me they haven't seen or heard from him since last Friday – this isn't good."

"Nick, let us handle this! I don't need you getting any further engaged. Understood?"

"Look, Tom, he'd have never even heard of the Jimenezes …"

"I understand. But you can better help by staying safe and in one place. We're on it."

Nick hung up the phone.

––––––––––

Tom Countryman, suspecting the worst, dispatched a team of investigators to Texas. He was convinced the Jimenezes were capable of foul play to protect their operations from public scrutiny. He obtained a fairly broad search warrant from a federal judge in Austin to search for evidence of the Jimenezes' operation, but failed to get a warrant to search the warehouse in Normandy. The building was not listed as an asset of the Delrio Corporation, and Countryman had no evidence that it was used for illegal activity.

The warrant did allow them to seize any security footage in possession of the corporation and it would be taken to a federal lab for clarification. Attempts to tail or eavesdrop on any member of the Jimenez family proved useless because none of them could be located. A stakeout was placed at every address for them on file. Upon the team's arrival at Marskey's apartment, the door handle was broken, the place torn up and there was dried blood in the hallway. The team's debriefing unveiled that their initial efforts had uncovered no leads. Countryman decided to fly to Austin.

When his plane broke the cloud cover over Washington National Airport, Nick wondered what he would do when he got on the ground. Denny Folgier had reluctantly given him Thursday and Friday off even though Congress was in session. Lisa had begged him not to go, then made him swear he'd call her every six hours. The only thing he knew was that he had a car rented at the Austin airport and he was going to help his friend.

As he descended the escalator in the airport eyeing signs to baggage claim, two men in dark suits looked toward him and said, "Welcome to Texas, sir." He looked behind to see to whom they might be speaking – there was no one. When he turned forward again, he saw that below him it was Tom Countryman they were greeting. Nick stalled long enough to fall behind them, then leaned in behind a large pillar by the baggage carousel and watched Countryman depart with his team in a sleek black town car.

He drove to the barbecue place where Bud had treated him to dinner hoping he might see Bud's friend, the cook. When he inquired and was told Abel was not working that night, the hostess was kind enough to give Nick his phone number. After eating, he pondered what to do; he had no plan and didn't know his way around town.

The Public Integrity Section had some clout, and the uniqueness of their investigations usually invited cooperation by federal and state law enforcement agencies. But the Austin Police had few leads on the Marskey case, and the local FBI knew little of the Delrio Corporation or its employees. They were aware of alien smuggling, but threw up their hands when asked about any border enforcement activity. Their inability to locate other real estate or physical property in Texas connected to the Jimenez family or the Delrio Corporation left few options.

Meanwhile, per a tip from a local fisherman, the team in Maryland had located the phantom fishing yacht. It was registered to Juan Jimenez, a foreign national and it sailed under the Mexican flag. The high-performance yacht was docked at a deserted home on the Severn River, and it did have a name — *River Walker*. Staunton was nowhere to be found. They'd tracked him Wednesday, but lost him heading toward the BWI Airport. Countryman couldn't justify tailing him, but investigators were allowed to observe activities within the purview of their investigation.

By late Thursday evening, Countryman had witnessed enough speculating and hand wringing in Texas. After dining with his team at a local steakhouse, he told them to prepare to travel by car first thing in the morning. Their whereabouts and destination would be on a need-to-know basis only.

——————

After dinner, Nick called Lisa to check in. He said his biggest discovery thus far had been that the smaller pork ribs were actually just as good as the big beefy ones at the restaurant where he'd previously dined. He told her of practically running into Countryman at the airport, and that he was hoping not to see him again. She asked if he'd been to Bud's apartment. They discussed his options and it seemed like the obvious starting place.

Nick found his way to the apartment building. Seeing the crime tape across the doorway was depressing. He tried the broken door handle, then looked around the grounds. No one could be seen. He backed up and crashed the door shoulder-first with all his weight. Nick slid to the floor with a painful thud.

Once again, reality and television proved worlds apart. As he lay on the concrete floor rubbing his shoulder, he looked up to recognize a small rectangular shape inside the hallway light. He stood and looked around, then checked inside the light fixture. It was a magnetic hide-a-key.

Once inside, he came to terms with the likely fate of his friend. Clearly, he'd been taken against his will. There were blood stains on the floor. He sat on the couch where he, Bud, and Lisa had talked well into the night months before about how to outwit Staunton and his thugs. He drove to downtown Austin and rented a hotel room.

He called the number given him at the restaurant, "Is this Abel? I'm a friend of Bud's."

"This Abel."

"This is Nick. I don't know if you remember me. Bud introduced us at the restaurant last fall." There was silence on the line. "I asked for American cheese and you laughed."

After a brief pause, "*Si*, I remember you – *da gringo* cheese guy – *si*?"

"That would be me."

"Okay then."

"Look, Abel, Bud is missing. I think he's in trouble. I've come to Texas to help him, but I don't really know my way around. I was hoping you might help..."

"I help you. *Bud es mi amigo tambien!*"

"Thank you. I think I know where to start, but it's a few hours' drive..."

"Come to restaurant at seven o'clock in the morning – I'll be there."

––––––––––

Bud Marskey awoke in a stiflingly quiet room. He was lying on a hard narrow pallet. His mind was in a fog, and his head ached. He tried to move, but little happened. He lifted his feet to the side of his makeshift bed. They fell onto a solid wood floor. Through the darkness, he could make out little of his surroundings. He stood and reached for the wall. His balance and perception were impaired. As he leaned toward the wall it seemed to fall away. The more he reached, the further away it got.

His mouth was parched. He discovered that his impaired vision was due to swelling around his right eye. He slowly recalled the encounter in his apartment. He'd been ambushed when arriving home from running errands. Some men had tackled him and taped his hands and mouth. He remembered being thrown into the trunk of a car and trying to figure out which direction he was being driven. They'd injected his arm with a needle – it hurt badly. He'd fought hard to stay awake. It seemed like a long time ago.

The Texan slowly walked the length of his room. It was long and narrow. The low ceiling magnified its cramped size. He knew the drugs were playing on his mind, but for his life he couldn't recognize anything resembling a door. A dim light at one end of the room appeared to come from the edges of a vent. He felt nauseous. He sat back down and tried to collect his thoughts. *Who were these people? What did they want?* He could remember no details of their faces or speech; in fact, he couldn't remember anyone speaking. The silence closed in on him.

Nick told as much of the history as he could to Abel during their drive through the Hill Country. Their language barrier was awkward at first, but improved along the way. They stopped at the taco stand on the side of the highway where Nick and Bud had been the previous fall. They sat at the same wood table under the same lone tree and ate. It was here that Nick had unloaded his woes on Bud about Congressman Staunton, and his friend hadn't hesitated to help.

Once back on the road, Nick asked Abel how he came to be in the U.S. Abel opened up, "My family worked a small farm near Oaxaca where I was born. We lived in a stone house attached to an old barn – looked out over many fields and the roof was covered with so many colorful vines. Our whole lives we had heard about America and the life and the money to be made here. It was like a symbol of hope. Mi padre never believed it. He'd been to America and worked the fields here before. He believed we had everything we needed in Oaxaca."

Abel rolled down his window. "But, then mi padre died. We had little money. A man visits us one day and promised many things in America. Madre paid him every peso. My brother, sister and me rode north in the truck for days then we're left in the desert. That desert's a bad place, Nick. My brother and I arrive here ten years ago. My sister's dead."

To Nick, Abel was a true-blue friend, and he certainly was not the enemy. It was Nick's government that wanted Abel for cheap labor, and enticed him with open borders, and then marked him as the bad guy for being here illegally. It was a half-baked government policy that was making him seem like the enemy. At a loss for words, Nick asked Abel if maybe his father had been right.

Abel looked out the window at the passing landscape. "Si – yes and no."

Road signs indicated an approaching border and additional language barrier: *Bar-f-que Sandwiches - $1.00* and *Learn to Speak Engish*. After riding in silence for a while they arrived in the small town of Normandy and parked several blocks from the Jimenez's building. It was a deserted street – any person was worthy of note. Once at the scene of his original crime, Nick got down to business. But, Abel, having personally experienced the likes of the Jimenezes, pulled him back.

"Nick, there security cameras in front of building – probably more 'round back."

"Right! How could I have forgotten? They're a big problem."

"Not worry that my friend – I be taking care of it for you."

Abel, looking away from the building while walking toward it, shimmied up a pole and pulled the wires out of the two front cameras. He then disappeared around back.

Abel returned, "Camera no problem now *amigo*."

They took a quick look in the front windows, then around back and up the stairs to where Nick broke in before. However, the Jimenezes had invested in a new metal door and large lock challenging what few criminal skills they had between them. After examining the door briefly, they descended the stairs to look for another way in. The ground floor door in the back of the building was neither new nor sporting a shiny new lock. However, it was solid and fairly thick. It had a small square window in its upper third, and Nick could see in if he stood on his toes.

The interior looked almost identical to how it had months before. It contained a few old rigs and jeeps and the tanker truck. There were some additional large obstacles to one side covered with tarps, and one contraption that looked like an overgrown boat trailer. They decided to case the rest of the building.

On the east wall, the one least exposed to public view, Nick noticed a piece of the aluminum siding was bent and pulled away from the framing. There was a pile of wood and assorted junk scattered on the ground. He situated himself between the pile and the siding and began to tug. However it was not as pliable as he'd hoped. He gave Abel a discouraged look.

"No worry," Abel offered again and disappeared around the corner.

Nick noticed a metal pipe within the junk pile and began using it as a makeshift crow bar to pry the aluminum further apart – some of the rivets shot out as if from a BB gun. Within ten minutes, he'd wrenched enough back to just get his head and shoulders in.

––––––––––

Countryman and his team barreled down the highway toward the border paying little attention to the speed limit. They arrived and parked on Mero Street two blocks from the Delrio building. They had telephoto lenses, high-powered binoculars, and an array of investigative tools, but no authority to enter the premises. Due to the company's penchant for security cameras, they all wore face masks. They split into teams; each went to a different side of the building. Abel saw them arrive from under the stairs where he'd scavenged a crow bar. Suspecting the worst, he ducked under a tarp.

The front building team reported that the door was locked, there was no response, and the office was empty. The west-side team reported the door atop the stairs was locked tight. The north team had tried the back door, it was locked, and there appeared to be no one inside.

Countryman, who stayed with the car, shook his head at his senior investigator and sighed, "Damn-devil. East team, anything to report?"

"Sir, it appears there may be some activity on the ground behind a junk pile. We can't tell if it's an animal sniffing around or what just yet."

"Well, find out! And, stay the hell away from those security cams!"

The sun was beginning to beat down as they approached the noon hour. Not a single other vehicle or person had passed them on the deserted street.

The east-side team reported in, "Sir, there appears to be a pair of legs sticking out of a small gap in the siding on the east wall of the building."

"Human legs?"

"Yes sir. Standby… actually they're moving. It looks from our vantage point like a man struggling. It's unclear if he's trying to get in or out."

Nick was sweating profusely due to the humidity inside the building. He'd managed to pry enough siding off to half fit through a small hole. He'd ripped his shirt on the pieces of torn aluminum and his pants were snagged on a bolt sticking out from the frame. The good news was he was halfway in; the bad news was he was stuck. There was not much to see straight ahead due to the placement of the tanker truck. But he could look slightly up to his right which is when he noticed the security camera focused on the building's interior. He wondered if their new photo of him would be better than his last.

Nick yelled at himself, "Great. They'll have another picture of me when they check the video in a few weeks. And at the rate I'm going, I'll probably still be here!"

He began to panic and flail and kick his way through the gap. As he did, the aluminum began to cut into his skin. The pain made him stop in his tracks. He realized it was futile. He decided to back out of the hole and start over.

"East team, anything concrete to report?"

"Yes sir. We are approaching the building. It looks like the legs of a male wearing jeans and farm boots. He appears to still be struggling into or out of the building. We also think we heard him talking."

Countryman snapped, "Back off and scan your perimeters, and do not engage the subject. He's not alone. I repeat to all units: scrutinize your perimeters for an accomplice."

He turned to his senior aide, "What have we got here, a random break in?"

Countryman and his investigator scanned their perimeter from the vantage point of the car with high-powered binoculars. He noticed for the first time something out of place. On that deserted, dilapidated street a few blocks away sat a brand-new, clean Chevrolet Impala. Looking at his aide, "Run the plates on that car immediately. Find out who it's registered to — use all priority authority you need."

"Yes sir."

"East-side team anything further?"

"Subject appears to be making little progress."

Countryman smiled, "Good Lord."

"Sir, the car is registered to Avis Car Rental, I'm awaiting information on the lessee."

"Very good. Let's just wait. All teams stand by."

Abel peeked out from under the tarp to see two men dressed in black camo, faces covered, and holding semi-automatic weapons. Unfortunately, he'd seen this movie before; he ducked back under the tarp.

"Sir, the car is rented to a Nicholas H. Taft, address, 3318 P Street Northwest Washington, DC, license number…"

Countryman waved him off shaking his head. He pinched the bridge of his nose, and exhaled.

––––––––––

Nick was convinced if he could just free his left hip from a thick slice of aluminum, he'd be able to wiggle his legs through. He promised himself to start working out more if he ever got home alive. But suddenly his heart stopped and adrenaline ripped through his body.

He heard a stern voice in perfect English, "What the hell are you doing?"

He laid perfectly still as sweat dripped off his nose, and prayed it was only an odd sound made by the aluminum bending or his boots scraping the ground. He waited in silence.

Countryman looked at his men then back at the pair of legs, "I said, 'what the hell do you think you're doing?'"

Nick who couldn't see who was talking and couldn't turn around or move at all for that matter, just stared at the concrete floor, "Who said that?"

Countryman chuckling, "That was the ghost of Hardy Boy nightmares past."

"Does this ghost have a name?"

"Yes. This is the ghost of nightmares present!"

"Well, I'm kind of in a jam here."

"I can see that. You remind me of my Lab trying to get his fat butt under our fence in Virginia."

"Tom? That is you – right?"

"It is."

Feeling relieved and embarrassed, "Well, I could use a little help."

"Are you asking for *my* help?"

"Yes sir."

Countryman barked, "Get him out of there."

27

Early October 1986   Normandy, Texas   89 Degrees Still

He didn't apologize to Countryman, but thanked his men for freeing him. After being lectured by Countryman and attending to several cuts with the help of a first aid kit, they got down to business.

"Well, since you're here, Taft, what have you discovered?"

Nick recounted his steps in Austin. Then admitting he had nothing to go on, made his case for continuing to look in the building.

"Look Tom, I'm certain something in there will give us a clue. This is where the smuggling operations are – that's all their stuff. Let's take a look."

Countryman's other men were coming out of the woodwork, "Nick, we don't have legal authority to go inside this building."

"What?"

"Our warrant doesn't cover it and we've got no probable cause to enter otherwise."

"For crying out loud, how do you people ever catch any bad guys?"

Several of Countryman's investigators nodded. Countryman snapped, "That's not worth debating right here and now!"

At that instant, half of Countryman's men trained their weapons on the back corner of the building, "*No te muevas, manos arriba* – hands up!"

His other men crouched and pointed weapons in all directions. Nick waved his hands, "Oh shit, don't shoot, don't shoot – he's with me!"

He ran to Abel who was frozen still with his hands up, "It's okay. They're friends – *amigos*." Abel kept his hands high.

They walked back toward Countryman. Nick explained Abel's presence and how he knew him through Bud. Countryman mumbled to Nick under his breath, "Is he legal?"

Nick was getting good at equivocating primarily because he'd heard so much of it in his short congressional career. "I don't know, Tom. He knows Bud and he's helping me look for him – all right?" Countryman ignored him.

"Getting back to our constitutional debate. It just so happens Nick, that you're not bound by any warrant restrictions and frankly you've already breached the break and enter standard, so there's nothing stopping *you* from continuing to look around."

"Really?"

"I'm not your keeper. Just don't let us see you. We'll be leaving now."

Countryman and his men began to walk away; he turned back and handed Nick a face mask and a radio, "Be careful."

———————

Nick wasted no time. He ducked in through the widened bent siding. Abel followed. They looked through everything, but noticed nothing unusual – some clothes and shoes, and empty water jugs. Abel confirmed, "This a smuggler operation for sure."

He motioned for Abel to follow him. He climbed the outside ladder of the tanker recalling how painful his descent from it had been months earlier. He had trouble seeing because the face mask Countryman loaned him was too big. He'd kept one hand free to continually readjust the eyeholes, but eventually just pitched it.

Once on top of the tanker, he tried to open the hatch like he had before. It would not move. There was a padlock on it. In his frustration, he banged on it several times then sat back on his knees. He climbed down the tanker and looked in the truck cab attached to it. It contained only maps and trash, but Abel noticed the key in the ignition. Just to mess with them in any way he could, Nick took the key. He slammed the truck door, and they headed back toward the hole in the wall.

However, as they approached the pulled back aluminum gap, Nick heard a noise behind him. They ducked behind the tarp and looked around. Then they both heard it again, a muffled thump, thump. They stood and moved slowly toward the tanker where the sound came again slightly louder – thump, thump.

Quietly approaching the side of the tanker, they listened intently. Nick pounded his fist on the exterior of the tanker, but couldn't even hear it hit the side. Abel scrambled for a piece of wood and then hit the side of the tanker hard. A muffled thwack was all he could manage no matter how hard he hit it. It was solid steel. They waited and listened.

Several thumps came back again in unison. Their faces lit up, "There are people in there! Hey, can you hear me?"

They ran back up the ladder, and Nick yelled at the hatch, "Can you hear me?"

Abel yelled, "*Está alguien ahi?*"

Their voices echoed around the interior of the metal warehouse. Nick realized the thickness of the tanker prevented any conversation. He scrambled back down the ladder and banged on the side again as hard as he could. This time many different muffled thumps came back.

They were ecstatic, even though he knew they couldn't hear them, Abel yelled out anyway, "*No se preocupen. Los vamos a sacar! No se preocupen, mis amigos!*"

Nick forgot about his radio and ran out of the building yelling, "Tom, Tom!"

Countryman appeared from nowhere and waved him over, "Shut up! Why don't you use a frigging megaphone for God's sake?"

"Sorry. But, listen – there are people in the tanker. I know it. We banged on the side; they all banged back several times. We've got to get them out."

"Did you try the hatch?"

"Yes, it's locked. Can your men help me?"

"Nick, I've told you, we can't enter that building."

"But you said probable cause would help. Isn't this probable cause – human smuggling? We know they do it."

"Look, unfortunately we don't *know* anything; and your illegal breaking and entering doesn't provide us a basis for entry."

"Oh, come on. It's right in front of our noses."

"You want to bust them just to watch 'em walk on a technicality? No probable cause to enter the premises and all evidence obtained thrown out. You went to law school – you know the exclusionary rule."

"Shit."

They sat in silence. Countryman's men were shaking their heads in frustration.

"You know, Nick, if that truck were outside of the building on a public street it would significantly improve our circumstances."

"I happen to have a key to that truck. But I don't have any way to open those huge back doors. Then again, what if I just drove it right through those flimsy doors?"

"I wouldn't want to encourage you to do anything illegal … but it would then be out in the open."

"Couldn't I get in a lot of trouble for that?"

"You're already in a lot of trouble."

"Right."

"It's up to you. But, if you want to think about it …"

"I'll do it."

"Taft, since you're going to drive it out, why don't you get it away from here while you're at it. Maybe up the interstate a few miles."

"Good thinking."

"And, remember – go north, not south."

"Got it."

"We'll be close behind."

––––––––––

Countryman and his men got into their cars and waited. Two held back in case there might be trouble with the doors. Nick and Abel climbed into the cab. Nick turned the ignition looking at the several shifter levers. He let the engine idle for a minute and pushed the clutch to the floor, Abel shifted one of the levers forward. Nick gave it some gas and let the clutch out. The truck jerked, rattled, and then stalled. They repeated their motions, but this time Nick let the clutch out more slowly. It started to move. He edged up to the doors, then powered on the gas, and let out the clutch.

The grinding of metal and the scream of the engine were deafening. The doors caught for a moment, then burst open. The big metal sheet on Nick's side flew back at the cab and scraped the truck's side before falling in slow motion to the ground. Nick steered into the open area behind the building. Once out, he put it in neutral and they jumped down to remove some pieces of aluminum hanging on the side. Nick gave the two investigators a thumbs-up and crawled back into the cab.

––––––––––

Tom Countryman's radio squawked in his car outside the Delrio building. It was his Maryland team reporting that Staunton's office administrator and two unidentified men had arrived at the house where the *River Walker* was docked. They sought permission to track them and the yacht should it leave the dock. They'd already secured a fast vessel for that purpose.

Countryman gave permission, but wanted clear photos and evidence of anything connecting Staunton to the unidentified men or the Delrio Corporation. Countryman put the radio down and then looked out the window with a gasp.

The radio on the seat next to Nick sounded off, "Nick, get the hell out of there, get out now – a car is coming in!" A car had just signaled and turned into the front lot of the Delrio building. Nick wondered, did he mean get out of there as in leave the truck or as in drive the truck? Abel put it in gear, and Nick put the pedal down. They wheeled around to the front of the building where three Hispanic men had exited their car. They stood with their mouths and eyes wide open as Nick and Abel drove past them onto Mero Street.

Countryman and his men were nowhere to be seen. Nick got the rig straightened out and he and Abel working as a team shifted into third, fourth, fifth, sixth, and seventh gears headed toward the only intersection in town. The Hispanic men jumped into a blue Buick sedan and sped after them.

Nick turned the corner as fast as he could and stomped on the gas once onto the interstate. They'd gone through ten gears to get up to seventy miles per hour. The radio squawked again, "Nick, watch yourself, these men are likely armed and dangerous."

Nick picked up the radio, "Yeah, and I'm counting on you to be armed and dangerous, too. Where the hell are you guys?"

"We're following them – and they're closing in on you. Nick, get as far away from your driver side window as you can. Try not to let them pass you."

"Right!"

The blue sedan pulled up behind the tanker. Shots rang out. They were trying to blow out its tires. Nick slammed on the brakes – the sedan braked hard, skidded sideways and missed the back of the tanker by inches. Nick and Abel struggled to get the truck back up to speed. They had to gear down and start over. A minute later Nick looked to his side, the Buick was already on him. A man was pointing a shotgun out the window toward his head. Nick held up his left hand as if to surrender. Within a flash, there was a loud blast and glass shot everywhere.

Countryman's men had blown out the back window of the Buick. Nick and Abel shifted gears again and put the accelerator to the floor. In his rearview mirror, Nick could see the sedan swerve from side to side and then straighten up again. But now an unmistakable maze of blue lights in the front grill of two black town cars were right behind it – on each side. Nick wasn't going to be the one to stop – he'd leave that decision to someone else.

He watched his mirrors. It appeared a gun battle was taking place, but he couldn't hear any shots. When Nick looked forward again, he was stunned. He stood on the brakes with all his weight – the truck's tires locked-up and smoked. The rig lurched hard and skidded toward the shoulder. Flashing lights were everywhere. Abel was thrown into the dash and onto the floor. It felt like a huge weight was pulling the cab off its chassis. Nick thought for sure they would flip over. Finally it came to a stop. He caught his breath and peeled his hands off the steering wheel. A large pistol was in his face, "Don't move – hands up – Now!" A gun was at Abel's head, *"No te muevas, mi amigo!"*

The Buick slid sideways toward them. Countryman's cars were right behind. Within an instant, three cars creating a roadblock wheeled around and surrounded everyone. Shots were fired – no windows or tires were spared. The men exited the blue sedan with their hands up. Texas State Troopers were in control.

Nick was escorted from his truck. Countryman waved the trooper off.

"You may be insane, Taft, but ... good work."

Abel was face down on the ground and an officer was cuffing him. Nick yelled, "Hey, what the hell are you doing? He's with us," as he looked to Countryman for confirmation.

Countryman reluctantly nodded, "It's all right – let him go. Nick, you better be right about him."

"Tom, he's Bud's friend – and now he's MY friend."

"That doesn't mean he's legal, Nick. Whose side are you on anyway?"

"I'm on your side – and he's on our side!"

Countryman clenched his jaw and gave Nick a cold stare. He barked, "Let's get that hatch open."

Two troopers climbed up on top of the tanker with bolt cutters. It took both of them to loosen the hatch after the lock was cut.

Once open, they looked in and yelled out, "Everyone alright?"

But they saw no one.

One trooper mumbled, "It's empty."

Nick, standing next to Countryman shook his head, "That's impossible."

He scrambled up the side of the tanker praying. "Please Lord don't let this thing be empty." He climbed in and walked to the very back, turned and looked forward toward the hatch. The troopers were watching him. He thought he saw something move. But it was just a bundle tucked up under a bench.

Nick said in a loud voice, "Anybody in here – *hola*?"

The bundle rolled out – it was a man.

"Oh my God! You old bastard. How'd you get here?"

Nick called up to the troopers, "Get Tom!"

A trooper and Countryman climbed into the tanker with a bottle of water and a medical kit.

Bud Marskey, whose mouth was too dry to speak, drank some water, "Who's the crazy son a bitch drivin' this thang?"

"Oh – that would be me," Nick acknowledged as he raised his right hand.

Bud smiled, "Well, I'm damn glad to see ya anyway."

He was helped out of the tanker by a police medic who tended to him. When it was all over, everyone was strangely calm. Countryman pulled Nick away from the crowd. They needed to get their stories straight. Nick volunteered to take the heat for any laws broken and Countryman promised to protect him. They gazed back at the scene: one sideways blue sedan riddled with bullet holes and shattered glass, five law enforcement vehicles pointing every which direction, and a jack-knifed tanker truck. Both counted their blessings.

Occupants of the sedan included Rudy Jimenez and two Delrio Corporation employees. They were arrested and charged with kidnapping, assault with a deadly weapon, and resisting arrest – for starters. They were transported pursuant to Countryman's request to the Travis County lockup. Bud Marskey per his request was taken to Seton Hospital in Austin where he was treated for dehydration and was required to stay overnight for observation. Nick remained in Texas for a couple of days to help Bud clean up his apartment and buy him and Abel a celebratory dinner. He flew back to Washington late on a Sunday night.

Lisa picked him up at Washington National Airport. He'd filled her in on all the events by phone, but she gave him a big hug as if to confirm he was okay. They went to a late-night diner in Georgetown, Au Pied de Cochon, and ate omelets and french fries. Nick gave her a step-by-step account of the whole experience. He was almost shaking when he recounted the highway chase.

Lisa put her hands on his, "It's become a dangerous world."

"I guess, but I think the worst is over. Countryman's men have the Jimenez family right where they want them."

They walked back to Nick's building, got his suitcase out of her car and climbed the narrow stairs to his apartment. It was a cool night, and the warmth of the building's old radiator heat felt good. After getting extremely well reacquainted, they had the best night's sleep in weeks.

28

October 1986   Capitol Hill   55 Degrees Cloudy

Denny Folgier took one look at Nick on Monday morning and chuckled, "Were you in an industrial accident or has the system finally beaten you down?"

"Well, not exactly beaten – yet."

"Good. Because I've got good news and interesting news."

"What?

"One, your *International Customs Waters* provision just got attached to the majority's big crime bill. They got wind of some polls showing concern over crime and drugs, and pieced together every pro-crime-prevention bill around into a new *Omnibus Crime Bill*. And the best part is you don't have to do anything – they're not even going to have a subcommittee or full committee vote. They're just packaging them together, scheduling a lot of press conferences, and passing them all on the floor in one big vote scheduled later this week. It won't be retroactive, but should become effective in January of next year.

"Unbelievable. They never even wanted a hearing on it. Now they're just going to pass it without any debate or amendments? You know what's the worst about all this, Denny? Everyone knows our legal process is supposed to be deceptive and that it produces often dishonest results. But most believe our congressional process is open, fair and democratic – we sell it that way. It's not even close. Even when it looks fair, they make the process so backward the result seldom is."

"Well listen to this, you might also have another shot at your triggered amnesty language. The Senate is taking the House / Senate Conference Report on the immigration bill to the floor for a vote. A Senator from one of those western states is angry that the Senate's triggered amnesty language got kicked out in the final conference compromise, and is threatening to offer it as an amendment on the Senate floor."

Nick came to life, "Really? Do you think it has a chance?" He sounded more excited than he actually was. "I thought you couldn't amend a conference report on the floor?"

"Well, not usually, but a few Senators are pretty upset about the House insisting that the Senate language be excluded, so I guess they're going to take a run at it. You know much about Senate procedure?"

"No."

"But, you know some people on the Senate Judiciary Committee – right?"

Nick knew a couple of counsels in the Senate, but the one he trusted was Ken O'Malley who was now at the Justice Department. Ken had worked in the Senate for years and knew the process well. Of course, Nick would have to buy another lunch in order to benefit from his friend's parliamentarian wisdom, but the advice was usually worth it.

Over mesquite grilled salmon he explained the history of the amendment in the House and the denial by the Rules Committee for an amendment on the floor. He asked for Ken's help in understanding a potential Senate strategy.

Ken nodded pouring a glass of wine, "My friend, the rules of procedure in the upper chamber are complicated."

"Oh please, just give me the scoop."

"You know what cloture is – right?"

The first time Nick heard that term was in a judge's chambers in Flamingo Beach. He wasn't sure what it meant then but it had worked to his advantage.

"Not exactly."

"Then let's start from the beginning. Despite that the bottom line is you can't amend a conference report, I'll give you some pointers. The people who control time on the Senate floor for any bill are the Majority Leader, the Minority Leader, the majority bill manager, and the minority bill manager. You better have one of those people helping or your amendment is not likely to even be heard."

"Okay."

"Depending upon how controversial the issue is as it moves to the floor, the first two things likely to happen are: one, the Majority Leader will file a motion to proceed which means the Senate will move to the bill; and two, if they do go ahead, the minority could force a cloture vote. Generally, the Minority won't do that on a motion to proceed, but will later on passage of the bill itself."

"And, what does that mean?"

"That means after a certain number of hours of debate, a vote on cloture – to cut off debate and vote on the bill – will occur. You need 60 votes to succeed on a cloture motion in the Senate, not 51% as is the case with most votes in the House. If you get your 60, debate is cut off and the legislation moves forward."

"Then how would we get this amendment offered?"

Ken, spooning foie gras onto a cracker, "All right, let's just cut to the chase. Unlike the House, where the Rules Committee drafts a nice, neat rule by which debate, including amendments, will proceed, the Senate is more like jungle warfare. Anything can happen at any time – well almost any time. Regardless, there's no rule to follow when considering a bill."

"So?"

"So, in the Senate, there are amendment trees – a device that limits the number of amendments that can be offered on a bill. Generally, if it is expected that many will be filed on a bill, the Majority Leader will likely use his prerogative and file the first underlying amendment, and then supporters of the bill will proceed to fill that tree with their own wish list thus locking out amendments not supportive of the legislation."

"Good Lord. How many does it take to fill the tree?"

"The number that can be pending at any time on any tree is eleven."

"Uh huh."

"And, you need to keep in mind that once cloture gets invoked, whether it's relevant to your language or not, then no nongermane amendments will be allowed. Is yours germane?"

"For crying out loud, can't we just deal with the substance of this amendment?"

"In Congress, Nick, process is substance. Cloture and the filibuster *actually* protect the minority party in the Senate – and, as *you* might appreciate, is one of the things that differentiates it from the House.[25] Now, is your language relevant to the text of the bill? Does it amend language in the underlying bill?"

"Well, it was in the original Senate-passed bill; it would create a Presidential Commission to determine if the U.S.-Mexico border is secure."

"What? Nobody's talking about securing any borders in that legislation. Look, this amendment probably isn't going to happen, it sounds like a lot of posturing to me. Democrats outmaneuvered Republicans on this in the House and during the conference. And friend, a little advice, stay away from the Senate process – you're not armed."

"Yeah, I've no business being involved with that effort. But thanks for your help."

"Always glad to educate someone from the lower chamber."

Nick paid the lunch tab – again.

One week after the Texas incident, Nick and Bud were able to laugh about parts of it on a telephone call. Bud described the local media's coverage of the grand jury impaneled to investigate the Delrio employees. That good news, along with Chairman Staunton's conspicuous absences in committee during the week, gave Nick a boost he'd needed for a while. He was able to focus for the first time on Maleva's immigrant status legal challenge. He talked with the immigration attorney in DC who had a partner in Miami. After reviewing Maleva's facts and the lawyer's initial investigation, Nick was told that the legal process would be somewhat routine, but the circumstances surrounding her case would likely benefit from some political help.

To celebrate the arrest of the Jimenez men, he and Lisa went to a small French restaurant, Tout Va Bien. It was creatively tucked into the old buildings on 30th Street heading down toward the Potomac River in Georgetown, and smelled of roasted duck. Afterwards, they strolled along the colorful streets of Georgetown. Nick took the slow pace of the evening to fill Lisa in on what he'd learned of Maleva's circumstance. He told of the need for some political help – and inquired about a potential letter from the Chairman of the committee that oversaw the INS.

"So, you want my help with Maleva – an illegal immigrant?"

"I would like to help her. If you could help me, it would be appreciated."

"Now, that's rich. The crusader to stop amnesty until the border is secure wants to help an illegal immigrant stay here despite the status of the border."

"One is a federal policy issue, Lisa, the other is an individual case."

"So, collectively you want to enforce the immigration

laws, but individually, enforcement depends upon a subjective standard of whom we're talking about? That's real consistent."

"Fair enough. Will you help me?"

"I'll need to think on it."

"You can by helping me get a letter from Staunton to the INS about her case."

"You're unbelievable! How hypocritical can you get?"

"I'm not concerned about my consistency – just Maleva's well-being."

Lisa sighed, "Let me see what I can do."

Back at his apartment they opened a bottle of wine. Lisa sat on one of the bar stools at his kitchen counter and he poured two glasses. He stood on the opposite side of the narrow wood bar.

Lisa changed the subject. "Well, here's to being alive."

"Salut!"

They clinked their stemmed glass rims together and to their surprise heard an unusual sound like broken glass. Each examined their respective wine glasses, then took a sip. The sound occurred again.

Nick looked toward the window that faced the alleyway behind his building, "What the hell was that?"

"I don't know."

"What's that on the window? It looks like ice."

He walked to the window and put his hand on it. Lisa swirled around on her barstool.

"Son of a bitch!"

He leaped toward Lisa, pulling her to the floor.

"What is it?"

"Someone just shot at us! That sound was the glass from the window. Those are bullet holes!"

"No."

"Yes. I'm telling you – damn it. Stay down!"

Crawling to his desk, Nick pulled the phone to the floor. He reached in his back pocket for Countryman's number.

It seemed only seconds before the DC police and Justice Department personnel were at his place. When Countryman arrived, he ordered the DC police to outside duty and his men to the inside. They measured the bullet holes and found the remaining fragments lodged in the thick wooden door frame of Nick's closet. Countryman's men searched from the window with high-powered infrared telescopes. They had men enter an abandoned building two and a half blocks away that had a line of sight to Nick's apartment.

They concluded three things. One, it was a skilled sniper shooting a pre-market prototype version of an L96A1 British sniper rifle firing 7.62 mm bullets. Two, whoever it was intentionally did not hit either of them. And, three, if they had intended to hit them, they would be dead. Lisa sat on the bed. Tears rolled down her face. Nick sat quietly beside, and put his arm around her.

Countryman started, "Look you two, they're trying to scare you. And I don't blame you for being rattled. I don't want you staying here tonight or you at your place, Lisa. Nick, you need to pack what you'll use for a couple of nights. Lisa, I'll have my men escort you to your place to get what you need. We'll get you rooms at the Hyatt Hotel on Capitol Hill. You will be safe there."

Nick and Lisa nodded. He packed his things and rode with Lisa to her place. They were given two rooms at the hotel, but stayed close together in one. Countryman instructed them to go to their respective offices on the next business day and carry on as if nothing had happened.

29

Columbus Day 1986   Maryland / Virginia   72 Degrees Calm

Chesapeake Bay was strangely flat on this unusually warm October day. Boaters were out for their last sail of the year. Seagulls glided for food in the slightest breeze over sun worshipers who hadn't stored their vessels for the winter.

The *River Walker* pulled away from its dock around eight o'clock in the morning and headed down the Severn River. As far as Countryman's men could see, passengers included Chairman Staunton, Judd Traynor, two unidentified men, and one bikini-clad woman.

The investigators' turbo-powered sport fishing yacht, the *Hammerhead,* tailed the chairman's vessel comfortably behind as they headed toward the bay. They carried considerable surveillance equipment and firepower if needed. Although their job was collection of intelligence only, they were prepared, if not anxious, for more. The team tracking Staunton for months had grown tired of keeping an arm's length so as not to draw the ire of the powerful congressman.

Finishing breakfast at the Annapolis waterfront restaurant, the girls were working on their second Bloody Mary. They chided their friend, Shelly, for not calling her secretive sugar daddy. It had been a boring three-day break so far, and they were looking for a fun Monday afternoon to salvage the weekend. These ladies had heard stories many times of his generosity with the nose candy and about his appreciative friends. Shelly finally obliged and left a message with his private answering service.

The *River Walker* made its way to the mouth of the Severn into Chesapeake Bay. It was cruising at a comfortable ten knots cutting through the glassy smooth water. Drinks were served and hors d'oeuvres put out. Chairman Staunton received a *shore to ship* call and returned it immediately. Although he'd never admit it, Shelley was his favorite. On the other hand, she knew she had him wrapped around her finger.

The *Hammerhead* hung back from view of the chairman's yacht. The investigators on board were speculating as to what Staunton and his henchmen were up to – the lead investigator was sure it was no good. Others on board considered him just a good time Charlie who lacked scruples.

Shelley took the phone call at the front desk of the restaurant, "Hey, sugar."

"What are you up to, darlin'?"

"Well, two of my best girlfriends and I are just bored to tears and wondered if you could come out to play."

"I see. Where are you?"

"I'm at Middleton Tavern in Annapolis. Where are you?"

"I'm on my yacht about a fifteen minute cruise away."

"How convenient."

"But we got some bi'ness to do on the boat just yet."

"Well, that's too bad – I was kind of hoping *the little chairman* was up for some bi'ness."

"That is very temptin'."

"How about your house here? Or is business being done there too?"

Staunton gritted his jaw. He wanted nothing more than to have Shelley to himself that afternoon. "Hold the line, darlin'."

Staunton conversed with Traynor and his boat captain. Traynor nodded his head and shook the chairman's hand.

"Darlin', you got your car?"

"Yes."

"I'll see you at the Annapolis City Dock in ten minutes."

Seventy-five miles west, Nick and Lisa spent the Monday holiday in the Virginia countryside. They just couldn't stay in their hotel rooms any longer regardless of the danger. Countryman said he'd allow them to move after the shooting inquiry was over and he could provide some minimum security, but the investigation continued. Taunting reality, they took their time driving out Route 50 to horse country. The sunny day highlighted the colors of the autumn leaves and made the usually scenic drive seem even brighter.

Over lunch at the Red Fox Inn, they discussed how they might get past their deepening predicament. It seemed it was all they talked about anymore, and just doing so made him tired.

Lisa began, "I don't think I'll ever have a normal life in Washington again – not that I ever really have."

"What do you mean? If Staunton and the Jimenezes weren't around, our lives would be totally normal. How the hell did someone like Staunton ever get into power anyway?"

Lisa, her palms flat on the table, "Who gave Staunton the power to enslave you? The voters – the core of your great American democracy!"

"Yeah, which is in jeopardy of becoming the great American plague."

"Listen to you. When we met you were taking on Congress and defending America's democracy to the point of obsession."

Nick, displaying his hard won armor of indifference, "Well, I've learned a few things. Like it's all bullshit and everyone should just look out for themselves. Speaking of which, I haven't heard back from Staunton's legislative assistant. I thought you said she could get a letter from him to the INS for Maleva? The immigration lawyer has asked me about it several times."

"Yeah, I need to tell you. I don't think it's going to happen.

Staunton's nervous about all that's going on with investigators snooping around and doesn't want to send any correspondence to any agency about any immigration related issues. Can you blame him?"

"Yes, I can blame him. You know, I have Judiciary Committee letterhead in my desk drawer with Chairman Staunton's name across the top. I could just write and send my own letter."

"You know the penalty for forging the name of a federal official?"

"You know the penalty for not helping someone like Maleva who's never asked for help in her whole life?"

"Well, don't come crawling to me when you're in federal prison wearing high heel shoes and learning how to dance."

It hadn't occurred to Nick that Lisa might balk at helping with Maleva's situation. "Maybe Countryman can help me somehow."

"Nick, you need to do a reality check on where you stand with Countryman, and how much more leverage you want him having over any more of your personal matters."

"How do you mean?"

"You've got to face the facts about this Justice Department investigation into Staunton and the Jimenezes. You're not going to simply walk away scot-free from all that."

"Lisa, I trust Tom. I think he'll help me ..."

"Yeah, in exchange for your testimony to a grand jury to help indict the Jimenezes and Staunton. I hope you don't think Tom's efforts to keep us out of harm's way are because he likes you. And you better watch what you say in any testimony so as to not indict the wrong person."

"No ... I understand. But I don't think I'll be in any legal jeopardy either."

"Look, I have no monopoly on reality here, but with regard to all of your ongoing efforts, you better hope Tom Countryman stays in his job and out of harm's way. I mean politically and personally. If Staunton or the Jimenez's put two and two together between you and Countryman, I guarantee you someone will take a fall."

––––––––––

The *River Walker* turned north toward Spa Creek. It cruised right by the *Hammerhead* whose crew snapped a hundred photos of Staunton's yacht as it passed. It sailed through Annapolis Harbor to the City Dock at the heart of the waterfront. The *Hammerhead* pulled back. Investigators had their telescopes and binoculars trained on the yacht, but there were plenty of obstacles in their view. The *River Walker* docked briefly and then reversed its engines. One person exited, but could not be identified.

"Shit. Are we supposed to follow the yacht or follow whoever that was?"

"Both," snapped the lead investigator, as he got on the radio. "We stay with the yacht. We can't confirm that Staunton is not on it."

The *River Walker* cruised back near them again heading south down the Chesapeake. A flurry of camera activity swept through the *Hammerhead* again. The captain slowly swung the 46-foot yacht around to follow their target. After clearing some random boat traffic, the skipper of the *River Walker* opened her up. Its big engines had her cruising at 27 knots. The *Hammerhead's* turbo engines allowed it to keep pace comfortably – but at a distance. Within a few hours, they were crossing Tangier Sound headed toward the south end of the bay.

————————

After lunch, they walked the antique stores on Main Street in Middleburg. Their lunch conversation had turned less than cordial when Nick perceived Lisa's warnings as patronizing. He knew the trouble he could be in, but took Countryman at his word – they'd been like partners in Texas. Nick wasn't sure Lisa understood how critical Tom's help had been or the loyalty he felt toward Tom.

Walking down different aisles in the stores, they kept their thoughts to themselves. Lisa fell in love with a large antique bird cage and pictured it in the great room of her grandparents' ranch. Nick saw a mahogany and glass gun case that he wished he could buy – then wished he had a home big enough to put it in. He caught Lisa's eye, pointed at his watch, and headed toward the exit. She opened the bird cage door, stared for a moment, and walked away.

They decided to skip an afternoon glass of wine at a local café, and drove back to Washington in occasionally interrupted silence. All the speculating in the world about their circumstances was meaningless until there was some resolution to the residual power of the Jimenez family and John Staunton. One other thing they couldn't begin to calculate was that forces greater than them were at work.

————————

The early afternoon sun grew brighter as the *Hammerhead* maintained pace with the *River Walker* which was covering a lot of ground. There were some tankers to dodge, and crab traps to avoid if they strayed from the channel, but the real task was to remain a constant distance and not be detected. By mid-afternoon they'd made it past Cape Charles at the southern end of the bay and were rounding the point toward the ocean.

The water was turning from brackish to a green-blue. The investigators, not exactly seasoned mariners, had no clue how far to sea they were headed but were grateful it was an unusually calm day.

By four o'clock the yachts were miles offshore in the Atlantic. The *River Walker* cut its engines and began to drift. As there were few boats that far into the ocean, the *Hammerhead* had to maintain an even greater distance to keep from being noticed. The captain cut its engines, and threw out some fishing lines as a ruse. They drifted at equal pace for half an hour. The investigators couldn't help but speculate what the *River Walker* crew was up to. Between coffee and cigarettes, their theories ran from engine trouble to monkey business below deck.

Out of nowhere a small plane flew overhead, banked a sharp turn around the *River Walker*, dropped two bundles out its rear door, and headed due east out of sight. The Department of Justice team snapped to attention. The captain fired the engines. The lead investigator got on the radio to the U. S. Coast Guard. The *River Walker* started its engines and headed toward the jettisoned bales. The *Hammerhead* set a course directly on them, but was twenty minutes away at full speed.

Judd Traynor and Juan Jimenez worked together with gaffes to snag the bundles and pull them to the boat. Their captain kept the boat alongside carefully working the dual controls. Once on board, they hustled the square groupers to the v-berths in the bow of the yacht and covered them with a tarp. As they tucked the excess under its edges, the captain yelled, "We've got company."

The *River Walker* took off due east full speed ahead. The *Hammerhead*, a lighter, slightly faster boat, was two miles away and closing. Traynor and Juan pulled a third man from below deck, duct-taped his hands in front of him and moved him to the stern. When the *Hammerhead* was within several hundred yards, they threw him directly off the stern into the chilly Atlantic Ocean.

"It's a risk, but just may buy us the time we need," snapped Traynor. My guess is they're not competition but law enforcement. If so, they'll stop and pick him up."

"Why did you leave him alive?"

"Well, it's one thing to throw a man overboard. It's altogether something else to murder him, now, isn't it? We have good lawyers, but maybe not that good."

"He could become a problem, you know."

"Oh come on, he's as loyal as the day is long; and that dumb son of a bitch couldn't tell 'em much if he tried."

The captain of the *Hammerhead* yelled into the yacht's intercom, "Man overboard, man overboard," as he pulled back on the throttles.

"Bullshit!" The lead investigator was incredulous. "What are you doing?"

"Picking him up, sir. We have no choice."

The *Hammerhead* slowed as it approached the man kicking frantically to keep his nose above water. "Get him out of there," ordered the captain.

The investigators hauled the heavyset man onto the swim platform off the stern and then into the boat. They took him below, wrapped a blanket around him, and removed the tape from his hands. He mumbled an inaudible thank you as he struggled to catch his breath. The *River Walker* had quickly put several miles between them. The captain was on the radio again with the Coast Guard giving coordinates. He returned the yacht to full power following directly behind their target again. The shoreline was fading from view.

The *Hammerhead* slowly began to gain ground. The radio squawked – the Coast Guard cutter *North Way* was reported to be within twenty nautical miles of the last coordinates the captain had given. He updated the information and gave their estimated location based on the speed and direction they were headed. The lead investigator went down to visit the man they'd rescued.

As he descended the steps into the galley, he heard conversation coming from below, "Dos basters twi to kiwl me!"

Once in front of him, he looked closer as he continued complaining, "Dougee?"

"Yeth?"

"What were you doing on that boat?"

"I dunno. They ask me who I tol' abou' the photo. Then they mosy ignorwed me."

"What were they doing on the boat?"

"Dwug pickup."

"Is Congressman Staunton on that boat?"

"Naw – he got off at da dock – he a nithe man."

"Shit."

The head investigator returned to the upper deck, "How we doing, captain?"

"We're closing on them slowly. We're also running into some choppy waters."

"I can see that."

"Where the hell's the Coast Guard?"

"We're headed in their direction."

––––––––––

The *River Walker* slowed to a crawl. Traynor, the captain, and Juan Jimenez brought up several large fishing nets from below. The *Hammerhead* closed the gap quickly. They stretched the nets out twenty yards across the stern of the yacht. And then, they waited for their pursuers.

The lead investigator was puzzled, "Captain, what's going on? They got engine trouble?"

"Maybe."

But before they could get too close, the *River Walker* took off again in a straight line headed northeast.

"We've got them now. We'll be on them in minutes, sir."

With that bold announcement hanging in the air, the *Hammerhead's* props let go a loud gurgle, the engines whined, and the boat slowed quickly, "Damn them," the captain yelled. "Sneaky bastards."

The Hammerhead's props were wrapped in yards of heavy-duty fish netting.

As they began to distance themselves again, Traynor and Juan smiled from the stern of their yacht. Traynor waved toward the *Hammerhead* and laughed, "Sometimes, it's best to be smarter than faster."

But, within minutes, their laughter turned to despair as they saw a Coast Guard cutter approaching from the north. It came out of the blue and was on them quickly.

Through a distant loudspeaker, "*River Walker*, this is the United States Coast Guard ship *North Way* requesting permission to come along side."

The captain increased to full power. The *North Way* came closer and repeated the request. With no response, the cutter followed protocol and radioed its Command on shore to seek permission via Mexico's U.S. Embassy to board the vessel flying under its flag due to a suspicion of drug trafficking. They kept abreast of the *River Walker* and awaited a response. Within minutes the embassy had telephoned Mexico, secured permission, and communicated back to the U.S. Command which radioed that permission had been granted.

Traynor and Jimenez watched with horror as the cutter suddenly moved closer, fired two rounds across the bow, and trained their guns directly on them. The *River Walker* stopped dead in the water. Coast Guard personnel boarded and seized the bundles of marijuana, cut two kilos of cocaine out of the middle of them both – then arrested all on board and seized the vessel.

After stopping briefly to ensure that the *Hammerhead* was operating under full power again, the *North Way* and all vessels headed to a Coast Guard station on shore.

––––––––––

October had been a bad month for Staunton and the Jimenez family. Three members of their Texas operation were indicted by a federal grand jury in the Western District of Texas. They would be tried for kidnapping, assault, mail fraud, forgery and resisting arrest. One editor in Staunton's district grabbed onto the story raining scandalous editorials down on the Congressman's political association with them every few days.

Juan Jimenez and Judd Traynor, although not indicted for drug trafficking in Maryland, had other legal problems. Their talented lawyer confirmed to the U.S. Attorney that the *River Walker* had in fact been boarded in international customs waters pursuant to permission from the Mexican government. But, such permission had been granted via ship to shore by radio and to the embassy via telephone which was insufficient per the antiquated federal statute that required such permission be in writing. Consequently, according to the most recent federal court decisions, the drugs seized would not be admitted as evidence against them, and the arrests made in connection with the drugs were illegal.

However, the facts leading to an attempted murder charge for throwing a man overboard at sea with his hands taped together was a sufficient basis for indictment. With the help of Dougee's heart-felt, if ineloquent, testimony, Judd Traynor and Juan Jimenez remained the subjects of a pending federal grand jury impaneled in Federal Court in Maryland to hear charges of assault and attempted murder.

Chairman John Staunton had no charges brought against him. He and the girls had slipped the investigator's tail in the narrow streets of Annapolis and spent the afternoon snorting, and cavorting. He was back in the committee chairman's tall chair the very next afternoon overseeing a hearing regarding the admission of evidence in federal drug cases.

Lisa Castile had been right about a few things. Nick was forced to testify to both grand juries about everything he'd learned regarding the Jimenez operations in Texas and Maryland. He was also required to check in with Countryman's office on a weekly basis and seek permission before traveling more than fifty miles from the District of Columbia – except of course to Texas or Maryland. The resolution of any potential charges against Nick would be determined only after the prosecution of all counts pending against the Jimenez family. The one recent bright spot was he'd opened a letter from his mother and it had contained a check for $1,000 from his father. Nick was grateful for it.

Although he'd been able to move from the hotel back to his apartment, Nick felt uneasy. He kept his blinds closed across the big windows that looked out over Georgetown. He'd also started using cabs to get around instead of his car. It made him feel safer; and the DC government had finally booted his car anyway due to uncountable unpaid parking tickets. There was a taxi stand just blocks from his house that he routinely walked to, a cab ride to most places was only five bucks. He was really looking forward to getting out of DC and down to Florida in a few days to attend Palmer's Election Night celebration.

The next day on Halloween afternoon, he walked amongst the fall leaves toward the cab stand. The late fall sun was almost blinding. Costumed kids celebrating early yelled *Trick or Treat* as he passed their door. An anxious Red Top Taxi driver quickly pulled to the curb, but there was already a passenger in the back. Nick, cupping a hand over his eyes, waved him on; but the cabby pleaded in broken English, "Don't worry, don't worry, I drop you first." Nick reluctantly agreed, but was immediately annoyed by a loose seat spring or something that snagged his shirt and pricked the back of his shoulder. A drowsy confusion made him temporarily forget where he was headed. The driver and passenger stared at him with curious expectation.

30

November 1986   In Between   45 Degrees Foggy

The captain's voice awoke him informing passengers they'd reached their cruising altitude. His flight would be arriving late, but he would have time to make it to Congressman Palmer's victory party. Nick wasn't carrying his usual optimism in traveling home. One, he hadn't sought permission from Countryman to travel to Florida. Two, although grateful to be out of DC where neither Staunton, nor the Jiminezes, were watching his every move, he was becoming increasingly paranoid. He kept seeing visions of his hands bound together and strangers staring at him.

In reality, strangers were staring at him. The man driving the cab Nick climbed into in Georgetown and the backseat passenger were two of Staunton's henchmen. The seat spring he felt that day was a hypodermic needle. He was, in fact, in a room at a remote hotel being fed a closely monitored combination of sodium penathol and heroin and was drifting in and out of consciousness. He was being harshly interrogated, but was feeling no pain.

Nick felt euphoric as he looked forward to seeing old friends, and confident that Palmer would be reelected, but was also dreading returning to Washington where a newly empowered Staunton would await him unencumbered by reelection distractions. He fell back to sleep and saw glimpses of Staunton's thugs in his face asking questions over and over.

Floating into the election party, colleagues whom Nick didn't quite recognize welcomed him. Mrs. Palmer, the best combination of political wife and down to earth lady gave him a big hug. As election night progressed, unexpected losses had people talking that Republicans might actually pick up a few seats for a change. Around ten o'clock, after toasting Palmer's victory with unusually colorful big bottles of English Ale, Nick and a friend walked two blocks to the County Commission building to check election results from across the country. Streaming down the familiar street, they came across a Florida State Representative stopped at a traffic light.

She yelled to them, "Quite a night, eh boys?"

"Yeah. Looks like we might win a few seats for a change."

"Win a FEW? You better look again. We're taking out Dems across the map!"

As the light turned and she drove down the street, her voice faded, "Nick, it looks like your boss on the Judiciary Committee is Texas toast ..."

"What'd she say?"

"Your loss on the issues in the city – messes the coast??"

"Now that makes a lot of sense. Drinking, no doubt?"

"What d' you think?"

They were suddenly in the County Center. The place seemed unusually quiet for election night. To their shock, the map on the screen was covered with small red squares and rectangles in almost every state across the country. The faces of nightly news anchors on every network were unusually reserved. Republicans had just pulled ahead in enough races to possibly take the U.S. House for the first time in decades.

A list of congressional casualties was highlighted at the bottom of the television map. Nick pushed mannequin-like people aside to get to the screen. He scanned the names like a robot, eyes locking onto Texas U.S. House 42ⁿᵈ : Staunton D 49.4%, Adams R 49.6%, precincts reporting 95%. Nick was in total disbelief. Looking again and again, he ran his hand across the screen until it all became a blur. He reached back past vague faces and grabbed his friend's jacket lapel, pulling him forward through the midst.

"What does that say?"

"Taft, you've lost it!"

He pulled him closer to the screen, "What does it say?"

"It says Staunton 49%, Adams 49% – no projected winner! Now, let go of me ya psycho."

No truer smile had crossed Nick's face. He was stunned, relieved, and confused. His friend suggested they get a drink. They had several.

At a dive on the beach, he fell off a bar stool spinning down and downward onto a wet floor.

He heard Lisa, in a whisper, "Nick?"

"Lisa, can you believe it? Staunton could go down?" Someone slapped him back into reality.

Staunton's thugs were tasked with finding out everything Nick knew about Congressman Staunton, his Texas operations, the Jimenezes and of Alec Sivore's murder. The injections were keeping him just beyond clarity – they figured some physical inducement might be helpful. Although Nick couldn't really feel the punches, he was bleeding from his nose and mouth and one eye was beginning to swell. Once again came the brief sharp of pain in his arm that he couldn't quite feel.

As the sun rose in his head and warmth surged through his body, Republicans were holding a slim majority in the House election. Of 435 seats, they would hold only a five seat majority in the next Congress. Nick thought, maybe with that close of a difference, the majority and minority will actually have to get a long for a change. One seat was still undetermined – Texas's 42nd District. With 98% of the votes counted, it stood at Staunton 50.8%, Adams 49.2%. Some absentee ballots had not yet been accounted for.

Although the media acknowledged Republicans had won control of the House, their focus was on the outcome of the Texas race. Whether the new majority would be in control by five or six seats wasn't all that exciting, but mudslinging and allegations of voter fraud in Texas were covered top to bottom. In the next instant Nick was watching all this unfold on a television in his parents' home in Florida. He kept trying to call Lisa but could never reach her. He checked the messages on his phone in Washington and there was one from the Major.

He returned Ity's call. His voice, as if under water, "Nicholas H. Taft, if you let Staunton weasel his way out and steal this election, he will never go down! You have friends – they need to let the public know Staunton is being indicted. You must shut this process down and put a stake through this scoundrel!"

Nick called the only person he thought could help, Alexi. They were seated on the roof deck of a seedy restaurant along U.S. 1 that had closed down several years before, but oddly were eating tasty steamers and conch fritters. He laid out his whole story from beginning to end, and apologized for not confiding in her sooner.

Her voice echoed, "Nick, that's a lot to dump on a girl. What do you want me to do?"

"I need you to help leak the story to the Texas and Washington press that this has gone down and that Staunton's about to be indicted."

"Good Lord!"

"Alexi, I need your help. You have any better ideas? And, I know, I know – I'll owe you."

She gave him a long hug and an unexpected kiss on the lips, "You owe me for a lot of things, but not this. Let me see what I can do."

Unfortunately, sodium penathol, known to many as the truth drug, diminished Nick's ability to protect himself or anyone else about what he knew. But unaware of the answers to so many questions posed by Staunton's men, he responded to them quite bluntly, "I don't know. Like I told you, I don't know!" When asked who else knew what he knew about Staunton, Nick answered truthfully, "My girlfriend, Lisa Castile." This brought a welcome interruption from the beatings and injections while phone calls were made. Nick drifted back out of consciousness.

The national networks announced a press briefing on the Texas election. The vote count now stood at Staunton 50.5%, Adams 49.5%. It started at high noon, and all channels carried it live. Staunton's campaign was hurling allegations so quickly against Adams, reporters couldn't write fast enough. It was alleged that he'd been arrested for abusing his wife and that he'd mismanaged funds as the U.S. Attorney, and that he was not really from Texas. Once the more tawdry allegations had been aired, Staunton took the microphone and gave an historical account of America's cherished representative democracy. He concluded with some well-

chosen words about the country's respect for the rule of law.

When he was done, the first question was, "Congressman, when were you planning to tell the voters of Texas that you're being investigated by a federal grand jury for smuggling illegal aliens and drugs across the Mexico border?"

John Staunton blinked for the first and last time in his long political career.

After more phone calls and bickering between Staunton's thugs over the uselessness of wasting any further time on Nick, they decided he'd given up all he could. They gave him a final lethal dose of heroin, untied his hands and threw him on the bed. They then turned out the lights and scrambled out of the trashed hotel room.

Suddenly Nick was back in DC feeling as optimistic as ever about life. The electoral process had worked, and his team came out on top for a change. Even his father congratulated him as if he deserved some of the credit. The outcome of Congressman Staunton's congressional election still appeared uncertain due to some ballots remaining uncounted. But victorious or not, he'd no longer be a powerful committee chairman since his party had lost their majority.

Nick's studio apartment didn't seem quite so small upon his return either. He still needed to replace the bullet-hole riddled glass pane, but that didn't bother him. The DC, DMV had finally towed away what remained of his car due to a record balance of unpaid tickets, and he'd have to pay a huge sum to get it back. However, in his newfound euphoria, it would be good to get a clean start on that front too. Maybe he'd just buy a new car. He curiously looked at the world with a new sense of hope.

To his surprise the Major knocked on his door — something he'd never done before. He kept shaking Nick's hand and repeating, "Are you back with us Nick? How do you feel?"

"Great, Major. I feel great. Were you as surprised as I was at our victory?"

31

November 1986   Georgetown   49 Degrees Clearing

Everything seemed to have a blurred frame around it. The room itself wasn't familiar, but he'd seen one like it before.

"Nick! Can you hear me?"

He saw the silhouette of white-lighted figures but couldn't make out their faces.

"Nick!"

Things came into focus, "Major, is that you?"

"Yes. It's me. Thank goodness, you're back with us."

"With you? What do you mean?"

Major Ity, perplexed by where to start, "You're at Georgetown University Hospital, son. We found you through a missing person's report filed by DC General Hospital. You looked like you'd dragged yourself into an army field hospital. You were a mess and have been in and out of consciousness for a while. The doctors say you were heavily sedated – you're lucky to be alive."

"DC General – when?"

"Early this morning."

"How long was I there?"

"No one seemed to know precisely, but we'd been looking for you for days."

"How many?"

"Three."

"What day is it?"

"It's Tuesday, November 4th."

"But – that's Election Day."

"That's right."

"That's impossible. The election already happened. We won! What's wrong with you?"

The doctor spoke up, "Son, you're suffering the side-effects of a heavy dose of narcotics."

"I've been out cold for over three days?"

Unbeknownst to Nick, he'd been mentally checked-out for over seventy-two hours. Once he'd given up all the information he could, Staunton's men had left him for dead in the Motor Hotel in southwest DC. The hotel, located in a wasteland near the DC Government inspection station, was one where rooms were usually rented by the hour, and the police seldom visited.

Fortunately for Nick, Countryman was ahead of the curve the moment Ity reported him missing. Nick was supposed to drive the Major to National Airport the evening of October 31st and Ity had offered to let him drive the Jaguar. He smelled trouble when Nick didn't show, and then Countryman's office received an anonymous tip from a woman that Nick had been abducted. They scoured the city for seventy-two hours. When a hotel maid found Nick unconscious and unable to be awakened, she called an ambulance which deposited him into the indigent system at the notorious DC General. The local police were eventually notified, and a missing persons report was published.

"Major...where's Lisa?"

"I'm not sure."

"Not sure?"

"I think Mr. Countryman has been keeping her informed."

Nick gazed around the room as if trying to get his bearings.

"The nurse informed Tom as soon as you became conscious."

The doctor spoke up again, "Young man, you need to rest. No more visitors today."

"When can I go home?"

"Not today."

Tom Countryman entered the doorway.

The nurse, taking Nick's blood pressure, "Sir, there'll be no questioning of this patient today or tonight."

"I understand. I just wanted to see for myself that you were all right. Glad you're back. You gave us quite a scare."

"Thanks, Tom," Nick said hesitantly. "Sorry I've caused so much trouble."

"No. I'm sorry we didn't do a better job of protecting you. By the way, I wanted you to know that Lisa's safe – she's in Texas. She left the day you went missing. If there's anything I can do, Nick, anything at all, just say it."

"I see. Well, actually there is something you can do for me, Tom. It involves a woman who's worked for my family for many years." Nick looked toward Countryman's assistant, and then said, "But can I talk with you about it in a couple of days when I'm back on my feet?"

"Of course."

"All right gentlemen, everyone out of the room. Visiting hours are over."

"No, wait … doctor, please let the Major stay. He's the only family I have here."

"Oh, I didn't realize. Sure, that's fine"

The Major gave Nick a wink and a smile.

"And, nurse, can we arrange for a television in this room – it's important?"

"Sure, Major. We can do that."

As the doctor departed, the Major turned back, "Nick, we'll have to watch the election returns tonight."

"Major, you don't understand. I just lived through this. It couldn't have all been a dream. It was so real, and Republicans took the House, and Staunton lost his chairmanship!"

Nick placed his intravenous-tubed arm on the metal railing that enclosed his bed. He saw the bruises where he'd been repeatedly injected by Staunton's men. "It *was* too good to be true . . . wasn't it?"

"Well, it sounds like quite a dream. But why don't we watch the returns tonight and see what reality has in store for us?"

"Yeah, okay." Nick felt very much alone, "I'd appreciate the company."

"I'm going home. Try to get some rest. I'll be back at seven o'clock."

He looked out the hospital window onto an empty, wet street in Georgetown. An entire election had passed through his brain – was he insane? The previous three days were completely lost to him. His head throbbed relentlessly and he'd declined pain pills in a desperate attempt to clear his mind. He requested a phone from the nurse to leave a voice message for Lisa at her office. After explaining as much as he could about what had happened, he emphasized he'd rather talk with her directly.

Upon trying to sleep, he drifted back onto the series of semi-conscious dreams he'd had, and thought of how they'd convinced him that one person *could* make a difference. He believed he had, and it gave him a renewed sense of prideful individualism. But now, he was in the dark again.

A slightly impatient nurse woke him at six o'clock to offer an unappetizing dinner. She informed Nick that someone had called who wouldn't leave their name. Major Ity showed up at exactly seven o'clock. He'd sneaked in a couple of ham sandwiches, chips, and some apple juice.

"Believe me, kid, I know how bad hospital food is – try one of these. I checked your answering machine like you asked. Your father left you a couple messages. You might give him a call."

Nick, with a long exhale, "Yeah – maybe not tonight, though."

He could taste the sandwich, but didn't have much appetite. Election returns began to mount up by nine o'clock. Palmer won reelection in Florida. Nick and Ity toasted with their hospital-issue paper cups. But as reality would have it, Republicans were not taking out Democrats across the country. In fact, it looked like business as usual for most of the nation. As reported by the TV news anchors, Democrats would retain the House majority by a large margin making it thirty-two straight years of political dominance.[26] Photos of incumbent committee chairmen were on the screen and Staunton's smiling face was prominent.

"Major, why do they get a pass? It all seems so useless."

"Nobody gets a pass. When the political pendulum swings back, your counterparts will surely be asking the same question. Look, there was a time when our media could have fortified their profession against the seductive path they chose. Their decision to sell out to advocacy journalism may render them irrelevant anyway. But, Nick you've been a good soldier for your party and you've had an opportunity to see behind the curtain, and having seen that makes you want to fight it. Why give up? In politics it's not just what you believe that matters, it's what you do."

"But Major, I came to Washington to get away from the uselessness of process. This charade surrounding our political system makes it worse than the law. At least in a courtroom the judge gets to hear and see the arguments of both sides – there's no party with all the power. In our political system – one has the right to speak but no right to be heard. The key players in a courtroom are the lawyers because they choose what arguments are heard. The key people in our political process are the news media who choose what they will and will not report."

"Perhaps things will get better. But if people like you don't stand up and fight, they will surely get worse."

As election results from the west continued to come in, Nick's dream of Staunton losing his powerful chairmanship was fading. By ten o'clock Eastern Standard Time, the Texas polls had been closed for two hours and the numbers were coming in on Staunton's race – he was winning with a solid 55%. Nick looked at Ity and shook his head. The often silent Major had dozed off in his chair. Nick decided to let his old friend sleep to rest and maybe fight again another day. This was not the election evening he'd anticipated. He gazed at the small TV screen and only half listened to the mundane chatter of the pundits until he fell asleep.

At eleven-thirty, the nurse woke them up, took Nick's temperature and told the Major to go home.

"Okay, I'll check on you in the morning, Nick."

Through half-open eyes, "Major, thanks for hanging out with me. Can you turn off the TV before you go?"

Ity reached toward the set, "Nick, look at this."

It was ten-thirty Texas time and Staunton's numbers had turned – he was suddenly losing by 4% rather than winning by 10%. With 99% of the precincts in Texas' 42nd district counted, the race was Adams 52%, Staunton 48%. The media pundits on all the stations were expressing shock that the venerable, if not sometimes irascible, House Judiciary Chairman was potentially in trouble. They acknowledged he'd been the subject of some ethics-related allegations, but no one expected him to ever lose his seat.

Nick yelled at the screen, "Potentially in trouble? With 99% reporting he's *in trouble*! Major, this is incredible."

By midnight Washington time, it was over. One hundred percent of the precincts had reported, and the majority in Texas' 42nd district had spoken: Adams 52%, Staunton 48%. Congressman John Staunton, in one of the few Democrat casualties of the night, had been defeated.

Nick was emotionally spent and losing his voice. The nurse had been in several times to quiet them down. By twelve-fifteen, she had lost her patience, "Major, I'm sorry but this is my last warning. And, Mr. Taft for the hundredth time, no woman has called, and you need to get some sleep." Turning to the Major, "And, *you* need to leave, now!"

Ity obliged, but not until he shook Nick's hand, "Congratulations young man I'm happy for you and pleased that the results will benefit your well-being."

"Major, those words are too familiar. It's like déjà vu? Hey, maybe I'm unconscious now – maybe this is a dream. And, maybe reality is..."

"Perhaps reality is somewhere in-between, Nick, but sometimes people deserve to have their faith rewarded. Now, try to get some rest."

One might have thought that Nick would crow in triumph at Staunton's defeat, but as it sank in he was surprisingly un-sanguine about the evening's results. He now knew that the next Chairman Staunton would be right around the corner. He watched election coverage until most channels ceased broadcasting, and fell into an exhausted sleep around two o'clock.

At nine-thirty that morning, Countryman and an assistant showed up in his room. After some talk about Staunton's defeat, he asked Nick to try to recount everything he could about his captivity. Even with remarkable recall, which he often had, all Nick could remember was his dream.

They showed him two photographs, "Do you recognize either of these men?"

"Yes." He pointed to the first photo, "That's the driver whose cab I got in – I'm positive."

"We arrested them this morning."

"Wow, that was fast!"

"We had help. Once the Jimenez crew was indicted in Texas, things quickly deteriorated between the Jimenez gang and Staunton's men. Apparently, the final straw was Juan Jimenez's indictment in Maryland for attempted murder while Staunton remained untouched by the authorities. They figured he'd cut some kind of a deal, and went after Staunton with a vengeance."

Countryman continued, "Always the survivors, the Jimenezes were ratting out everything on any Staunton activity in the Washington area. So, we had a treasure trove of anonymous tips. When an unconscious Caucasian male in his twenties was brought to DC General, it didn't take long. The missing persons report was a required formality when they couldn't identify you, but we had tips coming in within minutes of your admittance. One of the nurses had taken note of the bind marks on your wrists and the track marks on your arms. I'm sorry we didn't find you sooner."

Tom further reported that they expected Staunton to be indicted in Texas any day for conspiracy to smuggle drugs and humans into the United States, and were certain that his prosecution for tax evasion would go forward.

"Nick, I don't blame you for having doubts, but I believe you're safe now. The Jimenez operation has been dismantled, Staunton's days are numbered, and you're no longer a threat to them. There's renewed momentum for funding a task force on the border. A border agent was stabbed near Juarez yesterday – it hasn't gotten much coverage, but it may help us make our case and protect others in the future. If congressional politics doesn't get in the way again, we may actually start making some progress down there.

Countryman assured Nick there'd be no need to testify in

any further grand juries and that he could choose whether to participate in the pending criminal trials. Tom then rattled Nick's world by informing him that Lisa was being subpoenaed to testify to a grand jury in Texas.

"What?"

"Nick, I shouldn't be telling you any of this, probably lose my job for it, but feel like I owe you one – Lisa may be indicted."

"Indicted for what?"

I can't tell you that, but I can tell you it will be based in part upon your testimony."

"Tom, you can't do that!"

"Son, I'm afraid I can and I must. There's a bit more to this ordeal than you know. And that is all I'm saying about it. End of story. I've done all I can do at this point to keep you in the clear."

When Nick tried vehemently to question him further, Countryman abruptly shut him down, but hinted that a Texas judge, a drinking buddy of Staunton, was complicating matters by fraying the lines between judicial and political process. He thanked Nick for his help, and said to call if he could be of assistance.

Nick sat up in his hospital bed partially in shock. The doctor informed him his blood work looked better and that he would be released that afternoon. He slid to the edge of the bed, his feet about to touch the ground for the first time and thought about what Lisa might be doing. Suddenly it made sense to him that she hadn't tried to reach him.

Major Ity showed up and promised to drive him home and make sure he got situated. "Say Nick, when you're feeling better, let me host you at the club. We'll make it a celebratory event for your victory."

A little too bluntly, "No thanks, Major. I appreciate the

offer, but I'll pass."

"Well...okay. But, let's at least take the Jag out for a final spin before winter."

After a moment of reflection, Nick responded, "That I accept!"

The next day he cautiously walked the streets like a free citizen for the first time. His outlook was dimmer than the day he'd arrived, but it wasn't like he had a bad memory on every corner. Nick harbored no more enthusiasm for taking on entrenched politicians, and was happy simply to be left alone. He loathed politics as only one who has experienced it can, but at least he'd helped the voters in Texas replace one corrupt Member. Lisa was due back in Washington that night, and as always he looked forward to seeing her. He was still confused by the events of the past few days, and puzzled as to why Lisa must appear before a grand jury or possibly be indicted, but figured she had a good explanation. She always did.

Epilogue

January 2014   Washington, DC   32 Degrees Clear

Twenty-nine years later Nick journeyed down Pennsylvania Avenue toward the silhouette of the Capitol. Majorities in Congress had changed hands three times, but the same battles continued. Passing by the Justice Department, he thought of those who'd given their careers or, like his murdered colleague, Tomás Countryman, also their lives for the country. While the sight of the stately domed Capitol Building still inspired him, his experience of the process within it had not.

The legal process had continued to prove equally uninspiring. Lisa Castile was indicted for aiding and abetting the felon, John Staunton, during and after her employment with him. Thanks to a clever lawyer, she was not convicted and went on to head up the Texas Legal Aid Society. They talked in great detail just after her acquittal, but didn't speak again for ten years.

Approaching the regal House and Senate buildings, he sighed at the countless hours spent fighting in those arenas. Among other abject failures, the war on drugs was lost and his country's borders remained wide open. Ironically, enactment of the amnesty provision in the 1986 law which he'd tried to amend, allowed his friend, Maleva, to stay in the U.S. where she continued to reside with her family at the age of ninety-four. A new Congress was debating yet another immigration bill to provide amnesty to eleven million more people who'd entered since 1986, and entice still more to come in and live within the shadows. With the ornate buildings' detailed architecture in view, he considered the hardship his country's founders endured in forging the constitutional republic that had allowed democracy to flourish. He pondered what an idealistic, humanistic and revolutionary concept it was and how they all might have felt.

Driving past the reliable concrete barriers securing the Capitol's perimeter, he questioned the vulnerability of his country's unique theory of government – the requisite human element. Nick felt stupid knowing how many footsteps he'd followed to arrive at so obvious a place, so many steps that such disillusionment had long become cliché. He was disillusioned by those who took their country's security for granted, at leaders who ignored their most fundamental duties, and at how distracted America had become from its founding principles. He'd also learned that whether in a courtroom representing clients or in a political body representing constituents, to come prepared for an ugly and adversarial process. And he learned not to look to either forum for equity but for what is best primarily for the participants, clothed by journalists in what's best in it for them.

However, Nick would not be made wholly cynical by his education of democracy. In fact, it was its core principle that had saved him more than once. After all, what had allowed that which seemed so hopeless early in his career to somehow all turn around? What was it that had timely intervened to right the wrongs of those so powerful? The connection escaped him from time to time. But, after a quarter of a century, he'd discovered that in America's representative democracy, one cannot ignore the power or the final word of the ever-present and sometimes ruthless majority.

––––––––––

Acknowledgements

I would like to give special thanks to the following for their inspiration, help, encouragement, editing, reality checks and research on this book: Patrice Taylor, Joseph Gibson, Melissa Newman, Jim Haliczer, Bill Barloon, Joe McDonald, Linda Anderson, Stephanie Schaffer, Helen Wayne, Mark Borskey, Linda Willard, Matia Mejia, Linda Murphy, Abel Rodriguez, Joanne Fleming, Ron Kaufman, Chris Gallagher, Rob Quartel, Carey McKearnan, Wick Ferrell, Vicky Irvine, Jeff Bragg, Hance Haney, Jaime Horn, Chauncey Mabe, Alice Thomas, Patrick Cullen, Catherine Wallace, Chris Moore, Cathy Whelan and Alan Slobodin. Thanks also to the Sacajawea Hotel in Three Forks, Montana for the serenity of its front porch, and to the Coral Sands Hotel in Harbour Island, Bahamas for the peaceful quiet of its balconies.

Notes

1. In 1986, one Democrat and one Republican offered an amendment in the Judiciary Committee of the U.S. House to an immigration bill to delay amnesty for illegal immigrants in the U.S. until a Presidential Commission had determined that the U.S. - Mexico border was secure. See, 99th Congress 2nd Session, House of Representatives, Rept. 99-682 Part I, Committee on the Judiciary, HR 3810, The Immigration Control And Legalization Amendments Act of 1986. The amendment was briefly debated, and it failed not on a recorded vote, but on a voice-vote along party lines. See, "Congress Clears Overhaul of Immigration Law", Congressional Quarterly Almanac 1986, Vol. 42. See also, Transcript, Markup of HR 3810 Wednesday June 18, 1986, House of Representatives, Committee on the Judiciary, Washington, DC.

2. After Newt Gingrich stepped down in 1998 as the first Republican Speaker of the House in forty years, Dennis Hastert took over as Speaker and implemented what became known as the Hastert Rule. The Hastert Rule decreed that the House would only consider bills approved by a majority of the majority. Therefore a majority of the Republican caucus had to be behind anything that came to the House floor for a vote – effectively locking out many Democrats' ideas. The Hastert Rule is often cited as the reason Speaker Hastert did not allow a comprehensive immigration reform bill to come to the floor in 2006. The bill had the support of a large portion but not a majority of the Republican Conference. See, "Boehner Won't Revive The Hastert Rule," Congress Daily PM, December 17, 2010; but also see, "Democracy in the House," New York Times, January 10, 2013.

3. A study by political scientist, David Shirk, at the University of San Diego's Trans-Border Institute affirms that ongoing cartel activities trace their roots back to the 1980s. Shirk explains that through the middle of that decade, Mexico's drug trafficking organizations operated with impunity due to protection then afforded them by corrupt officials at very high levels in the Mexican government. During that same period, the relative influence of the Colombian cartels was declining, and the Mexican organizations' share of the global drug business expanded – a phenomenon that accelerated in the 1990s. See, Duncan Currie, "Progress Pains," *National Review*, July 5, 2010. See also, David Shirk, "Drug Violence in Mexico *Data and Analysis from 2001-2009*," January 2010, Trans-Border Institute, University of San Diego.

4. And eventually they did. See, for example, Clarence Williams, "Cops Bust 'La Familia' Members, *The Washington Post*, December 14ᵗʰ, 2010, and Jerry Seper, "ICE: D.C. Drug Plan Tied To Mexican Cartel," *The Washington Times,* December 20ᵗʰ, 2010. A federal grand jury in Washington indicted nine people in the nation's capital as part of an operation directed by drug cartel bosses in Mexico. The indictment said the drug operation was tied to La Familia, the Mexico based gang that killed 20 Mexican federal police and military officers in attacks in 2010. Based in the Mexican State of Michoacan, La Familia had quietly moved its drug operations across the border into the United States. All the men arrested were illegal immigrants. Note also, the U.S. State Department Travel Warning issued on April 26, 2011 to warn U.S. citizens away from several Mexican cities including the border towns of Sonora, Tamaulipus, Ciudad Juarez and Tijuana. The government agency warned that 34,612 people had been killed in narcotics-related violence in the previous four years and that more than 15,000 narcotics-related homicides had occurred in 2010 alone.

5. In the '80s, the media generally did not portray the border as a security risk. Regarding the 1986 Immigration Act, their focus was primarily on the higher profile issues of amnesty, employer sanctions and guest worker programs. In recent years – despite the documented realities of incalculable human trafficking, drug smuggling, gun running, murder, and gang violence along the border, and consequent U.S. State Department travel warnings – several press articles (citing border city crime statistics) seem to downplay the significance of those harsh facts. See, e.g., Alan Gomez, Jack Gillum, and Kevin Johnson, "On the U.S. Side, Cities are Havens From Drug Wars – Analysis: Spillover violence is exaggerated," *USA TODAY,* July 15-17, 2011; "Violent Crime Falls in U.S. Cities Along Mexico Border," *The Salt Lake Tribune*, November 4, 2012; and Ronald J. Hansen, "Crime Drops Along U.S.-Mexico Border," *The Republic*, February 26, 2013. Others argue that crime statistics reported by some local jurisdictions are not reflective of the grim reality playing out along the U.S. border. See, e.g., Richard Valdemar, Is Mexican Cartel Activity In the U.S. Exaggerated?, *POLICE Magazine*, August 30, 2013; and Sylvia Longmire, *Cartel: The Coming Invasion of Mexico's Drug Wars*, New York: Palgrave Macmillan, 2011.

6. By 2011, due to the U.S. government's failure to enforce immigration law, six states – Arizona, Alabama, Georgia, Indiana, South Carolina and Utah – enacted their own immigration laws attempting to enforce various aspects of federal law. The state laws included an array of the

following provisions: making it a state crime to be in the country illegally; making it illegal to work or seek work when not authorized; requiring state and local officers to determine the status of someone questioned, stopped or detained if it is believed the individual may be in the country illegally; and allowing warrantless arrests where probable cause exists to believe individuals have violated laws that would make them deportable under federal law. The federal government brought legal action against some states to prevent them from enforcing their own state laws. The U.S. Supreme Court, in an attempt to resolve those conflicts, took jurisdiction of a challenge to the Arizona law. The Court ruled in June of 2012 striking down parts of the Arizona law but upholding a state's right to determine the legal status of any individual detained by state authorities. See, Arizona v. United States, 567 U.S. __ (2012).

7. Though sparsely used after the statute was enacted in 1978, pressure to appoint independent counsels was brought more frequently on President Reagan's Administration. Eight fully-funded independent counsels were set in motion to investigate appointees of the Reagan Administration (Including, Ray Donovan, Secretary of Labor; Ed Meese, Counselor to the President; Michael Deaver, Chief of Staff; Iran/Contra to investigate those involved in the sale of arms to Iran where proceeds were diverted to the Nicaraguan Contras; and Lyn Nofziger, Assistant to the President). And still more were appointed in the years that followed to investigate the Administrations of George H. W. Bush and William Jefferson Clinton. While the first media account of the Iran-Contra Affair appeared in November of 1986, it did not become a full-blown Washington scandal until 1987.

8. By the mid-2000s, hundreds of millions of U.S. dollars were crossing into Mexico connected to everything from human trafficking to drug running to arms trafficking. In 2010, the Arizona Attorney General's Office forged an agreement with Western Union Financial Services which facilitates money wire transfers to Mexico. Western Union agreed to let law enforcement authorities from California, Arizona, Texas, and New Mexico monitor its wire transfers. That settlement meant that *coyotes* would have a harder time receiving and sending wire money payments. It also meant that actual cash would have to be moved back into Mexico. See, Terry Greene Sterling, *Illegal Life and Death in Arizona's Immigration War Zone*, Connecticut: Lyons Press, 2010.

Notes

9. The House Judiciary Committee voted on an amendment to cover Members of Congress under the law during consideration of legislation to reauthorize the Independent Counsel statute in 1987. It failed on a close to party line vote – Republicans mostly in favor, Democrats voting mostly against. A similar amendment was first proposed by former Democratic Congresswoman Elizabeth Holtzman of New York when a bill was considered by Congress in the 1970s.

10. Under normal order in the U.S. House, once a bill has been voted out of committee, a report is filed which explains the bill in detail. Then the Rules Committee may issue a rule which sets the terms for debate on the bill in the House. That rule will determine how much debate will be had on the legislation, how time for debate will be divided, and what amendments will be allowed to be offered. A member who wishes to offer an amendment during debate usually must appear before the Rules Committee to request that the amendment be allowed under the rule.

11. During the '80s, the media generally lauded the independent counsel statute as an effective tool for fighting abuse of power. See, e.g., "A Deaver-North Diversion," *Washington Post*, February 27, 1987; and "Look Who's Charging Impropriety," *New York Times*, February 26, 1987.

12. The independent counsel statute was considered by the U.S. House for reauthorization in the fall of 1987, and an amendment to include Members of Congress as covered individuals subject to independent counsel investigations was offered. It failed on a partisan vote, 243 to 169. See, Congressional Record, October 21, 1987, House Proceedings, Amendment No. 457, Record Vote No. 372.

13. A Democratic majority reauthorized the independent counsel statute in 1987. Ten years later when the target of several Independent Counsels was a Democratic president and Republicans controlled Congress, a Democratic minority agreed with a Republican majority not to reauthorize it again. The statute expired on June 30, 1999. Coincidentally, the media changed its perspective on the statute as well. When a Democratic president became the object of independent counsel investigations in the 1990s with the same powers, same unfettered discretion, and unlimited funding used to go after Republican presidents in the past, the media excoriated the law and the prosecutor it enabled. See, e.g., "Ken Starr's Misjudgments," *New*

York Times, February 25, 1998; Lenora Fulani, "Things Are So Bad . . . Clinton Looks Good," *Philadelphia Tribune*, February 17, 1998; Frank Rich, "Mixed Nuts," *New York Times*, February 28, 1998; and Ethan Bonner, "Starr's Wide Net Is Drawing Witnesses And Critics Alike," *New York Times*, February 14, 1998.

14. Congress considered an immigration reform bill in 1986. The title of the bill considered by the House then was the "Immigration Control and Legalization Amendments Act of 1986," also known as H.R. 3810.

15. The immigration bill passed by Congress and enacted into law in 1986 provided this authority. The report filed by the House Judiciary Committee (several other committees filed reports on the legislation as well) includes supporting views of the Reagan Administration's Department of Justice which reads in part: "Title II of the bill governs the legalization of unauthorized aliens already in the country. It empowers the Attorney General to adjust the status of unauthorized aliens to that of lawfully admitted aliens eligible for temporary residence if they apply, meet certain conditions, can establish that they illegally entered the United States prior to January 1, 1982 and have been residing here continuously since then. After one year in temporary status, the Attorney General can adjust the status to that of a permanent alien." See, Immigration Control and Legalization Amendments Act of 1986: Report of the Committee on the Judiciary, House of Representatives, on HR 3810 (Rept. 99-682, Part I) (July 16, 1986).

16. The Committee Report to H.R. 3810 states: "The committee believes that the solution lies in legalizing the status of aliens who have been present in the United States for several years, recognizing that past failures to enforce the immigration laws have allowed them to enter and settle here." See, Immigration Control and Legalization Amendments Act of 1986, Report of the Committee on the Judiciary, supra note 15.

17. See, e.g., Stephen Dinan, "Obama's Promised Push on Immigration Reform Sets up Early Test," *Washington Times*, January 7, 2013 ("President Obama, who strongly carried the Hispanic vote in his 2012 reelection drive, has vowed to push immigration [reform] early in the new year . . . Obama and Senate Democrat leaders want to handle the debate in one large bill – what they and advocates call 'comprehensive immigration reform' – which would include legalization of illegal immigrants.") Also see, Ed O'Keefe, "Senate Approves Immigration Bill," *The Washington Post*, June 28, 2013 ("The effort – to overhaul the nation's immigration laws achieved a victory – when the Senate

approved legislation that would allow millions of illegal immigrants the chance to live legally in the United States and eventually become U.S. citizens."); and see, Sara Murray and Janet Hook, "Immigration Bill Clears Senate," *The Wall Street Journal,* June 28, 2013 ("The Senate easily passed the most sweeping changes to immigration law in nearly 30 years sending the landmark legislation to the House ... to grant legal status to many of the estimated 11 million people living illegally in the U.S.")

18. Additional Views, submitted by one Republican and one Democrat, to the House Judiciary Committee Report on the bill reported by that committee in 1986 read in part as follows: "We strongly believe that legalization without increased immigration enforcement and border control activity will only encourage millions of new immigrants to come into this country illegally, and will require another amnesty program in the future ... Our border agents are virtually overrun. Overworked and under supported INS investigators cannot curtail the booming business in alien smuggling ..." See, Immigration Control and Legalization Amendments Act of 1986: Report of the Committee on the Judiciary, supra note 15.

19. In the fall of 1986, such an amendment was not allowed by the Rules Committee in the U.S. House. A member who supported it in committee, stated his opposition to the Rules Committee's decision as follows: "Mr. Speaker, I rise in opposition to the rule on the Immigration Control and Legalization Act ... During Rules Committee consideration of H.R. 3810, I urged the committee to adopt a rule allowing me to offer a "Triggered Amnesty" amendment to delay legalization until a Presidential Commission determines that our borders are secure ... The rule does not provide for its consideration." See, Congressional Record, October 9, 1986, House Proceedings.

20. The House leadership which, through the Rules Committee, had ensured that no vote would occur on a triggered amnesty amendment was aware that another amendment to remove the amnesty provision from the bill altogether was gaining momentum. They were also aware that allowing a triggered amnesty provision in both the House and Senate bills would make it difficult to remove the language during the House/Senate Conference that would craft the ultimate compromise to go to President Reagan for signature. See, "Congress Clears Overhaul of Immigration Law," *Congressional Quarterly Almanac,* 1986, Volume 42, and "Senate Votes to Revamp Immigration Laws," *Congressional*

Quarterly Almanac, 1985, Volume 41. See also, Congressional Record, October 9, 1986, Amendment No. 129, Record Vote No. 455, Recorded Vote: 192-199.

21. The Democratic cosponsor of the Judiciary Committee amendment to require triggered amnesty emphasized how out of control the U.S.-Mexico border was during debate on the rule for the immigration bill on the House floor in 1986 as follows: "As you know, I am greatly concerned over the fact we're still a long way from bringing the border situation under control. Last year, the INS located 1,348,749 aliens in this country who we deported under the Immigration and Nationality Act – millions more escaped detection. The agency has an average of only one agent on duty for every 9.8 miles along the southern border. Only one out of every two or three illegal aliens who come across the border are apprehended . . . No one knows for certain how many illegal aliens are already in this country. But estimates range between 3.5 and 10 million with more coming every day . . . In San Diego alone, we are averaging one arrest every 35 seconds. The INS estimates it will apprehend 1.8 million illegal aliens this year almost 5000 per day." See, Congressional Record, October 9, 1986, House Proceedings.

22. A Congressional report published ten years later estimates that the 1986 Immigration Reform and Control Act resulted in the granting of amnesty to 2,700,000 illegal aliens. See Report on The Activities of the Committee on the Judiciary During the 104th Congress, – 104th Congress, 2nd Session, House Report 104-879. It has been estimated since then that somewhere between 11,000,000 and 20,000,000 illegal immigrants have entered and settled in the United States. See, e.g., Brad Knickerbocker, "Illegal Immigrants in the US: How Many Are There?," *Christian Science Monitor*, May 16, 2006; Karin Brulliard and Krissah Williams, "Immigration Estimates For Region Vary Widely From Source to Source," *Washington Post*, June 11, 2006; Jay Seper, "Ridge Tapped for Immigration Views," *Washington Times*, December 11, 2003. Some experts have argued that the 1986 law, rather than discourage illegal entry, in fact encouraged decidedly more illegal immigration into the country: "The message to those [outside the United States] is that we are not serious about the laws prohibiting illegal immigration, so they may as well try their luck . . . In the past decade, we have seen sustained, high levels of illegal immigration that have not only replaced the entire estimated illegal population of 1986, but have exceeded that population by more than two times over." See, Testimony of Rosemary Jenks, Director of Government Relations, Numbers U.S.A., before the Subcommittee on Immigration, Citizenship, Refugees, Border Security, and International Law, Committee on the Judiciary, U.S. House of Representatives, One Hundred and Tenth Congress, First Session, April 19th, 2007, Serial No. 110-16.

23. The Immigration Control and Legalization Amendments Act of 1986 passed the House of Representatives in October of 1986 by a vote of 230 to 166. See, Congressional Record, October 9, 1986, House Proceedings, Record Vote No: 457. The Senate and House later agreed to a compromise version of the legislation in a Conference Report and sent it to the White House for signature. The bill passed by the Senate in that Congress (S. 1200) included a triggered amnesty provision, but during the Conference, the House position prevailed and it was removed. A key Senate sponsor of the 1986 law years later acknowledged that amnesty without border enforcement was a mistake: "There are simply no more excuses... for illegal immigration... Enacting any form of amnesty before... increased border enforcement [is] fully implemented, is wholly illogical." See, Statement of Alan Simpson, Former U.S. Senator from the State of Wyoming, Hearing Before The Committee On The Judiciary, U.S. House of Representatives, One Hundred Ninth Congress, Second Session, September 1, 2006, Serial No.109-142. On November 6, 1986, President Ronald Reagan signed The Immigration Reform and Control Act of 1986 into law.

24. The Pew Hispanic Center estimated that 8.3 million illegal immigrants were in the U.S. labor force in 2010, mostly in low-skilled jobs. The center also estimated that across the U.S. 40% of brick masons, one in four farm workers, and 28% of dishwashers were undocumented illegal immigrants. See, Paul Reyes, "Dobbs, Whitman Reflect Illegals Reality," *USA TODAY*, October 22, 2010.

25. In November of 2013, a Democratic majority in the Senate diminished the long-standing institutional protection once afforded the minority party there. The Senate, by a partisan vote of 52 to 48, changed the precedent regarding the threshold for cloture votes, depriving the minority of its leverage to filibuster any and all actions by the majority. Henceforth, invoking cloture for judicial and executive branch nominees (except for the Supreme Court) will no longer require 60 votes, but a simple majority vote. See, Congressional Record, November 21, 2013, Senate Proceedings, Rollcall Vote No. 243. See also, Todd Ruger, "Senate Changes Rules, Curbs Power to Filibuster," The Blog of LegalTimes, November 21, 2013 ("The Senate today ... stripped the ability of the minority party to block presidential nominations ... The 52-48 historic vote overturned a Senate rule that stood for more than a century.") Available at: http://legaltimes.typepad.com/blt/2013/senate-changes-rules-curbs-power-to-filibuster.html.

Notes

26. The Congressional elections of 1986, in fact, resulted in the Democrats picking up five additional seats in that midterm election for a total advantage over the Republicans of 258 to 177, making it thirty-two straight years of a Democratic majority in the U.S. House. In the midterm elections of 1994, Republicans won control of the House, placing the Democrats in the minority there for the first time in forty years.